LANGUAGE AND THE LANGUAGE ARTS

LANGUAGE AND THE LANGUAGE ARTS

James Flood
San Diego State University

Peter H. Salus
University of North Florida

Prentice-Hall, Inc., Englewood Cliffs, N.J. 07632

Library of Congress Cataloging in Publication Data

FLOOD, JAMES.
  Language and the language arts.

  Includes bibliographies and index.
  1. Language and languages. 2. Language arts.
  I. Salus, Peter H. II. Title.
  P106.F544 1984   372.6′044   82-25087
  ISBN 0-13-522979-0

Editorial/production supervision
  and interior design: Joyce Turner
Cover design: George Cornell
Manufacturing buyer: Ron Chapman
Cover photo by Linda Lungren
Page makeup: Diane Heckler Koromhas

Citations from the works of W. H. Auden
  appear through the permission of the
  Estate of W. H. Auden, Edward Mendelson, Literary Executor.

© 1984 by Prentice-Hall, Inc., Englwood Cliffs, New Jersey 07632

*All rights reserved. No part of this book may be
reproduced, in any form or by any means,
without permission in writing from the publisher.*

Printed in the United States of America

10 9 8 7 6 5 4 3 2 1

ISBN 0-13-522979-0

Prentice-Hall International, Inc., *London*
Prentice-Hall of Australia Pty. Limited, *Sydney*
Editora Prentice-Hall do Brasil, Ltda., *Rio de Janeiro*
Prentice-Hall Canada Inc., *Toronto*
Prentice-Hall of India Private Limited, *New Delhi*
Prentice-Hall of Japan, Inc., *Tokyo*
Prentice-Hall of Southeast Asia Pte. Ltd., *Singapore*
Whitehall Books Limited, *Wellington, New Zealand*

192783
BELMONT UNIVERSITY LIBRARY

Dedicated to our children
Johanna, Bartholomew
and Emily

CONTENTS

PREFACE xv
ACKNOWLEDGMENTS xvii

1 Looking at Language 1

Talking 2
Communication and Language 2
Linguistics 4
Anatomy 4
The Sounds of English 6
Vowels 9
Suprasegmentals 11
Form Systems: Morphology 12
Morphological Devices 12
Syntax 14
Semantics 17
Language Use 18
Exercises 19
Further Readings 20

2 Language Development 21

Learning to Talk 23
Historical Overview 23
Maturational Processes 24
Communicative Behavior 26
First Words and the Growth of Vocabulary 27
Telegraphic Speech and Pivot Grammar 28
Early Syntactic Development 30
Morphological Development 31
Syntax 33
Comprehension and Performance 38
More Syntax 39
Pragmatics 42
More Phonology 44
Semantics 46
Exercises 48
References 49
Further Readings 49

3 Language Over Time 51

Language Change 52
Languages and Language Families 53
The Germanic Languages 55
Loanwords 58
Coinages 60
Semantic Changes 60
Families of Words 62
Exercises 65
Further Readings 65

4 Teaching Oral Communication Skills 67

Oral Communication Programs 68
Listening 69
Critical Listening Skills 70
Factors Influencing Listening 71
Speaking 72
Speaking Skills 77
Factors Influencing Speaking 78
Interrelations of Listening and Speaking and the other Language Arts 78
Implementing a Listening/Speaking Program 79

Activities for Your Students 94
Exercises 98
References 99
Bibliography 99
Further Readings 99

5 Writing Systems 101

Reading and Writing 102
Kinds of Writing Systems 104
Beginnings of Writing 107
Phonetic Scripts 113
The Alphabet 114
Exercises 117
Further Readings 117

6 The Processes of Writing 119

Models of the Writing Process 123
Murray's Recommendations for Teaching Writing 124
Five Approaches to the Teaching of Writing 125
Six Steps to a Successful Writing Program 128
Designing Your Program 133
A Beginning Method for Teaching Writing to Young Children 139
Some Ways to Make Books 142
Types of Writing 142
Evaluation 149
Exercises 151
References 151
Further Readings 152

7 Handwriting 153

The Origins and Development of Writing 154
Guidelines for Establishing Objectives for Your Program 156
Handwriting Skills 157
Readiness for Handwriting 158
Why Begin with Manuscript Writing? 158
Teaching Manuscript Writing 159
Moving from Manuscript to Cursive Writing 160
Teaching Cursive Writing 161
Physical Factors Related to Cursive Handwriting Instruction 162
The Left-Handed Child 162

x   Contents

    Evaluating Progress in Handwriting 164
    Improving Performance 170
    Exercises 171
    References 172
    Further Readings 172

8 Looking at Spelling 173

    The Acquisition and Development of Spelling in Young Children 174
    The English Writing System 177
    Some Spelling Rules 177
    Basic (Spelling-Sound) Relations 179
    History of Spelling Instruction 181
    Objectives of Your Spelling Program 182
    Assessing Students' Strengths and Needs 182
    Curriculum Decisions 184
    Spelling Demons 190
    Grouping for Instruction 192
    Instructional Methods 192
    Common Errors and Corrective Measures 193
    Activities for Your Students 196
    Games for Your Students 197
    Exercises 199
    References 200
    Further Reading 200

9 Writing and Grammar 201

    Teaching Grammar 202
    Reference 202
    Agreement 203
    Formal Grammar 203
    Mechanics 205
    Exercises 217

10 The Process of Reading 219

    What Is Reading? 220
    Instruction in Reading 222
    Readiness for Reading 224
    Decoding 228
    Teaching Word Attack Skills 233
    Comprehension of Texts 246

Cautions About Using the "Literal, Inferential, Critical" Reading
  Trichotomy   249
Lessons   251
Questioning Strategies   254
Assessment of Reading   256
Exercises   257
References   258
Further Readings   259

11 Literature for Children and Adolescents   261

Importance of Familiarizing Children With Literature   262
Language Development   262
Personality Development   263
Contemporary Issues in Children's Literature   263
Teaching Children about Genres in Literature   264
Attitudes Toward Reading   279
Reading Interests   285
Reading to Young Children   286
Selecting Literature for Beginning Readers   287
Teaching Episodes   288
Organizing Your Children's Information Searching   291
Creating Stimulating Environments for Reading   291
Treasure Chest of Award-Winning Books   291
Caldecott Medal Books   292
Newberry Medal Books   293
Resource Books on Literature for Children   295
Exercises   295
References   296
Further Readings   296

12 Language Variation

Dialects   298
Language in Society   300
Varieties in the Classroom   300
Some Stereotypes   301
Dialect Differences   302
Some Alternatives   303
Black English   307
Interactions   309
General Guidelines   311

Teaching the Standard Dialect 311
Bilingualism 312
National Language 312
Intervention Techniques 313
Learning a Second Language 314
The Bilingual Child in the Classroom 315
Exercises 318
References 318
Further Readings 319

13 Students with Special Needs 321

Differences and Disorders 322
Speech and Language Disorders 323
Deafness 325
The Speech of the Deaf 326
The Language of the Cerebral Palsied 327
The Speech of the Retarded 327
Some Last Words 327
PL 94-142 328
Language Arts and the Exceptional Child 329
The Gifted Child 329
Teaching the Gifted 330
Exercises 331
Reference 332
Further Readings 332

14 Organizing and Managing Your Program 333

Defining Individualization 334
Designing an Effective Program 335
Exercises 352
Further Readings 352

APPENDIX: WORD GAMES 353

Easy Games 354
More Difficult Games 356

Advanced Games 359
Some Types of Games 359
Exercises 366
Further Readings 366

INDEX 367

PREFACE

The language arts include four main areas: speaking, listening, reading, and writing. Of these, speaking and listening are considered primary; reading and writing are secondary.

Most children arrive at the kindergarten door able to speak and to listen; few children read and write when they first come to school. While we can encourage and aid a child's listening and speaking skills, we actually shape his or her reading and writing skills. Since we learn everything through the medium of language, the language arts form the core of the curriculum.

Thus, you play a key role in the child's educational development. We believe that you will be better able to perform this role if you understand what language is, how children acquire language, and how our language (English) has developed; you would be less prepared if we only supplied you with methods and materials for your classroom. It is for this reason that we have included several chapters concerning linguistic topics and have then applied these concepts in the succeeding chapters.

The language arts concern *language;* we have therefore devoted several chapters to that topic. The language arts also involve *art;* thus, we also discuss oral skills, children's literature, creative writing, drama, and composition. Our belief in the importance of addressing both language and art is exemplified by our use of citations from the works of W.H.

Auden, a modern poet greatly concerned about and involved with words and forms.

Language and the Language Arts is intended for preservice teachers and inservice teachers who feel a need to further their education in the area of language arts. We hope this book will offer insights that will enable teachers to strengthen and/or develop a language arts curriculum that will meet every student's needs.

We have organized the book in the following manner: First, we talk about the nature of language as a human phenomenon and the development of language in the child. Next, we turn to oral language in the classroom.

From individual language, we turn to language as a group phenomenon—to language history—and, because of the importance of writing and reading in the language arts curriculum, to different kinds of writing systems and the history of our alphabet. The chapter on handwriting returns us to the individual and the classroom. We then go on to spelling. grammar, and composition. In these sections, we will make reference to the preceding material on language, language development, language history, and writing systems so that you may see how theory and practice are related to your classroom.

The chapters on reading and literature are also related to your classroom and to the experiences you and your children will have there. We offer the chapters on children from nonstandard dialect backgrounds as well as those on children from homes where English is not spoken and on children with special needs since we believe that understanding such phenomena will make you better able to relate to such children in the classroom and will help ensure that each child benefits maximally from the schooling received.

J.E.F. & P.H.S.

ACKNOWLEDGMENTS

We would like to thank our colleagues and students at Boston University, the University of Toronto, the University of North Florida, and San Diego State University, for their many comments, suggestions, and emendations; Ms. Susan Katz, our editor, for her patience, encouragement, and good counsel; our wives, Sharon and Mary, for their forbearance; and the many children who have tolerated what must have appeared to be a multitude of silly and meaningless requests.

Our special thanks go to Professor Edward Mendelson and the Estate of W. H. Auden for permission to quote the various poems and prose passages used as epigraphs.

Finally, we would like to thank our children, Emily, Johanna, and Bartholomew, who have inspired us over the years.

J.E.F & P.H.S.

LANGUAGE AND THE LANGUAGE ARTS

What we have not beheld or named as a symbol escapes our notice.

—W.H. Auden

1 LOOKING AT LANGUAGE

This chapter includes an overview of the field of linguistics, examining theories of the nature of language and communication. It also provides an overview of language study. It includes an explanation of the differences between language and communication, a definition of linguistics, and a brief description of phonology, morphology, syntax, semantics, and language use.

TALKING

It is obvious that almost everyone talks. This being true, one might ask what processes are involved in language and how to explain them. Understanding the development of language and the processes involved in language enables us to explain secondary phenomena. This understanding will make us better teachers.

By secondary phenomena, we mean reading and writing, for language (speech) is primary and these are secondary to it. Understanding language and its development helps us explain the complex processes involved in reading and writing.

COMMUNICATION AND LANGUAGE

Language is not the same as communication. Most animals are able to communicate with one another: Bees "tell" their hive-mates about food locations, dogs mark their territory with urine, peacocks spread their tails to lure peahens to mate with them, and boars snort and paw their assertions of superiority. However, the kinds of communicative acts most animals indulge in are of a limited sort; the kinds of messages conveyed are not very complex and the repertory is quite limited. Many animals communicate through odors, visual signals, or contact; some (such as birds and mammals) use sounds as well.

Except for some secondary forms (such as the sign language of the deaf), vocal communication appears to be richer and more varied than the messages conveyed by visual or chemical (taste or smell) media. But most

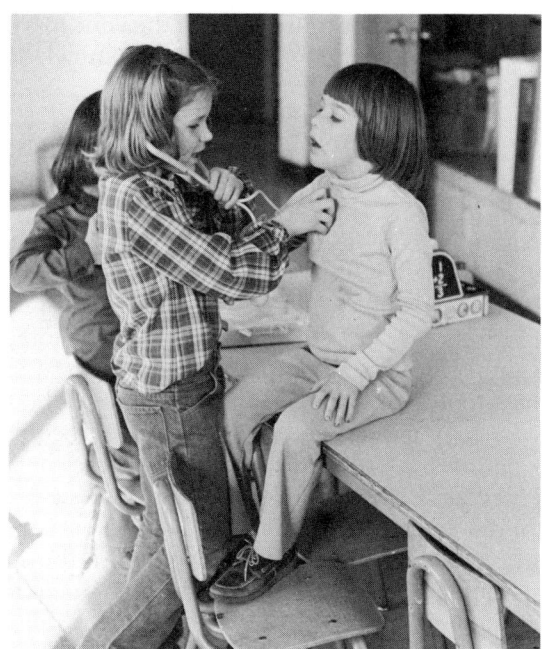

Language is not the same as communication. Human speech is the richest and most varied form of expression known. Children's play is filled with language. (*Photo by Linda Lungren*)

animals that make sounds use only a limited number of them, and their messages are not complex or extensive. Only human beings can talk.

Human speech is the richest and most varied form of expression known. Each of the more than four thousand languages spoken around the world preserves its own "flavor" and yet manages to convey all the ideas, hopes, fears, intentions, and observations its speakers wish to impart. No language is better than any other, nor worse than any other. Every known language has great complexity of form and expression. There do not appear to be any "simple" or "primitive" languages.

Every human language has a history, although this history may never have been studied or recorded. Every language, if it has more than a very few speakers, has social and regional dialects; every speaker of every language has several levels of language that he or she commands. Chapters 2 and 3 of this book deal with the variations of language within the individual, within groups, and over time. In order to present this information, we need to use some of the ideas and terms of linguistics, the study of language.

But before we do so, we might try to explain why we have included this theoretical material in the book. We believe that an understanding of oral and written arts in the classroom must be based on an understanding of language as a human phenomenon as well as on an understanding of the child's language development. We will examine this hypothesis in this chapter and later reuse some of the concepts introduced here to underscore the relationship between such basic knowledge and effective classroom applications.

LINGUISTICS

Linguistics is the study of language. This may seem like an unnecessary statement; however, the common confusion of the linguist with the polyglot—one who speaks many languages—provides good reason for begining with this sort of statement. Furthermore, it may be worthwhile to distinguish between linguistics and philology. Philology deals with language as a tool with which one gains access to the literature, anthropology, and sociology of speakers of a language. Frequently, the philologist is interested in the products of cultures where the language is no longer spoken (such as Ancient Greek, Sanskrit, Classical Arabic, or Classical Chinese). In these cases, the scholar is involved with the written, etched, carved, engraved, or printed word, but not with the spoken language.

The linguist is interested in language for its own sake and as a phenomenon of human behavior. As a result, much of modern linguistics might be viewed as a branch of cognitive psychology.

The essence of language is speech and the psychological realities underlying it. While writing is secondary, we are reduced to using writing systems to represent speech since sound is transitory and most scholarship is eye-oriented.

There are a variety of ways in which one can examine language. First, one might look at the noise itself, at the sounds of language. This study, called phonetics, can concern either the organs of speech (physiological phonetics) or the physics of sounds (acoustic phonetics). One might also look at the ways in which the sounds are relevant in a given language. This is phonology, the study of *relevant* speech sounds. Not all human noises are relevant to speech, and not all languages employ the same inventory of sounds. Before going on to other ways of looking at speech, it is important to examine sounds a little more closely.

ANATOMY

Human speech sounds are produced by passing air through the nose or the mouth, past the pharynx, larynx, and trachea, to or from the lungs. All the sounds of English are produced by expelling the air from the lungs into the outer world through the mouth or nose. Such sounds are referred to as explosive sounds. In some languages (for example, Zulu and Icelandic), there are sounds in which the air moves in the reverse direction. These are

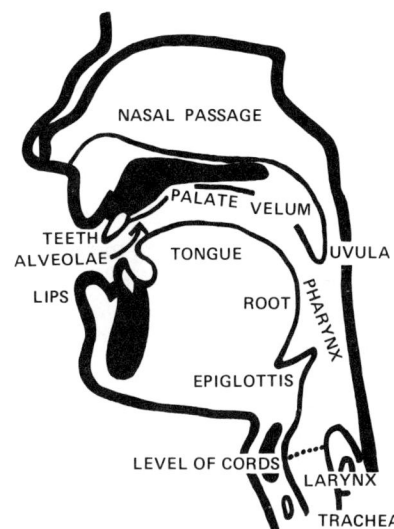

FIGURE 1-1. Diagram of Vocal Tract.

referred to as implosive sounds. Since we will be considering only English here, we will refer only to the explosive sounds.

The impetus for speech comes from the stream of air that we exhale. Normally, this is relatively noiseless, but we can make it noisy by putting obstacles in its path, thus causing the stream to vibrate. The most common way to cause this vibration is to use the vocal cords.

The vocal cords are part of the larynx (or "Adam's apple"); they are bands of cartilage running horizontally, back to front, across the trachea, or windpipe. When these bands are open, the airstream passes unimpeded; when they are tightly closed, the airstream is interrupted; when they are partially shut, the airstream sets them in motion and itself is made more turbulent. The vibration of these bands is called voice, and the speech sounds are said to be voiced. The space between the vocal cords is called the glottis.

You can tell whether or not a sound is voiced by placing your fingers against your larynx and uttering the sound: For example, you can feel the "buzzing" when you say *z-z-z-z-z,* but this is absent when you hiss *s-s-s-s-s.* The same distinction can be made between *p* and *b, t* and *d, f* and *v,* and *k* and *g,* where the first member of each pair is voiceless and the second is voiced.

There are only two other ways of varying speech sounds: constriction of the vocal tract (the nasal-oral cavity above the larynx) and closure of the vocal tract. The sounds produced by constricting the vocal tract at some point are called fricatives; the airstream at the point of constriction becomes turbulent, like steam escaping from the narrow nozzle of a steam kettle. The sounds produced by actual closure of the vocal tract are called stops, or plosives.

The part of the vocal tract immediately above the larynx is called the pharynx. Above the pharynx the tract forks, the upper branch leading to the nasal cavity, which is separated from the lower cavity (the mouth, or oral cavity) by the palate. The nasal cavity can be shut off completely by raising the soft palate, or velum.

In some ways, the mouth is the most important part of the vocal tract. Its shape can be altered extensively through movement of the palate, tongue, teeth, and lips—or, rather, movements of some of these with respect to the others.

The tongue is the most flexible of these organs, as it can be moved to the front or back or up and down. The lips can be rounded or spread, they may contact the teeth, or they may be closed completely to stop the airstream. The teeth, in contact with the lips or the tongue, may be used to restrict the airstream in various ways. Finally, the palate, the roof of your mouth, is divided into three parts: the alveolar ridge (the bony ridge just behind your front teeth), the bony hard palate, and the muscular soft palate behind it.

All the sounds of English are produced with the organs discussed above.

THE SOUNDS OF ENGLISH

If we put together a list of words such as

pill	till	kill	chill
bill	dill	gill	Jill
mill	nil	fill	ville
will	Lil	sill	hill
rill			

you will note that they differ only in their initial sounds. If we put together another list such as

pet			Chet
bet	debt	get	jet
met	net		vet
wet	let	set	het
	yet		

we find that while there are some slots we cannot fill (there is no English word *ket, an asterisk before a word means that it is hypothetical or ungrammatical), there is also an item for an unfilled slot in our first list (there is no *yill in English).

If we arrange these words in pairs, such as *pill:bill* or *wet:yet*, we can clearly demonstrate that the difference between the first sound in each word is relevant to the sound pattern of English. When words differ in only one sound, we say that they form a minimal pair. Such a minimal pair demonstrates the relevance of a sound distinction in a language. The first list illustrates seventeen distinctions in English; the second list, fourteen. However, the second list adds *y* to our inventory.

It is not necessary to use initial sounds to demonstrate relevance or to establish a minimal pair. Sequences such as *bill:bell:bull:ball* or *hit:hid:hip:his:hiss* might also be used.

The smallest relevant sound of a language is called a phoneme, and the distinctions between *pill* and *bill* or *debt* and *get* are referred to as phonemic. The difference between the initial sound of *kill* and *cow* or between the two *k* sounds of *key* and *ski* is not relevant in English and is called nonphonemic. You can demonstrate the difference between the *k* sounds of *key* and *ski* by taking a thin strip of paper and holding it in front of your lips. When you say *k-k-k*, the paper will flutter; when you say *sk-sk-sk*, it won't. This is because the *k* in *kill* has a slight puff of air accompanying it; this puff is not present when the *k* is preceded by another consonant in the word. The *k* sound of *kill* is pronounced a bit further forward in the mouth than that of *cow*. However, this difference is not relevant in English—there are no words differentiated by front versus back *k* or aspirated versus unaspirated *k* as there are words differentiated by *k* versus *p* or *g*. Incidentally, although the *k* sounds of *kill, skill, cow,* and *scow* all differ from one another, the differences are automatic for any English speaker.

Although we are concerned only with English, it is important to note that sounds are phonemic or nonphonemic only as they relate to specific languages. In Hindi, for example, the distinction between the *k* in *ski* and in *key* would be relevant; in Arabic, the difference between the *k* in *key* and that in *cow* is of importance. (The further-back *k* sound is the one frequently transcribed as a *q* in Arabic place names, for example, *Iraq* or *Aqaba*.)

Since referring to sounds as "the *k* in *key*" or "the initial sound of *key*" is rather cumbersome, symbols are usually used to specify the sound meant. In this symbolism, phonemes are enclosed in slash marks, / /, and phonetic elements are enclosed in square brackets, [ ]. Most consonants are represented by their alphabetic symbols. Thus, in English we have the following set of consonants:

Symbol	Initial Occurrence	Final Occurrence
/p/	paste	lap, rope
/b/	baste	lab, robe
/t/	tot	feet
/d/	dot	feed
/k/	kale	lack
/g/	gale	lag
/f/	ferry	knife
/v/	very	knive
/m/	moon	loom
/n/	noon	loon
/ŋ/	---[1]	long
/r/	rope	poor
/l/	lope	pool
/w/	wet	---[2]
/y/	yet	---[2]
/θ/	thigh	bath
/ð/	thy	bathe
/č/	cheap	catch
/ǰ/	jeep	cadge
/s/	sow	bass
/š/	show	bash
/z/	zoo	close
/ž/	---[3]	rouge
/h/	hill	---[2]

We can now redraw our mouth and locate these consonants on it as regards place of articulation:

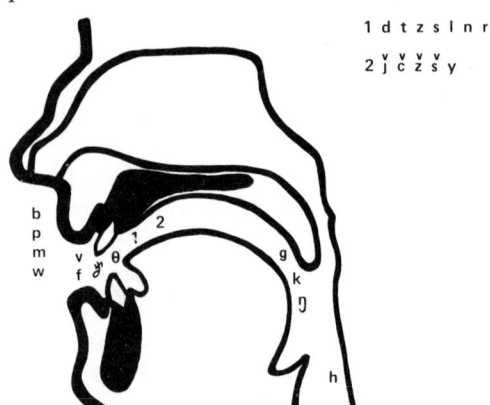

FIGURE 1-2. English Consonants: Place of Articulation.

[1] /ŋ/, called engma, never occurs at the beginning of a word in English.

[2] /w/, /y/, and /h/ never occur at the end of a syllable in English as consonants. They are frequently used to indicate parts of diphthongs (see the discussion of vowels below).

[3] /ž/ does not occur initially in English, except in a few foreign names, for example, *Zhukhov*.

Alternatively, we can label these sounds on a grid:

English Consonants: Place and Manner of Articulation

	Bilabial	Labio-dental	Dental	Alveolar	Alveo-palatal	Velar	Glottal
Stops							
Voiced	b			d		g	
Voiceless	p			t		k	
Affricates							
Voiced					ǰ		
Voiceless					č		
Fricatives							
Voiced		v	ð	z	ž		
Voiceless		f	θ	s	š		h
Resonants							
Lateral							
Voiced				l			
Nasal							
Voiced	m			n		ŋ	
Median							
Voiced	w			r	y		

There are a few more symbols with which you ought to be familiar, although they are not phonemic in English. The puff of air after an initial /p, t, k/ is known as aspiration. It is signified in phonetics by a small raised *h*, as [kʰ] for the initial sound of *cat* or *king* or [pʰ] for the initial sound of *pike*. The sound used in some dialects of British English and in New York City for the *tt* in *bottle* or *little* is called a glottal stop and is symbolized by a [ʔ] (a question mark without the dot). Finally, the *ts* of *cats* or *hats* is sometimes transcribed using [¢] (the cents sign). It occurs initially in English only in some pronunciations of *tse-tse fly* and *tsar* (or *czar*).

VOWELS

The principle of minimal pairs can be used to establish a set of vowels for English, just as it can be used for consonants. A series such as

| bit | bet | bat | beat | bait | bout |
| boat | boot | but | bought | bite | bot |

will establish the fact that there are twelve distinctive "vowels" that occur between /b/ and /t/ in English. If we try to refine our classification a bit more, we may notice that *bit* and *beat* appear to have something in common. That is, the beginning of the vowel sound of *beat* is like that of *bit.* When we compare *bet* and *bait,* we may note that here too the beginning of the vowel sound of the second word is like the vowel sound in the first. Moreover, there is something similar about the last part of the vowel sounds of *beat* and *bait*—and we can add the vowel of *bite* to this list also. Finally, we may note that the last parts of the vowel sounds of *bout, boat,* and *boot* have something in common.

Conventionally, we consider the vowel sounds of *bit, bet, bot, bat,* and *but* to be fundamental, while the vowel sounds of the other words have something added to them. We call this additional component a glide, and the resulting combination of sounds is termed a diphthong. Most linguists agree that English has two glides, /y/ and /w/, and many would add a third, /H/, to nine "basic" vowels. Theoretically, all the vowels could occur alone or with any of the three glides, making a total of thirty-six vowel sounds in English. However, no dialect makes use of more than half of these possibilities, and the following are sufficient to describe most varieties of American and British English:

/i/ bit   /iy/ beat
/e/ bet   /ey/ bait
/a/ bot   /ay/ bite   /aw/bout
/o/   /ow/ boat
/u/ book   /uw/ boot   /uH/ tour
/æ/ bat   /æy/ maid   /æH/ salve
/ə/ but
/ɨ/ childr*e*n
/ɔ/ cot (in New England)

æ is called ash (its name in Old English), or digraph, ə is called schwa, ɨ is called barred *i,* and ɔ is called open *o.* These vowels are frequently represented schematically on a trapezoid, the shape standing for the oral cavity. We refer to the lips as the front and the rear of the cavity as the back, and we describe the position of the tongue and the openness of the mouth by terms such as *high, mid, low,* and *open.* We can thus plot our "basic" vowels as follows:

	Front	Central	Back
High	i	ɨ	u
Mid	e	ə	o
Low	æ	a	ɔ

If we wish, we can also redraw these on our mouth diagram:

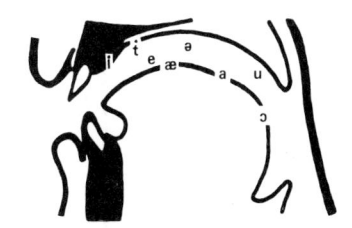

FIGURE 1-3. Vowel Locations.

SUPRASEGMENTALS

The sounds we think of as consonants, vowels, and glides or "semi-vowels," are known as segmental phonemes. Each can be thought of as a discrete piece of speech. However, there are other things relevant to a language's phonology. Among these are pitch, stress, and intonation. Such factors are referred to as suprasegmentals, things that occur on or above the segments themselves.

While /p/ plus /a/ can be pronounced in a variety of pitches or tones or with a variety of intonations, no pitch or tone or intonation can be pronounced without a segment "supporting" it.

In some languages, such as Chinese and Thai, tones also play a role; however, since tones do not yield a difference in meaning in English, we will not discuss them in detail. We will only mention intonation as relevant in marking the difference between questions and statements.

A suprasegmental known as juncture is of particular interest. Juncture is the result of several different phonological phenomena. One such phenomenon is referred to as pause. As you look at the following list,

giant's eyes   giant size
Mikey's   my keys
candlesticks   (the) candle sticks

you will notice that in each word or phrase there is a longer hiatus—a greater pause—in the item in the right-hand column than there is in the corresponding item in the left-hand column. The longer pause is called open juncture; it is frequently indicated by a plus sign (my + keys). Note that there is a similar pause in sentences such as

> Not every white house is the White House.

and

> Crows are black birds with black wings, whereas blackbirds have red wings.

FORM SYSTEMS: MORPHOLOGY

The study of the sounds of language is called phonology; the study of the forms of language is known as morphology. Just as we consider the phoneme to be the minimal relevant unit that distinguishes words in the sound system of a language, so we consider a morpheme to be the minimal meaningful unit of a language.

A morpheme is usually a sequence of phonemes, although it can be a single phoneme in length. Not every sequence of phonemes is a morpheme, however. */grib/ is not a morpheme in English; it lacks meaning. It is pronounceable, however, and might someday become a morpheme, just as *radar* and *Kodak* were added to the language. A sequence such as */pzkflsr/ could never become an English morpheme because it violates the possible structure of English words.

If we think of a morpheme as a minimal meaningful unit, then it cannot be further divided without destruction of its meaning. *Porch* is an English morpheme; if we further divide its phonemes, the fragments bear no discernible relation to the meaning of *porch*. Many English morphemes contain only one syllable: for example, *boy, chair, star, -ing, -ness, -ly, un-, pre-*. Others are polysyllables: *elephant, Saskatchewan, language*. Still others are less than one syllable, such as the *-s* of *hats*. Here both *hat* and *-s* are morphemes, for each carries meaning. Perhaps we should point out that many morphemes are not words: In a form such as *ungentlemanly*, there is a general buildup of forms—*un-* plus *gentlemanly; gentleman* plus *-ly; gentle* plus *man*. Note that this sort of analysis will not work with a form like *Mississippi*, for this word is monomorphemic—the name has nothing to do with *miss* nor *is* nor *sip* nor *pi*, although each is a morpheme in English.

MORPHOLOGICAL DEVICES

Just as phonemes embrace variants called allophones, morphemes have variants called allomorphs. Most morphemes (for example, *Alaska, -ing, semi-*) are invariant and do not depend on context or environment. Some, however, do vary. A good example of a morpheme with several different forms is the English plural, *-s*. This is realized as /-s/ in *hats*, as /-z/ in *heads*, and as /-ɨz/ in *bushes* and *roses*. Despite the variations, English speakers know that the forms are the same, and our spelling system aids in this identification. The rule is rather simple: /-ɨz/ occurs after words ending in /-s, -z, -š, -ž, -č,* and *-ǰ/* such as *hiss, rose, bush, garage, match,* and *ledge;* /-s/ occurs after all other voiceless sounds, such as those in *hip, rat, fork, cuff,* and *faith;* and /-z/ occurs after vowels and all other voiced consonants, such as the final sounds of *pie, shoe, cub, head, leg, stove, lathe, home, pin, ring, pole,* and *car*.

While this rule takes care of most of the plurals of English, it does not cover all of them. We are still left with *ox:oxen, sheep:sheep, child:children, mouse:mice, goose:geese, datum:data, index:indices,* and even *cow:kine* or *cow:cattle.* Although the *-s* plurals might be called morphologically conditioned, it is not possible to make a neat statement about all of these.

Morphology also includes all the phenomena to which traditional grammar gives the names declension and conjugation. English morphology includes such paradigms, despite their limited scope. The English noun, for example, has the paradigm

        book   books
        book's   books'

which is obviously not highly diversified. In the present tense, the English verb is inflected for the third person singular as follows:

I write   I jump
you write   you jump
he (she, it) writes   he (she, it) jumps
we write   we jump
you write   you jump
they write   they jump

The verb also differentiates the present from the past:

I jump   I jumped   I write   I wrote
you jump   you jumped   you write   you wrote
he jumps   he jumped   he writes   he wrote

Again, this is not a very diverse pattern. Classical Greek contains over six hundred forms of each verb. Sanskrit verbs have about a thousand forms.

Affixes are morphological devices that occur widely; they include morphemes such as *-ed, -ing, pre-,* and *un-*. When they are added to the beginning of a word, they are called prefixes; when they are added to the end of a word, they are called suffixes. There is a third type (which does not occur in English) in which the affix is inserted into the middle of another morpheme. This occurs in Latin, for example, in the present tense of *touch— ta-n-go,* ''I touch''—where the nasal infix does not occur in other forms of the verb (for example, *tetegi, tactus*). Infixation is a common device in many languages of the Pacific, for example, Samoan.

A type of morpheme that does play a major role in English is the replacive form, as in *sing:sang, goose:geese,* and *man:men,* where a portion of the word is actually replaced by something else. The extreme case of replacement is called a suppletive, where the entire form is replaced: *am:be:is:was, go:went.*

There are many other types of morphological devices, but we will not discuss them here.

SYNTAX

Traditionally, syntax deals with the arrangement of words into sentences. Within modern American linguistics, the grammar of a language is seen as something that "generates" or "enumerates" the sentences of a language by means of a set of rules. While we do not wish to expound even a small portion of the theory of transformational-generative grammar here, we will supply some background that may be useful both later on in this book and in reading other works that use the terminology.

If you were given a number of sentences such as

> John has a sailboat.
> Sarah broke the glass.
> The dog chased the squirrel.

and asked to divide them each into two parts, you might very well put *John, Sarah,* and *The dog* in one group and *has a sailboat, broke the glass,* and *chased the squirrel* in the other. You would then be dividing the sentences into their noun phrase (NP) and verb phrase (VP) components. The basic rule of transformational grammar is

$$S \rightarrow NP + VP$$

(read "Sentence is rewritten as noun phrase plus verb phrase").

This can also be written as

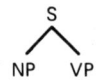

```
     S
    / \
   NP  VP
```

We might, in turn, note that *a sailboat, the glass,* and *the squirrel* have something in common and that they share something with the NPs we have already labeled. In fact, since we can turn the sentences around and make these elements subjects *(A sailboat is owned by John, The glass was broken by Sarah,* and *The squirrel was chased by the dog),* we might consider them NPs, too. Our tree would then look like the following:

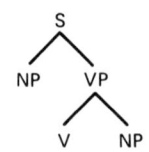

```
        S
       / \
      NP  VP
         / \
        V   NP
```

We have inserted V here, for *has, broke,* and *chased* are verbs in the ordinary sense of the word. However, we still have to account for several other things in our three sentences: *the, a,* and the past tense. Before we draw another tree, let us note that we can also have sentences such as

>That blue boat sailed to Block Island.

and

>John owns this blue boat.

In other words, we must try to account for demonstratives (*this* or *that*) and prepositional phrases *(to Block Island)* as well as adjectives *(blue)*.

Our more elaborate trees would look like the following:

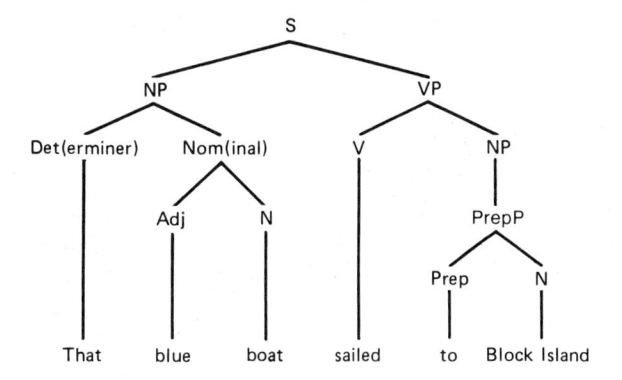

```
                      S
                    /   \
                  NP     VP
                 /  \   /  \
            Det   Nom  V    NP
           (erminer) / \    |
                   Adj  N   PrepP
                                 / \
                              Prep  N
            That  blue  boat sailed to Block Island
```

and

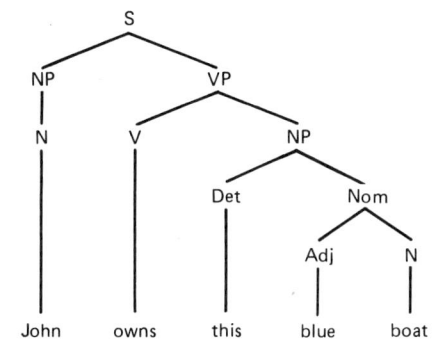

```
              S
            /   \
          NP     VP
          |    /   \
          N   V     NP
                   /  \
                 Det   Nom
                       / \
                     Adj  N
         John  owns this blue boat
```

But let us look at two other sentences:

>The glass was broken by Sarah.
>Was the glass broken by Sarah?

Again, it is clear that these two sentences are related in some way and also that they are related to

>Sarah broke the glass.
>Did Sarah break the glass?

and

>Break the glass, Sarah!

Modern linguistic theory relates these sentences to one another through a set of transformations. The theory postulates, for example, a passive transformation that derives *The glass was broken by Sarah* from *Sarah broke the glass,* effectively making the object NP of the active sentence into the subject NP of the passive sentence, switching the active subject NP and the passive object NP, adding a form of *be* and a preposition, *by,* and changing the form of the verb. The trees involved would be of the following types:

ACTIVE

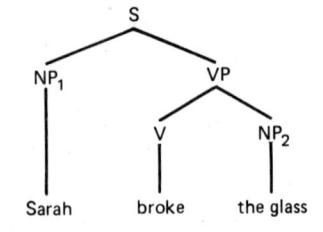

```
          S
         / \
      NP₁   VP
       |    / \
     Sarah V   NP₂
           |    |
         broke the glass
```

PASSIVE

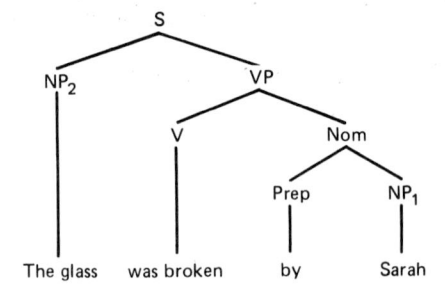

```
              S
             / \
          NP₂   VP
           |    / \
       The glass V   Nom
                 |    / \
             was broken Prep NP₁
                        |    |
                        by  Sarah
```

Was the glass broken by Sarah? would involve applying a question transformation to the passive sentence, moving the *be* form to the front of the sentence to produce what is known as a yes/no question. The general notion of the theory of transformations is that they can add things (such as *be* and *by*), rearrange things (such as NP₁ and NP₂ in these sentences), and delete things. We have not yet considered deletions.

Another notion is that forms such as pronouns, which stand for other word classes, do not exist in the "base" of the tree; rather, they arise as a result of transformations. Thus, if we had a sentence such as

> Fred washed himself.

we would postulate an underlying form

> Fred washed Fred.

in which the second *Fred* is deleted and the reflexive pronoun is put in its place. Similarly,

> The children danced and played.

would be derived from the conjoining of two sentences:

> The children danced.

and

> The children played.

Here, the common NPs cause one to be deleted leaving only a VP to be added to the first sentence. Furthermore, identical VPs can be deleted and the results conjoined:

> Fred flew to Seattle.

and

> Agnes flew to Seattle.

conjoin to yield

> Fred and Agnes flew to Seattle.

There are many other aspects of transformational grammar, but we intend to use only a few of these notions later in the book. Therefore, we present here only a highly simplified presentation of the theory.

SEMANTICS

It must be obvious that the really important thing about language is that it means something. The study of linguistic meaning is called semantics. As a formal study, semantics is a relatively young science, and there are only a few things about it that can be said with any certainty. In the next chapter, we will discuss the growth of word meaning in the developing child, but we will avoid a lengthy discussion of theories of meaning here.

18   Looking at Language

The really important thing about language is that it means something. Even this child's finger puppets have language. (*Photo by Linda Lungren*)

LANGUAGE USE

Basically, we use language for only a few purposes:

>   To request (or ask or inquire)
>   To command
>   To inform

There are a few types of utterance that do not fall into these categories, and we will return to them shortly.

Requests are basically questions. *How are you? Is it raining? What is the height of Mt. Everest?* and *Do you know how to calculate the volume of a sphere?* are examples of requests for different kinds of information.

Commands generally take the form of imperatives: *Get out!* and *Set the table!* are examples of such sentences. However, it is important to recognize that many things that appear to be imperatives are not really commands. *Drop dead!* is a good example. It means "no"; it is not an order to expire.

Most of what we say is intended to inform our hearers of something. *I'm fine, No, it's not raining,* and *Four-thirds pi r cubed* are examples of such statements. So too are sentences such as "I have a headache" or "Cubs 3, Astros 7."

Further, the meanings of utterances are not the sum of their parts; the meaning of a sentence is not the additive meaning of the individual words in the sentence. In an exchange such as

>What's new?
>My dog got hit by a car.
>Wonderful.

The last remark does not indicate pleasure. In

>What's new?
>I won $136 in a bingo game last night.
>Wonderful.

it does. Much of the import of an utterance such as "Wonderful" is conveyed by intonation; some is conveyed by context. A teenager telling a friend

>When I graduate, I'm going to play for the Yankees.

and being told

>Yeah, yeah.

in response, is being greeted by disbelief, not by affirmation, even though the customary meaning of "Yeah" is affirmative.

The study of meaning can be looked at either from the formal or practical standpoint. Some of the most interesting work on the everyday uses of language has been done by Dwight Bolinger, and several of his works are listed under Further Readings.

EXERCISES

1. List words to establish that the following are phonemes of English. Attempt to use the sounds both initially and finally. For example: for [č] and [ǰ]: *choke:joke; catch:cadge;* for [s] and [z]: *sip:zip; bus:buzz.*
2. How many morphemes are there in each of the following?
   a. Saskatchewan
   b. hats
   c. illegible
   d. undistinguished
   e. beginning
   f. avalanche

3. The prefix *in-* (not) has a number of allomorphs in English: Some examples are *ineligible, incredible, indelible, impossible, irreligious,* and *illegible.* Can you think of others? What is the determining factor as to which allomorph is used?
4. List the NPs in each of the following:
    a. The white house on the hill is on fire.
    b. Sam lost his new green jacket.
    c. Gerbils are rodents.
    d. "Peanuts" is my favorite cartoon character.
    e. Happy families are all alike, but each unhappy family is unhappy in its own way.

FURTHER READINGS

BOLINGER, D. A. *Aspects of Language,* 2nd ed. New York: Harcourt Brace Jovanovich, 1975. One of the best introductions to the field of linguistics.

BOLINGER, D. A. *Language—The Loaded Weapon.* London & New York: Longman, 1980. An excellent essay on the use and misuse of language.

BOLINGER, D. A. *Meaning and Form.* London & New York: Longman, 1977. A valuable set of insights into the nature of the lexicon and discourse construction with great attention to actual usage.

FROMKIN, V. A., and RODMAN, R. *Introduction to Language,* 2nd ed. New York: Holt, Rinehart & Winston, 1978. Probably the best and most straightforward "survey" of linguistics.

JESPERSEN, O. *Essentials of English Grammar,* 1933. Reprint: University of Alabama Press, 1963. Although nearly half a century old, this may be the finest statement on the whole of English syntax.

LANGENDOEN, D. T. *Essentials of English Grammar.* New York: Holt, Rinehart & Winston, 1970. An excellent introduction to modern syntactic theory for the nonspecialist.

SCHANE, S. A. *Generative Phonology.* Englewood Cliffs; N. J.: Prentice-Hall, 1973. A good, brief introduction to modern phonological theory.

SOMMERSTEIN, A. H. *Modern Phonology.* Baltimore: University Park Press, 1977. An extensive investigation of modern phonological theory.

*Talkative, anxious
Man can picture the Absent
and Non-Existent.*

—*W.H. Auden*

2 LANGUAGE DEVELOPMENT

Over the course of the child's first few years, talking and walking are perhaps the greatest milestones. This chapter traces the child's linguistic development from nonverbal behavior, through babbling and one-word utterances, to articulate speech.

Over the course of the child's first few years, talking and walking are perhaps the greatest milestones. (*Photo by Linda Lungren*)

LEARNING TO TALK

People talk.
Infants don't talk.
Children learn to talk.

These three simple sentences encompass the scope of the field generally known as developmental psycholinguistics, or first-language acquisition. No infant is born talking, yet every child—unless grossly abnormal in some psychological, physiological, or neurological way—acquires the language around him or her in a relatively short space of time.

While the general lines of the child's language development are known, the mechanisms involved are far from clear. In this section, we will discuss the child's language development up to the middle school years.

HISTORICAL OVERVIEW

St. Augustine (354–430 A.D.) appears to have been the first author to consider the child's acquisition of speech. He believed that children acquire language without direct instruction and by means of an inborn, God-given capacity. This was not a popular view of learning and language acquisition for most of the next fifteen hundred years. Still, the concept of an innate and universal mechanism possessed by all humans that enabled them to acquire speech flourished in, for example, the philosophical works of Descartes and his followers (from the late seventeenth century on). However, Descartes's belief in an innate language capacity did not gain currency among developmental psychologists and linguists until recently.

Yet, even a century ago people were interested to learn what route the child followed in acquiring speech. There are interesting articles on the subject by Charles Darwin and Hippolyte Taine in the philosophical journal *Mind* in 1877; and perceptive insights can be found in the works of Preyer (1889) and Stern and Stern (1928). There have been many works on the evolutionary nature of child development, on "genetic epistemology" (Piaget), on the problems of "deviant" populations, on the language of the deaf, and on the problems of those who lost the power of speech through psychological or physiological injury. We will not involve ourselves with these questions, but will look only at the basic question of normal child language acquisition.

While many authors organize work on language acquisition into sections on phonology, morphology, syntax, and semantics, we would like to look at the child at various stages. For this reason, we will discuss syntax several times—dealing with both early and later developments—for it is clear that a child is involved with learning the sounds, the forms, and the meanings of language simultaneously, not attacking each aspect of language one after the other.

MATURATIONAL PROCESSES

From physiological research, we know that the human infant is born with both an immature musculature and an immature nervous system. However, the central nervous system (the brain and the spinal cord) is more mature than the peripheral nervous system (both the sensory system and the nerves that control voluntary movement). As time goes on, the infant learns to control its muscles, and with the maturing of its nervous system it becomes more and more capable of discriminating sounds, shapes, and colors. There has been much research on the developmental nature of the infant's sensory abilities; this—together with observation—enables us to suggest a schedule of times at which certain types of gross linguistic performance occur:

Chronological Stages of Verbal Output

Age	Type of Vocalization
Birth	crying
1–2 months	cooing as well as crying
3–6 months	babbling as well as cooing and crying
9–14 months	first (single) words
18–24 months	first "sentences"
3–4 years	most simple syntactic structures
4–8 years	most speech sounds correctly articulated
9–11 years	most semantic (meaning) distinctions established

We can conclude that at birth the infant is incompletely equipped to perceive and produce speech and that the newborn infant does not produce articulated sounds. However, there is quite a range in time as regards when each stage occurs in the infant's life, although the stages appear in the same order in every child.

Try to imagine the process that is occurring. Here is a newborn infant, immature neurologically and physiologically, exposed to a vast variety of auditory, visual, and tactile stimuli. In a relatively short time, the infant learns to identify his or her care-giver's voice (mother, father, nursemaid, grandparent, and so on) and to distinguish human noises from other environmental noises. The infant also learns to recognize faces, and to dis-

Even the immature brain is capable of taking the verbal stimuli of its environment, analyzing them in some way, and constructing a "grammar" suitable to decoding and encoding in the environmental language. (*Photo by Linda Lungren*)

tinguish between one human voice and another. Soon the infant begins to produce obviously human noises, and in a short time he or she is able to comprehend many utterances and even to produce a few. This is true of every "normal" human infant, regardless of the culture to which it is born. Children brought up in German, Korean, or Swahili environments learn to produce the sounds of those languages, no matter what their ethnic background. Further, children in every known language community achieve the stages in the table at about the same age and in the same order.

Although no two human beings are identical, all have a great many features in common. Thus, just as not all birds or all fish can interbreed, so too not all higher apes can interbreed. However, all humans—whatever their color or stature—can interbreed. A consequence of this phenomenon seems to be that human brains (and other organs) are quite similar to one another and are capable of performing the same functions. American children are not born better-attuned to learning American English than, say, Spanish; nor are Thai children better-attuned to learning Thai. The human brain, even the immature brain, is capable of taking the verbal stimuli of its environment, analyzing it in some way, and constructing a "grammar" suitable to decoding verbal input (speech) and encoding suitable outputs (speech) in the environmental language.

It must be pointed out, however, that an infant's first communicative acts are not speech or language; the infant communicates hunger, discomfort, and other internal states quite effectively long before the advent of babbling, much less speech. Researchers in the area of nonverbal communication and of mother-child interactions have shown quite convincingly that infants and their care-givers communicate quite a bit by contact, mutual gaze, and attitude (facial expression and posture).

If we were to think of the child as being immersed in the sea of words and other noises each of us confronts daily, we might well wonder just how the infant sorts out enough to make a sensible analysis of the data. The answer is quite simple: The infant is not confronted by a flood of language. Most speech addressed to infants is reduced in complexity, trivial in vocabulary, and spoken more slowly than speech between adults. We use a special language, called "baby talk register," in talking to infants and even to older children. (Other "registers" are discussed in the chapter on dialects.) It was previously thought that a great deal of what the child must learn is not immediately obvious from the stream of speech to which he or she is subjected. It now appears that this stream of speech is extensively reduced in several ways and that the child thus has much less to sort through.

Despite the preceding, we must admit that each infant is still confronted by a formidable task: developing a coherent verbal communicative ability. We must also recognize that almost every infant is capable of this task.

COMMUNICATIVE BEHAVIOR

At birth, infants can eat, sleep, excrete, and cry. They cannot see very well. Within the first month of life, they "learn" how to see; begin to recognize familiar faces, objects, and voices; and modulate their cries into several different kinds (most mothers have no difficulty in distinguishing between "I am awake and I want attention" and a cry indicating true distress or illness). This is the beginning of human communication and goes along with playing "peek-a-boo" on the diapering table. But this phase does not last long. Soon the infant is able to coo and chuckle as well as cry and to distinguish mother's voice from other voices. Most children turn their heads toward the familiar voice by the time they are two months old.

Over the next few months, children begin making all kinds of verbal noises, but they have no recognizable words at this stage, which is referred to as the babbling stage. Although a number of scholars (beginning with Allport in 1924) have proposed that babbling is a "bridge" to communicative speech, there is no evidence of a continuity between babbling and speech. In fact, there may be a sharp discontinuity at both ends of the babbling phase. Whatever role babbling plays, it is far behind the scenes.

FIRST WORDS AND THE GROWTH OF VOCABULARY

Between the ages of nine and fourteen months, the infant has been lying in its crib and crawling on the floor and has been wheeled and carried about while being subjected to a great deal of (reduced) verbal stimuli and other environmental noise. For the last part of this first year of life, the child has attempted to make noises of his or her own that relate, egocentrically, to her or his wants or needs. Finally, with a still-immature neurological system and imperfect muscular control, the first words are produced, much to the delight of parents and grandparents.

It has been pointed out that *mama, papa, dada,* and so on, are frequent first words. Others are *byebye* and *dawdy* or *gawgy*. For some children, the last two mean "daddy" or "doggie." In terms of phonological structure, all these utterances have two syllables, and each syllable has a C(onsonant) V(owel) shape, with the same consonant in both syllables. In fact, most early words have this CVCV shape. Only after several more months do "closed" syllables—those ending in a consonant—appear. At first, too, all these words have a wide range of meaning. First words such as *mama* or *dada* frequently refer to any human or any supplier of X as well as meaning "Come here" or "I'm hungry." It is only with a growing vocabulary that the child differentiates more and more finely the objects and activities of the world.

One child, for example, at about eighteen months of age, may have /gʌki/, *duck,* for any bird; /fis/ for anything in the water; and /gawgi/, *doggie,* for any four-legged animal. This would mean that crabs and lobsters are /fis/ and that a cat or a squirrel is a /gawgi/. But within a few months, each of these classes becomes multiply subdivided (the child acquires *cow* and *horsie* and *kitty* as well as retaining *doggie,* for example). It is of great importance to note that adults' use of the baby talk register is full of CVCV constructions—*dollie, daddy, mommy, goody*—as are nicknames (*Betty, Billy, Katie, Johnny, Sammy, Sally*).

Most first words are nouns or personal names; they are used to indicate familiar or desired objects in the child's environment: *juice, milk, mommy, car, fish,* and so on. Other words may be verbs, for example, *go, pick up, ride*. A very few may be prepositions such as *up* or *down* or quantifiers such as *more*. However, most early words are nominals (about 60 percent of the first fifty to sixty words) and most of the remainder are verbs. There are many content words in the child's vocabulary and very few function words.

> Four legs... bigger than cats... friendly... wet nose... nice doggy! nice doggy!

TELEGRAPHIC SPEECH AND PIVOT GRAMMAR

The child produces first words somewhere between nine and fourteen months of age; within six months of producing the first word, the inventory grows to fifty items or more. At this time, when the vocabulary is of the magnitude of fifty to sixty words, most children begin putting words together. A large number of these early combinations are of a form that is usually called telegraphic: that is, they omit articles, prepositions, and auxiliary verbs. Samples of such utterances are

> Two boot.
> Hear tractor.
> See truck mommy.
> There go one.
> Put truck window.
> Adam make tower.

It has been suggested that children use such forms for precisely the same reason that adults use "telegraphese": to economize. The adult wishes to save money and therefore eliminates the items considered unnecessary to the message as a whole. The child needs to economize because of limitations in vocabulary and memory (not in dollars). Yet the results are very much the same. As vocabularies grow, children change the ways in which they put their words together.

Soon after their vocabularies reach the "critical" size of fifty or so items, children begin using some of the words as pivots. That is, some of the words are fixed points to which other ("open") words may be attached. We often find utterances such as the following:

byebye daddy
byebye mommy
byebye truck
byebye birdie
byebye bottle
byebye banana
byebye blocks

or

allgone banana
allgone milk
allgone taxi
allgone daddy
allgone bedtime
allgone candy

Such utterances seem to indicate that the child has divided up the vocabulary into object words and function words, or something of that nature. Presumably, it is these divisions that later give rise to the truly functional divisions we think of as word classes (nouns, verbs, adjectives, conjunctions, and so on).

Slobin has shown that such pivot structures occur in a variety of languages, including Russian and German. In other words, we are considering something that children do in acquiring articulate speech, not something that is confined to children acquiring American English.

In the three sets of utterances listed above, we have used standard spellings for the child's words. It must be understood, however, that the child's pronunciation is far from the adult version. In fact, the child only achieves a good approximation of adult pronunciation at nine or ten years of age. Between one and ten years of age, the child produces comprehensible utterances that are seriously deficient in phonology, syntax, vocabulary, and semantics (or meaning). Yet, these utterances still convey intentions to parents, teachers, and peers. The child, with help, reduces the richness of language, yet retains certain basics to guarantee a reasonable amount of intelligibility. The very young child, with a limited vocabulary, small phonetic inventory, and telegraphic approach to syntax is, in fact, frequently unintelligible. Each of us has witnessed a scene where a parent is trying to guess what it is a teary child desires: "Do you want a drink? Your doggie? Your doll?" This occurs because the small child's speech has a great many possible meanings packed into each sequence of sounds.

The pivot phase is transient. Some children appear hardly to use these forms; others use them for several months. In any event, the class of pivots soon begins to break down; that is, the words the child has used as pivots are soon reanalyzed into other classes. First articles (such as *the* and *a*) and demonstratives (such as *this* and *that*) are separated out. Subsequently, adjectives, possessives, and other words (such as *one*, *more*, and *all*, which might be called quantifiers) become separate word classes. This might be represented in a tree diagram in the following way:

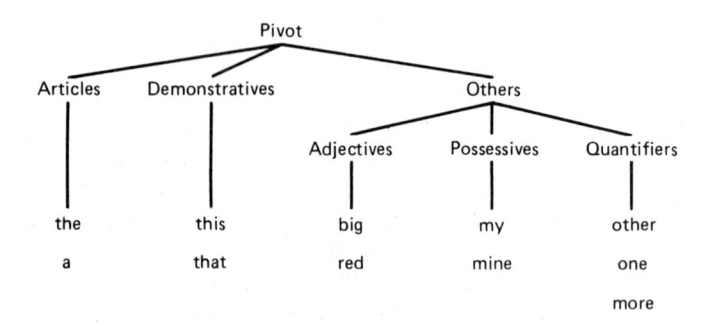

```
                         Pivot
          ┌────────────────┼────────────────┐
      Articles      Demonstratives        Others
         │                │         ┌───────┼────────┐
         │                │     Adjectives Possessives Quantifiers
         │                │         │         │         │
        the             this       big        my       other
         a              that       red       mine       one
                                                       more
```

EARLY SYNTACTIC DEVELOPMENT

Roger Brown and his co-workers at Harvard University have studied the development of the child's language on the basis of length of utterances. Stage I is the period during which a child's utterances have an average length of more than one morpheme, but less than two (this measure is referred to as the "mean length of utterance," or MLU). The relationship between linguistic stage and MLU is shown in the following lists:

MLU	Stage
to 1.75	pre-I
1.75 – 2.25	I
2.25 – 2.75	II
2.75 – 3.5	III
3.5 – 4.0	IV
over 4.0	V

This does not mean that the Stage I child uses only one- and two-word sentences. On the contrary, many Stage I children use utterances of up to seven morphemes in length. But we are talking about mean length, the average length of the child's utterances. Brown has shown that while children vary enormously in their speech development, and thus in what they know and don't know at a given age, their abilities are fairly uniform at a given MLU. In other words, while children of the same age may represent a variety of linguistic levels, children with the same MLU appear to have the same grammatical attainments.

Until the MLU passes 1.50, the utterances appear to be confined to what are known as two-term relations on the semantic level: agent-action, such as *daddy hit;* action-object, such as *hit ball;* and experiencer-state, such as *I hear.* But once the MLU passes 1.50, we begin to hear three-term relations: agent-action-object, such as *mommy throw ball;* and action-object-locative, such as *put ball here.*

There are two types of development involved here. The first is what might be thought of as the gluing together of earlier two-term relations: *daddy throw* plus *throw ball* equals *daddy throw ball.* The second involves the expansion of an earlier two-term relation: *sit chair* (action-locative) becomes *sit daddy chair* (action-possessive-locative).

With Stage II, the child begins to acquire both the inflectional system of the language and the syntactic system.

MORPHOLOGICAL DEVELOPMENT

We will use three studies originating from Roger Brown's group at Harvard to illustrate our discussion of the child's acquisition of morphology.

In one of the earliest experiments involving the child's learning of English morphology, Jean Berko Gleason (1958) showed children a picture of a cartoon figure and assigned it the nonsense name *wug,* saying "This is a wug." She then told the child that another one had come along and that there were now two of them. She showed a picture and said: "Now there are two _____," expecting the child to supply the plural *wugs* /wəgz/. She carefully set up nonsense words so that all three phonological realizations of the English plural morpheme (/-s/ as in *cats* /-z/ as in *dogs,* and /-ɨz/ as in roses) were included. Berko Gleason found that children in the age range between four and seven years made 67 percent errors with the /-ɨz/ forms, but only 25 percent errors with the /-z/ forms. She also determined that the children did have /-ɨz/ forms in their vocabularies, for 91 percent of the children had the correct plural for *glass.* This shows that while the children were acquiring the appropriate plural forms for English, they had not completely analyzed and incorporated forms that actually existed in their grammars. In linguistic terms, while a word such as *glasses* existed as a frozen form, it was not "productive" in the children's language.

In another study, Courtney Cazden (1968) examined the acquisition of the plural and possessive inflections on nouns and the present progressive, the regular past, and the present indicative inflections on verbs in three children. She found that two of the children used plurals before possessives, while the third achieved them at the same time. Cazden also found that all three children used plurals within noun phrases (as in *some crayons*) much more accurately than they did across noun-phrase boundaries (as in *those my crayons*). With the possessive, all three children used the inflection less reliably in everyday forms (for example, *that's daddy's hat*) than in elliptic forms in which the final noun is deleted (for example, *that's daddy's*).

The data concerning the possessive are of great interest when compared with information on children's use of English plurals. Just as children were less reliable in using the possessive when the second noun was present, so too were they less reliable in using the plural markers when there was a numeral present (*some boys* but *two cow*). In other words, with both the plural and the possessive forms, children tended to pay less attention to the production of the correct (or appropriate) inflection if there was information elsewhere in the phrase or sentence that made the inflection redundant. In doing this, the children showed great economy in using their limited resources.

As regards verb inflections, Cazden's study showed that the present progressive (the *-ing* form) was achieved satisfactorily between Stage II and Stage III. By Stage V, one of the children was using both the regular past and the present indicative with 90 percent efficiency. Of the other two children, one had achieved the past and one the present indicative at this stage. The following table illustrates Cazden's comparison of inflections and stages:

Acquisition of Inflection on the Basis of MLU

			Stage		
	I	II	III	IV	V
Eve*	—	—	*-ing*	Plural Poss. Past	77% Present indicative 18% Auxiliaries
Adam	—	—	*-ing* Plural	—	Poss. Present indicative 91% Past 23% Auxiliaries
Sarah	—	Plural	*-ing*	Poss. Past Present indicative	79% Auxiliaries

*These were not the real names of the children.

Ursula Bellugi, working with the same children as Cazden, found that while one child used auxiliary verbs systematically before Stage IV, the other two children did not achieve this usage until Stage IV. Only one child used tag questions (for example, "You have it, don't you?" or "You can do it, can't you?") by Stage V. None of the children used function words (articles, prepositions) more than approximately 85 percent of the time, even in Stage V.

From these investigations (and similar ones), several things become clear about the acquisition of English morphology: First, there appears to be a definite order of acquisition (plurals precede possessives; *-ing* precedes past; past precedes present indicative); and second, while the time of onset—in terms of MLU or Stage—is clear, the inflections and inflectional categories are used quite unreliably for a while.

SYNTAX

Looking at syntax in the child is difficult for what may seem a strange reason: Since everything the child utters must be assumed to have a syntax, an arrangement of elements in time and space that relates to the things spoken about in a logical way, we are overwhelmed by material. In the following pages, we present a selected number of topics in developmental syntax. We will discuss them briefly, but will make no attempt at formulating a comprehensive syntax.

The three areas we will look at are negation, questions, and relative clauses.

Negation

Klima and Bellugi, working with the same three "Harvard" children we mentioned earlier (Adam, Eve, and Sarah), analyzed the early development of some syntactic elements.

In Stage I, they found utterances such as

> More . . . no.
> No sit there.
> No play that.
> No fall!
> No heavy.
> No want stand head.
> No Mom sharpen it.

They noted that at this point "there are no negatives within the utterances, nor are there auxiliary verbs. The element which signals negation is *no . . .*, and this element either precedes or follows the rest of the utterance."

In Stage II, Klima and Bellugi found the following:

> I can't catch you.
> I can't see you.
> We can't talk.
> I don't want it.
> I don't like him.
> No... Rusty hat.
> Book say no.
> Touch the snow no.
> Don't leave me.
> That no fish school.
> That no mommy.
> There no squirrels.
> He no bite you.
> I no want envelope.
> I no taste them.

In these utterances, while there are obvious "hangovers" from the older system of either prefixing or postposing the negative marker *(no)*, there is a real tendency to put the negative between the NP and the VP of the utterance. In the child's language, though, since items such as "fish school," "mommy," or "squirrels" are not what we would normally think of as VPs, we might be better off thinking of these sentences as being composed of a topic and a comment, or a subject and a complement. In any event, the negative marker appears between these two parts of the utterance. Finally, in this stage of development the children use two notable auxiliary verbs, each with an attached negative: *can't* and *don't*.

In Stage III, the child's use of the negative is closer to the adult standard. Klima and Bellugi reported the following:

> Paul can't have one.
> I can't see it.
> I didn't did it.
> I don't want cover on it.
> You don't want some supper.
> You didn't caught me.
> I didn't see something.
> I gave him some so he won't cry.
> Donna won't let go.

Here, the negative auxiliaries are no longer limited to *can't* and *don't*. Further, the auxiliary verbs appear in sentences unattached to the negatives, so that they may be considered as separate elements. As Klima and Bellugi note,

> Indeterminates now start appearing in the children's speech, in affirmative utterances such as *I want some supper* or *I see something.* The children's negative sentences have the form *I don't want some supper* and *I didn't see something,*

rather than the adult, 'I don't want any supper' or 'I didn't see anything.' The negative versions are clearly not imitations of adult sentences, and indicate that the complex relationships of negative and indefinite has not yet been established.

From this, we can see that what the child does first is to attach *no* or *not* to two or three word utterances. At the next stage, the child begins to form auxiliary verbs with attached negatives, and generally inserts the negative between the subject of the utterance and the complement of the "sentence." In this stage, however, remnants of the earlier stage may still be found. In Stage III, the use of auxiliaries is extended further. The use of the emphatic *"No"* at the beginning of sentences (parallel to the negative attached to a verb in the sentence) also comes at this time, but the proper sorting out of the indeterminate elements in sentences and appropriate use of *some/any* has not yet occurred.

It may be worth remarking here that the range of ages in other experiments where children used the negative with *do* was two years and three months to two years and eleven months; for negative with *be*, it was two years and four months to three years and one month. As a result, we can state that the normal child acquires the use of negative plus auxiliary during the third year of life.

Questions

English has two ways of forming questions: One way is to begin the sentence with a verb; the other is to begin a sentence with a *Wh*-word: *who, what, where, when, why, which, whose,* and so on. The first type of question is frequently called a yes/no question, for "yes" and "no" are the typical answers to these verb-initial questions. For example:

> Is the coffee ready?
> Do you like Chinese food?
> Will you marry me?
> Have I missed the train?
> Can you help me with this?

On the other hand, *Wh*-questions are called information questions, because they typically request substantive information:

> What sort of food do you like to eat?
> When will the coffee be ready?
> When does the train leave?

When children learn to ask questions, they do so first by incorporating the rising intonation typical of English questions into the same sentences they use for statements and demands. In one study, of 71 questions, 64 (just over 90 percent) were marked solely by intonation, while only 7 (just under 10 percent) contained verb inversion. But somewhat later, when the children were two years and five months old, of 157 questions, 86 (nearly 55 percent) were marked by intonation and 71 (just over 45 percent) were verb inversions. At three years and one month, there were 43 percent intonation-marked questions (69 of 162). Still later (age range three years and four months to three years and eight months), of 311 questions recorded, over 81 percent had verb inversions (252 of 311). All the children also had two *Wh*-words, *what* and *where,* but these appear to have been rigid forms, not part of the question-making system.

The Klima and Bellugi data yield further information on the acquisition and development of interrogative structures in English. At Stage I, the children used questions such as the following:

> Mommy eggnog?
> See hole?
> I ride train?
> Sit chair?
> Ball go?

The first group are marked merely by intonation. The *Wh*-questions, as Klima and Bellugi point out, "only superficially resemble those questions in which the object of a verb has been questioned and preposed, and they [the children] do not understand this construction when they hear it." The last point is of some importance, for Klima and Bellugi were careful to analyze what the children comprehended as well as what they produced. Thus, exchanges such as

> What did you hit?
> Hit.

and

> What did you do?
> Head.

show that the child neither comprehends this kind of interrogative nor is able to produce it.

At Stage II, interrogatives such as the following occurred:

> See my doggie?
> That black too?
> You want eat?
> I have it?
> Where my mitten?
> Where me sleep?

Here we can see that the use of pronouns, articles, and modifiers is much more frequent than it was earlier. Some inflections are now present (plurals and the *-ing* forms), but there are only two negative auxiliaries (*don't* and *can't*) and no indefinite or indeterminate forms. However, Klima and Bellugi note that by this stage the child has "appropriate answers to most questions. The responses reflect that the child understands that the object of a verb or preposition is being questioned."

Some questions recorded in Stage III include:

> Does the kitty stand up?
> Does lions walk?
> Is Mommy talking to Robin's grandmother?
> Did I see that in my book?
> Oh, did I caught it?
> Will you help me?

Here, yes/no questions occur for the first time, and the auxiliary *do* takes on a special function in inverted questions and in negatives. The system is now similar in many ways to the adult system, although auxiliaries are still not inverted in questions with *Wh*-words, nor is *do* present in such questions.

Even here, with a small number of examples and a very brief exposition, you can see what is happening in the child's language. As with negatives, first the entire sentence is questioned, so that a *Wh*-word is simply affixed to a declarative sentence. When they do emerge, auxiliaries are always associated with negatives such as *can't* or *don't*. However, exchanges in Stage II such as

> What d'you need?
> Need some chocolate.

and

> Who are you peeking at?
> Peeking at Ursula.

show that the child's comprehension of full forms (not present in Stage I) is now adequate, even though such forms are not used actively. The child's comprehension precedes the child's performance here, as in so many things.

Relative Clauses

The last area of syntax we wish to look at is that of relative clauses. It must be recognized that most relative clauses are introduced by the same *Wh*-words used in asking questions. Among the eight words reported by Wick Miller as those used to introduce relative clauses by the children studied, only *that* is not a *Wh*-word. Furthermore, *what, where, when,* and *that* accounted for 80 percent (121 of 151) of the children's recorded samples. *When* was the only word used more frequently and earlier as a relative-clause marker than as an interrogative.

Sentences such as:

> What daddy do when get home?

apparently occur before

> When we go visit grandma?

Miller notes that while one might expect children to apply question inversion to relative clauses, since interrogatives are much more common, the children he investigated did not do so.

Miller's work would lead us to believe that children acquire proficiency with relative clauses before they enter elementary school. The later work of Carol Chomsky demonstrates that many children do not have full comprehension of relative clauses until quite late. We will come back to this after a brief digression.

COMPREHENSION AND PERFORMANCE

In most cases, it appears obvious that the child understands much more than he or she produces. Just how much more the child understands is, unfortunately, unclear; yet, it is fairly safe to assert that comprehension precedes production.

That the above is true is apparent from the child's (appropriate) responses to the questions or commands of adults, even when the child is in Stage I or Stage II. However, it is equally apparent that adults simplify both their vocabulary and their syntax when addressing young children, and that when more difficult vocabulary items are used, children do not act appropriately.

Several years ago, one of the authors (PHS) was at an afternoon party at a colleague's home. His older daughter was romping on the living room furniture. When the other guests began to arrive, her father said, "Alice, stop being obstreperous and go play outside."

The child went into the back yard but came back, crying, in about fifteen minutes. When asked what was wrong, she replied, "The swing was 'streperous and knocked me down."

From this, it is obvious that all the child understood of her father's remark was "You are behaving improperly. Go outside." The meaning of *obstreperous* was irrelevant; to her, it was "not doing what you're supposed to" or "being bad" or "behaving improperly." Thus, when she fell off the swing, the swing was not performing as it ought; it was "being bad" or "behaving improperly." Alice was performing without (full) comprehension—something that many of us do, sometimes with embarrassing results.

It can also be shown that, in general, children do not understand passive sentences; they tend to interpret the first noun of a sentence as the subject and the second as the object, unless this results in an interpretation that is nonsense in the child's cognitive world. Thus, a conversation such as

> "Do you see that dog?"
> "Uh-huh."
> "Daddy was bitten by that dog."

will be interpreted correctly, while

> Billy was kicked by Fred.

will be interpreted as *Billy kicked Fred*. The passive here is not "recognized" by the child. It was interpreted correctly in the earlier exchange because the notion that daddy bit that dog is not possible. Who kicked whom is an open question; in the child's world, Billy is just as likely to have been an aggressor as a victim.

There are many syntactic structures (just as there are vocabulary items) that the child does not comprehend; but there are also many that the child does not use, even though they are comprehended. On another level, each of us comprehends more than we produce: Our passive vocabularies are vastly larger than our active vocabularies.

The fact that a child does not produce plurals correctly does not mean that the difference between one and more-than-one is not understood; nor does the child without the past tense inflection necessarily fail to comprehend the difference between past and present. At the very least, the child needs at least partial comprehension before attempting production. This can most readily be seen in the ways in which children comprehend things incompletely or incorrectly and then use them inappropriately. Overgeneralization of words (for example, *daddy* for all men or *doggie* for all animals) and of morphological features (for example, *sheeps, mans, goed*) occurs with great frequency within the speech of all children.

MORE SYNTAX

As you may have noticed, most of the work reported here concerns young children. Yet all of us know that five- and six-year-olds do not have complete mastery of any aspect of the language they are acquiring. Carol Chomsky has performed several experiments dealing with the syntax of older children, from six to ten years of age.

Chomsky found that many eight-year-olds are confused by or react inappropriately to instructions such as

> Tell Janet what to feed the dog.

and

> Ask Fred which piece to move.

(Chomsky's experiments all involved children manipulating dolls, puppets, and other toys.)

She also found that instructions such as

> Make the car hit the bus.

and sentences such as

> The car was hit by the bus.

are interpreted identically. Even eight-year-olds apparently assume that the first NP of a sentence is the subject, except when such an interpretation results in something that is counter to the child's reality (as in the notion of daddy biting the dog).

Chomsky also experimented with the comprehension of sentences such as

> Is the doll easy to see?
> Make the doll easy to see.
> Make the doll hard to see.

using a doll and a blindfold. She found that when the blindfolded doll was lying on the table, most children would tell her that it was "hard to see" and that when asked to make the doll easy to see, they removed the blindfold: The distinction between "easy for the doll to see" and "easy for you to see the doll" was not present for many six- and seven-year-old children. Further, a few at age eight still interpreted the construction incorrectly. Here are two of Chomsky's conversations.

Peter R.: (six years and nine months)
Is this doll easy to see or hard to see?
  Hard to see.
Why?
  'Cause she got a blindfold.
Will you make her easy to see.
  (Removes blindfold)

>
> Will you explain what you did.
> I punched her. (An accurate description)
> How did that make her easier to see?
> It punched off the blindfold.
>
> *Ann M.:* (eight years and seven months)
> This is Chatty Cathy. Is she easy to see or hard to see?
> Easy.
> Would you make her hard to see.
> So you can't see her at all?
> OK.
> (Places doll under table)
> Tell what you did.
> I put her under the table.

Chomsky also conducted experiments concerning the understanding and use of *promise,* of *ask/tell,* and of pronouns. While her overall results are not easily described, we will generalize from her findings so as not to overburden this chapter with statistics and details.

As regards *ask/tell,* most five-year-olds were not able to sort out the differences appropriately; but up to and including the ten-year-olds, no group reliably fit into a fully competent developmental pattern. With *promise* and *easy to see,* none of the youngest children were able to perform adequately; the six-, seven-, and eight-year-olds were mixed; the nine-year-olds all knew the constructions involved. As regards pronouns, all the children over five years and six months knew the constructions, while the youngest children did not. This can be tabulated in the following way:

1. *Promise* and *easy to see:*   mixed from five years and six months to nine years
   success from nine years on
2. *Ask/tell:*   mixed at all ages
3. Pronominalization: failure below five years and six months
   success from five years and six months

When children come to school, they are far from having a complete command of their language. As can be seen from the examples involving the passive, much of their interpretation of syntax has to do with their knowledge of the real world. It is during the elementary-school years that children gradually become able to manipulate linguistic propositions and to rely upon the information presented to them verbally. The preschool and elementary-school child arrives in the classroom with a set of procedures he or she uses to assign meanings to utterances. Most of these procedures arise from context (the physical surroundings) and from interpersonal relationships, combined with common sense derived from their prior experience. It is in the classroom during the early school years that children acquire the ability to see beyond the interpersonal cues to the language itself and to derive implications from utterances, rather than from their limited acquaintance with the world at large.

PRAGMATICS

We have said that in learning about words and sentences the child takes his or her cues from the environment, rather than from the language itself. That is why even nine- and ten-year-olds frequently misinterpret passives and other sentences in which the first noun is not the "deep" subject of the sentence.

In other words, confronted by

Tom hit Fred.

a child knows that *Tom* (the first noun) hit *Fred* (the second noun). But given

Fred was hit by Tom.

It is in the classroom during the early school years that children acquire the ability to see beyond the interpersonal cues to the language itself and to derive implications from utterances. (*Photo by Linda Lungren*)

the child will assume that *Fred* (the first noun) hit *Tom* (the second noun). The pragmatics of the child's grammatical system lead to this simplistic attitude: The thing mentioned first is the actor; the thing mentioned second is acted upon. It is due to the same analytic tactic that children misinterpret words such as *easy:* Given a blindfolded doll and asked to make the doll "easy to see," most children removed the blindfold. When asked to make the doll "hard to see," some children hid the doll, while others replaced the blindfold. Apparently, the differentiation of things such as

Make it easy for the doll to see.

and

Make it easy for me to see the doll.

is not clear until the child is in grade three or four.

Similarly, given a toy truck and a toy car and asked to make the car hit the truck, even most five-year-olds knock the truck over with the car. However, asked to hit the car with the truck or to make the car be hit by the truck, most older children hit the truck with the car.

A notable exception to this occurs when interpreting the first noun as the actor results in something contrary to the child's knowledge of the real world. If you ask the child to represent

The tree was hit by the truck.

the child will move the toy truck against the toy tree. It is not possible in the child's universe for the tree to move in such a way as to collide with the truck. The same sort of response can be elicited by sentences such as

Daddy was bitten by that dog.

because the child's universe cannot cope with an interpretation that would result in daddy's biting the dog.

It is fairly clear that it is social interactions with communicative partners that lead to language behavior. Even early peek-a-boo games and smiles are part of the interpersonal communicative exchanges that develop into conversations. It is social interactions that are, in effect, the pragmatics of language.

Thus, the social interactions with stationary as opposed to moving objects within the child's world are what lead him or her to reject the notion of the tree hitting the truck. It is the child's knowledge of daddy's social behavior that forces the conclusions that the dog was the biter. In other, less clear-cut, situations, the child uses the strategy: Noun one is the actor, noun two is acted upon.

In many cases, we must try to ascertain what the child means, not what the child says. In listening to a story about summer camp being told by a ten-year-old girl, one can overhear the following: "Some guys got away from a refinery and all the counselors were put on night patrol." "Refinery?" "You know, where there are bad kids who aren't old enough to go to jail." "Do you mean reformatory?" Pause. "Yeah, I guess so. They got out of a reformatory."

As another example, a six-year-old wanting to watch a special on TV was heard to say: "No! I wanted to go to bed earlier!"

Neither of these children had fully established the meanings of the words they used. Polysyllables such as *refinery* and *reformatory* are similar in sound. Also, they are both special places. In some ways, officers of penal institutions, one supposes, hope that their charges will become refined in some way. For the other child, the difference between *earlier* and *later* was not yet fully established.

However, it must be noted that in both cases the actual meaning is transparent. No one supposed the camp counselors would care about people from a refinery, and it would make no sense to have a tantrum about going to bed earlier. In general, even adult malapropisms or errors are interpretable in their social context: Constable Dogberry's "comparisons are odorous" (in *Much Ado About Nothing*), or Reverend Spooner's "You have hissed my mystery lecture" are comprehensible (and funny) because of our pragmatic knowledge. The developing child is more context bound, while the adult is more language bound. But like the child, we never stop using social and physical context to help us with meaning.

MORE PHONOLOGY

In the beginning of this chapter, we remarked that there appeared to be a break between babbling and first words in the infant. This discontinuity is apparent in the development of the sound system of the child as well. For example, while it seems that back consonants (for example, /g/ and /k/-like sounds) emerge first in babbling, front consonants (for example, /p/, /b/, and /m/-like sounds) emerge first in speech. Charles Ferguson has noted that this observation seems to be true cross-culturally, not merely in English.

Roman Jakobson (1941; Jakobson and Halle, 1956) noted that the child's first articulate attempts at producing speech sounds are directed toward maximal oppositions in the speech tract. Thus, the first consonants to emerge are /p/, /b/, or /m/ (produced by cutting off the airflow completely with both lips, with or without voicing and with or without velar closure), the furthest front consonants; and the first vowel to emerge is /a/, a low back vowel. If you look back at the mouth drawings in Chapter 1 (pp. 5 and 8), you will be able to see what this means in terms of articulation. It is for this reason, says Jakobson, that first words and the words for caregivers are so frequently of the /mama/, /papa/, /baba/ type.

Jakobson would then derive the large inventory of speech sounds from these maximal contrasts by means of a series of binary oppositions:

Consonants	dental vs. labial
	/t/ vs. /p/
Vowels	high vs. low
	/i/ vs. /a/
High Vowels	front vs. back
	/i/ vs. /u/
Back Vowels	rounded vs. unrounded
	/u/ vs. /a/
Consonants	velar/palatal vs. labial/dental
	/k/ vs. /t/
Consonants	palatal vs. velar
	/š/ vs. /k/

While such a scheme does not fulfill the needs of the consonant inventory of English, it does give a notion as to how such a theory might account for the consonants and vowels of the language.

No matter what the mechanism, however, children do start with only a few recognizable language sounds and gradually develop these into the full inventory for their language community. Berry and Eisenson have given the following order for the correct pronunciation of English consonants. We say "correct" here, because Berry and Eisenson are writing for speech pathologists, who are concerned with judging the adequacy of children's productions.

Years	
3 1/2	b p m w h
4 1/2	d t n g k ɔ y
5 1/2	f
6 1/2	v ð ž š l
7 1/2	s z θ r

It is most important to note here that the child in the early school grades cannot be expected to articulate all the consonants of English appropriately. In addition, the range for acquisition of any language phenomenon is quite broad; thus, neither the primary teacher nor the anxious parent need be worried by a young child's lisping or having trouble with *th* until well into the child's school career: The best person to assess whether or not there is a problem is a trained speech pathologist.

In general, however, by the time a child reaches kindergarten or first grade, he or she has a fairly good grasp of the phonological inventory of the language. Even if some of the distinctions are lacking, there are enough clues in the context so that what the school-age child says is rarely ambiguous or incomprehensible.

Among the phenomena that are present in children's speech, one should be aware of the following:

1. Weak-syllable deletion. There is a tendency among children to drop one or more unstressed syllables from a long word or phrase. Examples of this are *potamus* for *hippopotamus* and *raff* for *giraffe. Getti* for *spaghetti* and *plice* for *police* are other examples. However, this is a common phenomenon in many languages. Adult English examples include *burger* for *hamburger, phone* for *telephone,* and *Coke* for *Coca-Cola.*

2. Cluster simplification. Many English words have consonant clusters in them, and many of these clusters appear to offer some difficulty to children acquiring the language. As a result, children tend to simplify clusters in a variety of ways. First, elements may be deleted: *poon* for *spoon* or *bella* for *umbrella* (which also shows weak-syllable deletion). Second, extra vowels may be inserted: *terain* for *train.* Third, one of the elements may be altered: *chrain* for *train* or *twee* for *tree.* Finally, the elements may be switched around (metathesized): *aks* for *ask* or *pisgetti* for spaghetti (which shows both metathesis of the first two consonants and insertion of a simplificatory vowel between them). Innumerable other examples could be provided.

3. Assimilation. Assimilation literally means making one sound more like another (usually adjacent) sound. It is a common phenomenon in many languages and familiar in English in the case of the negative prefix *in-* (for example, *in̲decision, in̲credible, im̲possible, il̲legible, ir̲responsible*). Words such as *dod̲dy* for *dog̲gy* and *pop̲pamus* for *hip̲popotamus* (also showing syllable deletion) are examples from children's speech. (Many other examples of these and other phonological processes may be found in Salus and Salus, 1974.)

SEMANTICS

The final topic to be considered in this chapter is semantics, or the growth of meaning. It is clear that a young child has neither words nor names for all the things perceived or all the activities engaged in or observed. It is equally clear that as the child grows older, he or she is able to distinguish objects or activities from one another with greater accuracy; this discrimination applies as well to ideas that are neither things (or nouns) nor activities (or verbs). Color words, prepositions, and words indicating size and directionality all become more specific with the child's cognitive development. Yet, despite the wealth of observation as to what the child does, there is a definite dearth of information as to what processes are involved; and although there are a number of theories, none has gained wide acceptance.

One attractive theory of semantic growth is that suggested by Herbert Clark (1970). He proposed resolving some of the dilemmas in the area of semantic development by adopting a theory incorporating the Jakobsonian notion of binary opposition in the establishment of semantic distinctions. It had been pointed out earlier that at a certain stage many children interpret *less* as though it means *more*. Clark argued convincingly that in learning polar adjectives and comparatives, children first learn that both members of the pair (for example, *more/less, big/little, near/far*) refer to the general dimension. That is, *more* and *less* both mean "some" or "having extent." The child then learns that there is a dimension involved and identifies both terms with the positive pole, thus *less* equals *more*. Finally, the child learns that the dimension is polar and distributes the terms appropriately.

Such an attitude toward a child's view of meaning is most productive when we look at less-easily-tested items than adjectives or locatives. For example, when a child uses /dawdi/ for both *doggy* and *daddy,* only "animate object other than me" is being distinguished. When the dog and the father are discriminated, presumably it is on the basis of human and nonhuman, *daddy* referring to all males. Only later does *daddy* come to mean "father." At about the same time, *doggy* stops meaning "four-legged beast" and is assigned to "dog," other animals receiving appropriate names.

Whatever device we accept as determining the child's acquisition of language, it must take a great many factors into account. The child has been taking in his or her surroundings and organizing them for about a year before attempting speech. Observations continue to be absorbed and "rationalized" during the second year, when verbal communication emerges and Stage II and Stage III utterances are observable. The child's organization of the real world is obviously the basis for his or her first hypotheses (or guesses) about word meanings. This would appear to motivate the overextensions and generalizations with which every observer is familiar.

It now seems clear that our model of language acquisition will have to take more than just language into account. The child's nonlinguistic knowledge appears to be highly structured according to certain built-in principles; It is these principles that enable perceptions to be organized and categorized into a coherent whole onto which linguistic data is then mapped. To paraphrase Clark, the child acquires spatial expressions by applying the words to his or her prior knowledge about space, and temporal expressions by expressing space in terms of a metaphor about time.

The actual nature of the language acquisition device will have to wait until we know much more about the neurological and physiological bases of higher mental functions.

The above should not be interpreted as meaning that we know nothing: As can be seen, we have a very good idea about the acquisition of the sound system (phonology), the form system (morphology), and the syntax of whatever language the child is acquiring. There has been enough research on the acquisition of languages other than English, and of languages quite different from the standard Western European type, for us to make good generalizations about the development of language in the child. We also know a good deal about the growth of word meaning and the growth of vocabulary.

While it seems most likely that humans are "prewired" in some way to acquire language, what that prewiring is, and how it works, is the object of much research at the present time, and is the foundation underpinning the research concerning the cognitive and communicative abilities of primates (chimpanzees, gorillas, and orangutans) over the past dozen-or-so years. If we can understand the abilities of man and of other creatures, we may be able to come to grips with the differences between them. It may be of importance to mention at this point that despite the intensive "teaching" that has gone on, no ape has yet been trained to express an original sentence, whether using plastic symbols, American Sign Language of the Deaf, or a modified computer keyboard.

The expressive instrument that is language still appears to be solely human, although our experiments have taught us much about nonhuman intelligence.

EXERCISES

1. Observe a young child (three to five years of age) for an hour or so. How much of the information conveyed is the result of immediate context and gesture, and how much the result of actual verbal behavior?
2. The "trick-or-treat" of Halloween is a ritual in children's language. Can you think of other rituals and formal exchanges?
3. Jean Berko Gleason tells a story about a mother getting onto a bus with a weeping, screaming child, who carried on for the entire trip. As the mother disembarked with the still-hysterical child, she said: "There, wasn't that fun?" What was the mother "teaching" the child? What discrepancy is noticeable between the words and the behavior?

REFERENCES

Allport, F. H. *Social Psychology.* Cambridge, Mass.: Houghton-Mifflin, 1924.
Bellugi, U. *The Acquisition of Negation.* Ph.D. dissertation, Harvard University, 1967.
Berko Gleason, J. "The Child's Learning of English Morphology." *Word* 14 (1958): 150–177.
Berry, M. F., and Eisenson, J. *Speech Disorders.* New York: Appleton-Century-Crofts, 1956.
Brown, R. *A First Language: The Early Stages.* Cambridge, Mass.: Harvard University Press, 1973.
Cazden, C. B. "The Acquisition of Noun and Verb Inflections." *Child Development* 39 (1968): 433–448.
Chomsky, C. S. *The Acquisition of Syntax in Children from 5 to 10.* Cambridge, Mass.: The MIT Press, 1969.
Clark, H. H. "Word Associations and Linguistic Theory." In J. Lyons, ed., *New Horizons in Linguistics.* Baltimore: Penguin, 1970.
Jakobson, R. *Kindersprache, Aphasie und allgemeine Lautgesetze.* Uppsala: Almkvist & Wiksell, 1941.
Jakobson, R., and Halle, M. *Fundamentals of Language.* The Hague: Mouton, 1956.
Klima, E. S., and Bellugi, U. "Syntactic Regularities in the Speech of Children." In J. Lyons and R. J. Wales, eds., *Psycholinguistics Papers.* Edinburgh: University Press, 1966.
McNeill, D. A. *The Acquisition of Language.* New York: Harper & Row, 1970.
Salus, M. W., and Salus, P. H. "Rule-Ordering in Child Phonology." *Canadian Journal of Linguistics* 19 (1974): 29–39.
Slobin, D. I. "Universals of Grammatical Development in Children." In G. B. Flores d'Arcais and W. J. M. Levelt, eds., *Advances in Psycholinguistics.* Amsterdam: North-Holland, 1970.

FURTHER READINGS

Brown, R. *A First Language.* Cambridge, Mass.: Harvard University Press, 1973. The best summary of the work of a single research group.
Dale, P. S. *Language Development,* 2nd ed. New York: Holt, Rinehart & Winston, 1978. An excellent overview of the field of child language.
Menyuk, P. *The Acquisition and Development of Language.* Englewood Cliffs, N.J.: Prentice-Hall, 1971. Another very good overview of the field of child language.
Terrace, H. *Nim.* New York: Knopf, 1979. At the same time, the best recounting and best critique of chimpanzee-language experiments.

Nature, consistent and august,
Can't teach us what to write or do:
With Her the real is always true,
And what is true is also just.

—W. H. Auden

3 LANGUAGE OVER TIME

We can tell from studying literature that our language has changed over time. Shakespeare's English is different from Emily Bronte's; Jane Austen's is different from James Baldwin's. This chapter will detail the ways in which English has changed over the centuries and discuss the ways in which new words enter our language.

LANGUAGE CHANGE

If you have ever glanced at *Beowulf* or *Gawain and the Green Knight* or the works of Chaucer, it is obvious that Old English and Middle English are quite different from the language of Shakespeare or Dickens or Saul Bellow. In fact, it is quite obvious that Shakespeare's language is different from that of Dickens, while Dickens's differs from that of Bellow or Philip Roth. This is more than a matter of style; it is the very essence of the living language.

Just as we now differ from the infant we each developed from, and from the senior citizen each of us will become, languages grow and develop and change over time. In fact, languages are born and they die, in many ways displaying an organic life of their own.

In the middle of the seventeenth century, the first Dutch settlers landed in South Africa. Over the years, their language diverged from the Dutch spoken in the Netherlands, each developing in its own way. Three hundred years later, we consider the Afrikaans of South Africa to be a different language from the Dutch used by the subjects of Queen Beatrix. At the other end of the scale, literally hundreds of North and South American Indian languages have vanished, overwhelmed by English, French, Portuguese, Spanish, and other aboriginal languages such as Nahuatl. On the European continent, the language known as Old Prussian was spoken in the eighteenth century; today, no speaker of that language survives. The last known speaker of Dalmatian, a Romance language, died in 1898.

In the course of time, languages change their phonologies, their morphology, and their syntax. They borrow words and coin new words; other words become obsolete and fall out of use; some words change their meaning.

The history of a language tells us something of the history of its speakers. Had the Norman French not invaded England in 1066, we would not have borrowed *beef* or *veal* or *pork* from their language. If the Vikings had not raided the British Isles, we would not have *ski* or *sky* or *skull*. If the Dutch had not been a great maritime nation, we would not have taken up their words *keel* or *yacht*. If the Pilgrims had not come to North America, English would lack *skunk*; if the Spanish had not invaded Mexico, we would lack *tomato*. Had imperial Britain not annexed India, we would not know *khaki* or *calico* or *curry*. Without the Arabs, there would be neither *algebra* nor *alcohol*; without the Chinese, no *tea*; without the Malay, no *ketchup*. Names, too, become words. Where would exercisers be without the nineteenth-century French acrobat Jules *Léotard*? What fish fancier would not be unhappy without the contribution of Reverend *Guppy*? And think of the mischief caused by factory workers throwing their wooden shoes into the machinery—we call it *sabotage*, for a *sabot* is a wooden shoe. In this chapter, we will discuss some of the history of the English language and how this history can be used in the classroom.

LANGUAGES AND LANGUAGE FAMILIES

We can go further with our biological analogy and talk about languages being related to one another, about there being families of languages. Thus, many of the languages of eastern and southern Africa are called Bantu languages; many of the languages of central Asia are Uralic-Altaic; and most of the languages of Europe, including English, are Indo-European.

Even before the fifteenth-century voyages of exploration and the colonization of the Western Hemisphere, Australia, and New Zealand that lasted into the late eighteenth century, the Indo-European family was widespread. The easternmost relative of English was a language called Tocharian, spoken in what is now the Chinese province of Sinkiang in the early centuries of the Christian era. Up to 1492, the westernmost relative was Icelandic, spoken on an island in the North Atlantic Ocean.

If we look at the word for mother in a number of ancient and modern languages, we can see that some languages are more closely related than others:

Thai	maa
Turkish	anne
Japanese	haha
Nubian	en
Russian	mat'

Armenian	mayr
German	Mutter
Latin	mater
French	mere
Spanish	madre
English	mother

It would appear from this superficial measure that Thai, Japanese, and Nubian are not as closely related to English as the other languages listed. The chart on pages 54 and 55 supplies an extensive list of the Indo-European languages. Extinct languages are marked with an asterisk (*).

It must be understood that such a chart is only a beginning; it does not list all the languages. It omits the "medieval" stages of historical development, and it tends to distort some facts (for example, Modern Greek is not a direct descendant of Classical Greek; there were a number of other Italic languages—Oscan and Umbrian, for instance—contemporaneous with Latin). Nonetheless, the table does serve to show the types of relationships within the Indo-European family and to list a number of the languages that are still spoken.

Because our focus is on English, we would like to look more closely at the Germanic branch of the Indo-European family tree.

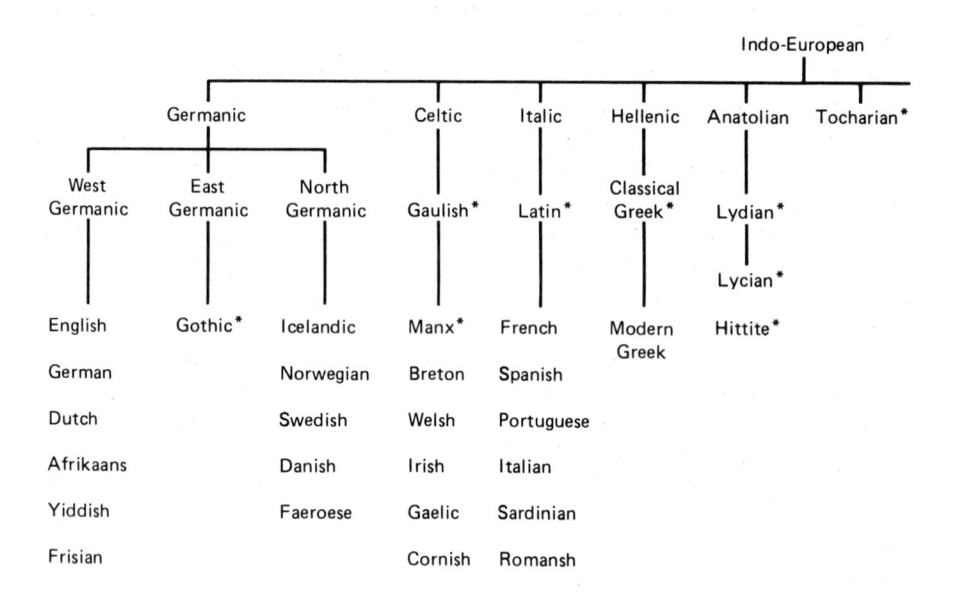

```
                                                          Indo-European
                                                                |
         ┌──────────┬──────────┬──────────┬──────────┬──────────┐
      Germanic     Celtic    Italic    Hellenic   Anatolian  Tocharian*
    ┌─────┼─────┐    |         |          |          |
  West   East  North Gaulish*  Latin*  Classical   Lydian*
Germanic Germanic Germanic                          Greek*     |
    |     |      |                                           Lycian*
 English Gothic* Icelandic  Manx*    French    Modern      Hittite*
 German         Norwegian   Breton   Spanish    Greek
 Dutch          Swedish     Welsh    Portuguese
 Afrikaans      Danish      Irish    Italian
 Yiddish        Faeroese    Gaelic   Sardinian
 Frisian                    Cornish  Romansh
```

THE GERMANIC LANGUAGES

Although the Roman historian Tacitus (about 55–117 A.D.) wrote a book about the Germanic tribes in 98 A.D., the earliest real records we have of a Germanic language are the fragments of a Bible translation and a commentary by the Visigothic Bishop Ulfila (or Wulfilas) in the fourth century. From about the same period we have a number of inscriptions in Old Norse, in a writing system we call runic. The earliest actual manuscript of Gothic dates from the sixth century, and of Old Icelandic from the twelfth century. West Germanic languages are recorded from the last centuries of the first millennium, both in Old High German (an ancestor of modern German) and in Old English. The earliest records of Old English date from the eighth and ninth centuries.

All of the Germanic languages differ from the rest of the Indo-European languages in several ways, but the most notable differences involve the treatment of certain consonants. If we look at Latin or Greek, for example, we find that the words for "fish" have a "p" in them, that the word for "thin" has a "t" and that the word for "hundred" has a "k." Furthermore, the "p" "t" and "k" sounds of English tend to correspond with "b" "d" or "g" in Latin. These correspondences were noted at the

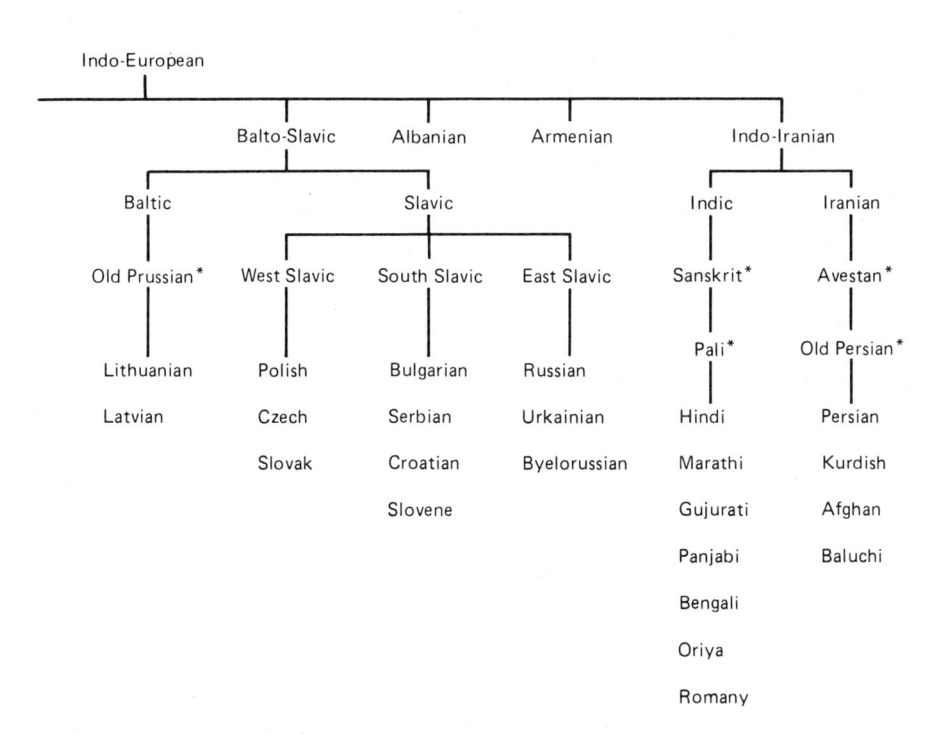

```
Indo-European
    ├── Balto-Slavic
    │     ├── Baltic
    │     │     ├── Old Prussian*
    │     │     └── Lithuanian
    │     │         Latvian
    │     └── Slavic
    │           ├── West Slavic
    │           │     ├── Polish
    │           │     ├── Czech
    │           │     └── Slovak
    │           ├── South Slavic
    │           │     ├── Bulgarian
    │           │     ├── Serbian
    │           │     ├── Croatian
    │           │     └── Slovene
    │           └── East Slavic
    │                 ├── Russian
    │                 ├── Urkainian
    │                 └── Byelorussian
    ├── Albanian
    ├── Armenian
    └── Indo-Iranian
          ├── Indic
          │     └── Sanskrit*
          │           └── Pali*
          │                 ├── Hindi
          │                 ├── Marathi
          │                 ├── Gujurati
          │                 ├── Panjabi
          │                 ├── Bengali
          │                 ├── Oriya
          │                 └── Romany
          └── Iranian
                └── Avestan*
                      └── Old Persian*
                            ├── Persian
                            ├── Kurdish
                            ├── Afghan
                            └── Baluchi
```

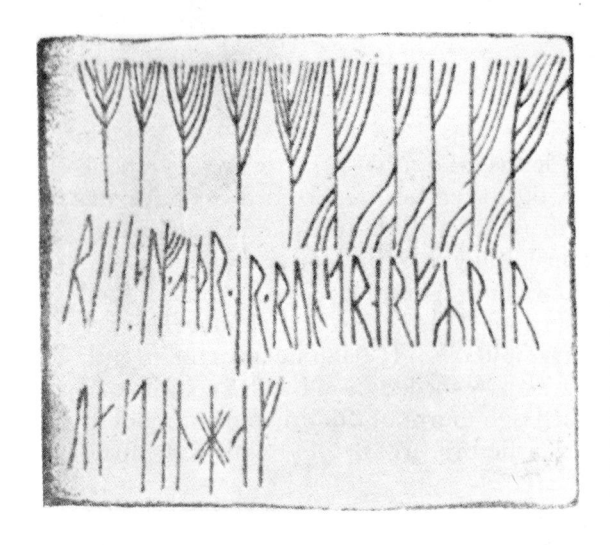

FIGURE 3-3. An inscription from Maeshowe in the Orkney Islands. Two different styles of runes: above, in "branch runes": these runes; below, in "standard form": were carved by he who is the most rune-knowledgeable in the north sea.

beginning of the nineteenth century by a Danish scholar, Rasmus Kristian Rask, and formalized by Jacob Grimm in the 1830's. They are known as "Grimm's Law" or the First Consonantal Shift.

Our earliest records of English reveal a language much like that of the Frisian records of the twelfth century. Frisian is still spoken by about 500,000 people in part of the Netherlands and in a few islands along the North Sea coast. But the language differs from the Old High German records. Historical linguists therefore postulate an Anglo-Frisian branch of West Germanic and a Continental branch (German, Dutch-Flemish, Afrikaans, and Yiddish).

Old English (ca. 700–1050) is recorded in several dialects. It is a highly inflected language, with special forms for case endings on nouns and pronouns and elaborate verb inflexions. Here is the Lord's Prayer in Old English:

> Fæder ure þu þe eart on heofoum, si þin nama gehalgod. Tobecume þin rice. Gewurþe þin willa on eordan swa swa on heofonum. Urne gedaeghwamlican hlaf syle us to dæg. And forgyf us ure gyltas, swa swa we forgyfad urum gyltedum. And ne gelæd þu us on costnungen ac alys us of yfele. Sodlice.

Although there are a number of words in it we can recognize, especially since the text as a whole is a familiar one, the language is, for the most part, incomprehensible to the modern reader—even the educated modern reader.

But, as we have said, languages change over time, and external history plays a major role in language change. When England was converted to Christianity in the beginning of the seventh century, the language acquired words such as *abbot, altar, cap, chalice, hymn, relic, sock, beet, pear, oyster, cook, lily, rue, school, verse,* and *meter.* During the Scandinavian (Viking) invasions of the ninth through eleventh centuries, words such as *birth, sky, trust, take, skirt, disk,* and *dike* entered the language. Thus, up to the Norman Conquest in 1066, there had been Latin and Scandinavian borrowings into English. With the Battle of Hastings came a flood of French borrowings and, more important, a tremendous French influence on the language as a whole. Among the French borrowings were *court, battle, nation, enemy, crime, justice, beef, pork, veal, roast, mutton, charity,* and *miracle.* We refer to the English of about 1050 through 1400 or 1450 as Middle English.

Toward the end of this period, following the separation of Normandy and England in about 1200, there was a growing sense of Englishness. The advent of major poets such as Chaucer in the fourteenth century was both a result of this and an important impetus to its development. Here is the Lord's Prayer in the Middle English of Chaucer's day:

> Oure fadir that art in heuenes halowid be thi name, thi kyngdom come to, be thi wille don in erthe es in heuene, yeue to us this day oure bread ouir other substance, & foryeue to us oure dettis, as we forgeuen to oure dettouris, & lede us not in to temptacion: but delyuer us from yuel, amen.

Though this is not yet modern English by a long shot, it is much more comprehensible than the Old English. It was not merely roast beef that the English acquired from their Norman conquerors. By the time Henry IV ascended the throne in 1399, England had a national identity and a national language that we can recognize as ancestors.

Historically, it was the Hundred Years' War (1337–1453), followed by the advent of printing, that forged this identity. It was in 1476 that William Caxton produced in Bruges the first book printed in English. The next year he returned to England, set up his press in Westminister, and in December 1476 produced the first known piece of printing in England. His first English book appeared on November 18, 1476. It was *Dictes and Sayings of the Philosophres.* Perhaps Caxton's best known and most successful work was Malory's *Le Morte Darthur*, which appeared in 1485. All in all, Caxton printed about a hundred different works before his death in 1491, at which time his press passed on to Wynkyn de Worde, who had been his foreman. It is more than merely a bad pun to say that Caxton's work made a lasting impression on the English language.

Printing, among other things, led to the standardization of spelling and increased the number of writers and readers. Caxton's achievement occurred less than a century before Shakespeare's birth; with the reigns of Henry VIII and Elizabeth I came plays and poems and learned books. At this time, English borrowed large numbers of Latin and Greek "learned" words and also coined many new words. *Anachronism, allusion, atmosphere, capsule, dexterity, halo, agile, external, insane, adapt, erupt, exist,* and *extinguish* all entered English at this time. We generally refer to the language of this period (ca. 1450–1700) as Early Modern English. A version of the Lord's Prayer from the seventeenth century is

> Our father which art in heaven, hallowed be thy Name. Thy kingdome come. Thy will be done, in earth, as it is in heaven. Giue vs this day our dayly bread. And forgiue vs our debts, as we forgiue our debters. And leade vs not into temptation, but deliuer vs from euill: For thine is the kingdome, and the power, and the glory, for euer. Amen.

This is obviously the same language that we speak, although there are differences that may make us a bit uncomfortable.

In addition to the things we have mentioned here, English has borrowed words and expressions from a variety of sources. Their imperialist activities from the middle of the seventeenth century brought the British into contact with more and more peoples and more and more parts of the world, including India, Africa, Australia, New Zealand, and North America. But rather than narrate, we will here merely list a number of sources and some English words imported from them. It is these imports that supply the paprika, curry, and tabasco to our speech.

LOANWORDS

Before getting into the variety of loanwords English has adopted over the past millennium and a half, it might be worth noting that about 25 percent of our vocabulary is traceable to Old English, although this is most likely a false impression since about 40 to 50 percent of our most basic words are inherited. But there are some Greek and Latin words, that antedate the Scandinavian invasions of over a thousand years ago.

Although the majority of Greek words in English are scholarly or learned creations such as *antibiotic* ("against life") or *telephone* ("distant sounder"), there are two other routes by which Greek words have come into English: One is through the mediation of Latin including words such as *church, bishop, box, school, martyr,* and *butter,* all of which entered our language as a result of the Christianization of the British Isles; the other route is also through Latin (or French), but by a more "popular" path. Examples of such words are *treasure, chamber* and *camera, hour, machine, chair, place, govern, cream, fancy,* and *fantastic.*

Most Latin words have come to us through the intervention of French or some other Romance language. But there are several types of words that have entered English directly. These are words that entered English with the coming of Christianity (*street, cheese, cheap,* and *shrive*); learned words (*agenda, quorum,* and *alibi*); and cultural words, borrowed—for the most part—during the Renaissance (*stimulate, dedicatory, simplification, pontificate,* and *provide*).

The number of English words derived from French is vast. In addition to the various food and cooking words we have already mentioned, words such as *valet* and *chauffeur, emotion* and *action, stamp* and *envelope, taxicab* and *beast,* are all from French.

From Italian we have borrowed *design, opera, aria, piazza, portico, stanza, violin, volcano, maccaroni, alto, piano, spaghetti, torso, cello, broccoli, vogue, pizza, serenade, confetti, cash, carnival, ravioli, cartoon, studio,* and *solo.*

From Spanish, *alligator, banana, canoe, cocoa, cockroach, hammock, hurricane, mosquito, tobacco, ranch, rodeo, mesa, canyon, potato, cork, tornado, sombrero, arroyo, mustang, lariat, lasso,* and *armadillo*

From German, *sauerkraut, delicatessen, hamburger, frankfurter,* and *dollar.*

From Dutch, *chapter, yacht, schooner, boor, drawl, deck, boom, cruiser, furlough, landscape, tub, scum, freight, jeer, snap, cookie, toy, switch, cole slaw,* and *yankee.*

From the Scandinavian languages, *sky, skull, skirt, ski, fee, firth, hell, narwhal,* and *skill.*

From Portuguese, *pagoda.*

From Arabic, *hazard, artichoke, alcohol, algebra, zero* (and *cipher*), *candy, lemon, orange, spinach, sugar, alkali, assassin, syrup, sofa, divan, mattress, magazine,* and *sherbet.*

From various Indic languages, *palanquin, curry, loot, pundit, calico, chintz, punch, coolie, bungalow, cot, polo, thug,* and *khaki.*

From Hebrew, *camel, ebony, cherub, seraph, cabal, rabbi, bagel,* and *sapphire.*

From Japanese, *kimono, samurai,* and *kamikaze* (to say nothing of *bonsai, jiujitsu* and *harakiri*).

From Chinese, *tea, fantan,* and *chow mein.*

From Malay, *caddy, ketchup,* and *orang-utan.*

From African languages come *gorilla, zebra, voodoo, jazz,* and *chimpanzee.*

From American Indian languages English has borrowed *skunk, moccasin, raccoon, totem, woodchuck, caucus, teepee, hogan, tomahawk,* and place names such as *Chicago* ("the place of stinks"), *Peoria* ("the place of fat animals"), and *Manhattan* ("where everyone got drunk"). From Eskimo come *kayak* and *igloo.*

There are tens of thousands of English words borrowed from Latin, Greek, and other languages that we have not listed here. These include words such as *kangaroo* and *wombat* from Australian languages, *kiwi* from Maori, *emu* from Moluccan, and *teak* from Malayalam. One of the virtues of English is its willingness to adopt new words.

But not all new words are borrowed from other languages. On occasion, an individual becomes identified with some thing or some act; thus we have *boycott* and *lynch, leotard* and *bloomer, guppy* and (for discoveries and inventions) *pasteurize, Listerine,* and *Birdseye.*

COINAGES

Sometimes, brand names become identified with a product: *Frigidaire, Kodak, Xerox,* and *Scotch Tape* are examples of this. Abbreviations, too, become words: for example, *UNESCO*, to *"emcee," WHO,* and *BART* (for the San Francisco Bay Area Rapid Transit system).

On occasion, someone actually coins a new word that becomes part of the language: *chortle* (from "Jabberwocky" in *Through the Looking-Glass*) and *blurb* (coined by Gelett Burgess) are examples of this.

New words come into our language in other ways as well, for example, through the phenomenon known as backformation, in which a new word is derived from an old age. Middle English had a vegetable, *pease*; since this obviously sounded like a plural, a new singular form, *pea*, was created. In a similar way, our language has derived *edit* from *editor*, *peddle* from *peddler*, *pub* from *public house*, *cad* from *cadet*, and *pup* from *puppy*. Sometimes, only parts of older words are used: *motorcade* from *cavalcade; litterbug* from *jitterbug; telethon* and *sell-a-thon* from *marathon; washateria* from *cafeteria*. We also combine words: *smoke* plus *fog* equals *smog; motor* plus *hotel* equals *motel*.

Language is a living thing. In order to stay alive, a language must change. It takes in new words and new forms while others fall into disuse or drop out entirely. *Fallout, countdown, astronaut,* and *rock* and *disco* have all been added to English in the past thirty-five years; *23-skidoo, cool cat,* and *bobby sox* have vanished. Some other words have remained but have changed their meaning.

SEMANTIC CHANGES

There are a variety of ways in which a word can change its meaning. Some words generalize, that is, their meanings broaden in scope. Other words specialize, their meanings narrow. Some words come into being as euphemisms, words designed to make things better or nicer or fancier than they are. Some words elevate their denotations—they come to stand for better and better things as time passes. Others degenerate, they become worse as time passes—or, rather, they come to stand for worse and worse things. Let us look at some examples.

Front, from Latin *frons*, originally meant "forehead." It then came to mean "face," and has generalized to its present meaning, "forepart."

Hazard was originally the name of a dicing game. It has generalized from "fall of the dice" to any "risk" at all.

Zest originally meant "a piece of lemon peel." It now means "anything added to impart flavor or relish."

A word such as *room* is a good example of specialization. Like the German *Raum*, it originally meant "space." However, as a result of use in phrases such as "sleeping room" and "eating room," it came to mean, as early as the fifteenth century, "a section of space in a building," the meaning we still use today.

Fowl once meant "any kind of bird," but now has narrowed its meaning to "domestic fowl." *Meat*, which once meant "food in general," now means only "food from animals." *Cattle* (from the same Latin stem that gave us *capital* and—by way of French—*chattel*) meant "stock," was narrowed to "movable property," and finally narrowed yet further to its present meaning of "bovine livestock."

Examples of contemporary euphemisms are *sanitation engineer* for *garbage collector; passed on* or *lost* or *departed* for *dead; beautician* for *hairdresser;* and *mortician* for *embalmer* or *undertaker*. Train and bus *dispatchers* have become *transportation supervisors, sweat* has become *perspiration,* and *crazy* and *mad* have become *insane* or *deranged*. Such euphemisms originated at all stages of our language. It is obvious that ancient taboos on using names are the reasons for our use of such items as *the Lord, the Creator, the Savior,* and *the Redeemer.* Somehow, *nude* seems more genteel than *naked,* and *soiled* is better than *dirty.*

Many words have suffered degeneration over the centuries. *Specious,* which once meant "beautiful, fair," now conveys the meaning "without real merit." *Charity*, which originally meant "love," now has overtones of a patronizing attitude and is yielding most of its meaning to *benovolence* ("of good will"). *Boor* once meant just "farmer," *wench* originally merely designated any "girl," and *knave* meant "boy" (compare German *Knabe* "boy"). In attitude, *stupid* once meant "amazed," and *sullen,* "solemn."

Elevations are also interesting. *Prestige* originally had to do with "magic." *Boudoir* literally meant "sulking room." *Fame* originally meant merely "report" or "common talk."

In some way, the elevations and the degenerations seem to cancel one another out in our vocabulary. If *childish* and *puerile* have come down in the world, *boyish* and *youthful* have been elevated; if *cheap* and *vile* have descended, *costly* and *precious* have ascended; if rash (meaning "quick" or "swift," originally) has become "foolhardy," *sturdy* and *stout*, which originally meant "reckless" and "foolish," have compensated for it.

We have already mentioned personal names that have become words; on occasion, place names do also. As a result, we have *frankfurters, hamburgers,* and *wieners* (Wien is the German name of Vienna) as well as *vienna sausages*. But we also have *Danish pastry* (called "Viennese bread" in

Danish) and *Swiss cheese* (which does not seem to differentiate among *Emmenthaler, Gruyere,* and *Appenzeller*). Finally, we have our Thanksgiving *turkey,* which does not seem to have originated in the Near East.

It might be worth pointing out that all personal and place names have their own histories, as do family names. There are a number of handy lists of common given names, many of them in the form of "Baby Books"—lists purporting to assist parents in choosing names for their children.

We have gone into considerable detail on the history of the language because we have found that children in all grades are fascinated by the stories behind the words they use every day and behind their names and the names of their friends. In the Appendix, we will suggest some materials, games, and puzzles that can be used to get schoolchildren interested in language. However, before concluding this section, we would like to discuss one more topic: families of words.

FAMILIES OF WORDS

At the beginning of this chapter, we listed a number of the Indo-European languages and discussed briefly the fact that English is but one member of a very large and widespread group of related languages. As a result of this situation, there are a large number of related forms in English and a large number of related words in other languages. The lists of words presented in the preceding pages gave you some idea as to the vast range of sources of our vocabulary. By looking at a few families of words, you can see how the same basic forms have entered English by a variety of routes. Let us look at such a family tree. (We will begin each tree with its hypothetical Indo-European form, reconstructed by the methods of historical linguistics from the oldest recorded forms.) Each of these hypothetical forms will be marked with an*.

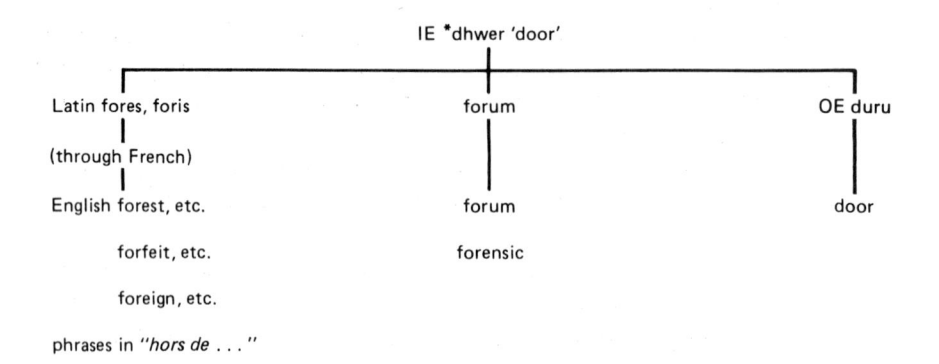

```
                         IE *dhwer 'door'
        ┌───────────────────────┼───────────────────────┐
Latin fores, foris            forum                  OE duru
     │                           │                       │
(through French)                 │                       │
     │                           │                       │
English forest, etc.           forum                   door

     forfeit, etc.             forensic

     foreign, etc.

phrases in *"hors de..."*
```

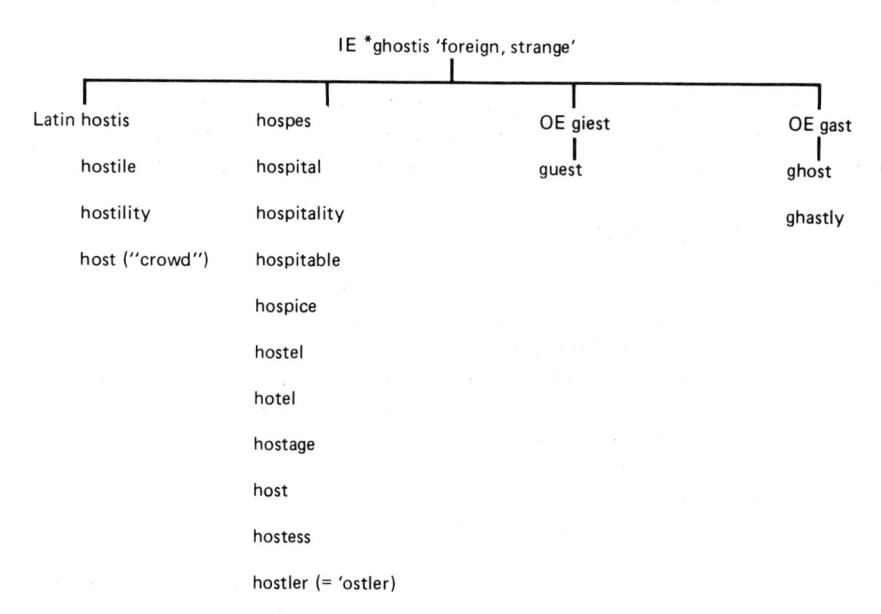

```
                        IE *ghostis 'foreign, strange'
         ┌──────────────┬──────────────┬──────────────┐
    Latin hostis      hospes         OE giest        OE gast
       hostile        hospital         guest          ghost
       hostility      hospitality                     ghastly
       host ("crowd")  hospitable
                      hospice
                      hostel
                      hotel
                      hostage
                      host
                      hostess
                      hostler (= 'ostler)
```

A tree like this one gives us a lot to think about: a *guest* is someone we take in, and act as a *host* toward; but certainly invaders are *guests* of a different sort, and those with whom we would engage in *hostilities,* unless we were injured and taken to a *hospital.* Certainly, too, a *ghost*—the returned spirit of a dead person—is a *guest* of a different sort, a rather *ghastly* one. A *hostage* is, in certain ways, both a person with whom we are on *hostile* footing and a *guest.* But let us look at another tree:

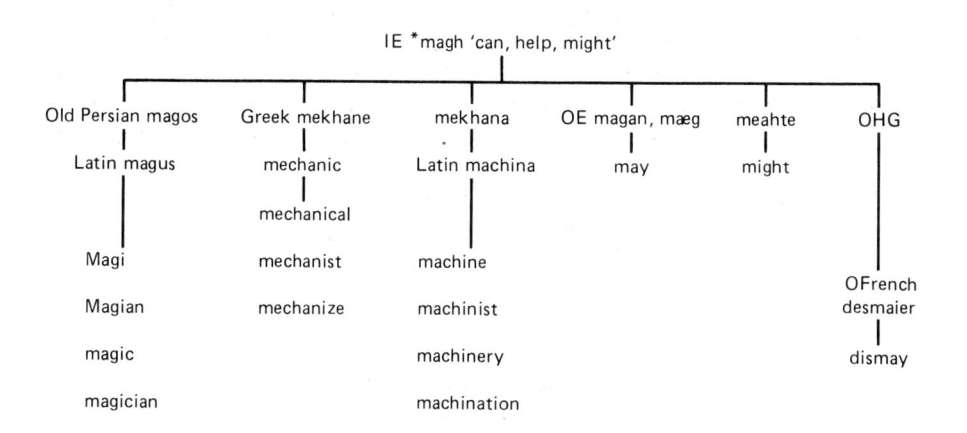

```
                              IE *magh 'can, help, might'
    ┌──────────────┬──────────────┬──────────────┬──────────────┬──────────────┐
Old Persian magos  Greek mekhane   mekhana      OE magan, mæg   meahte        OHG
    Latin magus      mechanic    Latin machina      may          might
                    mechanical
     Magi           mechanist     machine
                                                                          OFrench
    Magian          mechanize     machinist                              desmaier
     magic                        machinery                                dismay
    magician                      machination
```

Through different routes, we have *magician, mechanic, machinist,* and *might* ("strength" as well as "perhaps"). But do not let this *dismay* you! Look at two more trees before ending this chapter. The first is a simple *mouse,* but note how many different animal words are related to it:

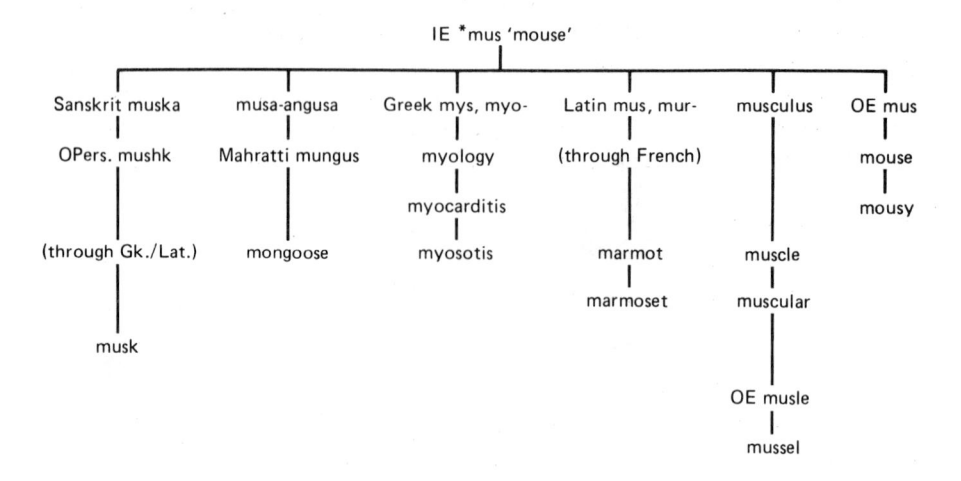

```
                              IE *mus 'mouse'
        ┌──────────┬──────────────┬────────────┬─────────────┬──────────┬─────────┐
   Sanskrit muska   musa-angusa   Greek mys, myo-   Latin mus, mur-   musculus   OE mus
        │              │              │                │                │          │
   OPers. mushk    Mahratti mungus   myology      (through French)    muscle     mouse
        │              │              │                │                │          │
        │              │         myocarditis           │            muscular    mousy
   (through Gk./Lat.)  │              │                │                │
        │          mongoose        myosotis         marmot              │
        │                                              │             OE musle
      musk                                          marmoset             │
                                                                       mussel
```

Finally, let us look at the digit *ten*:

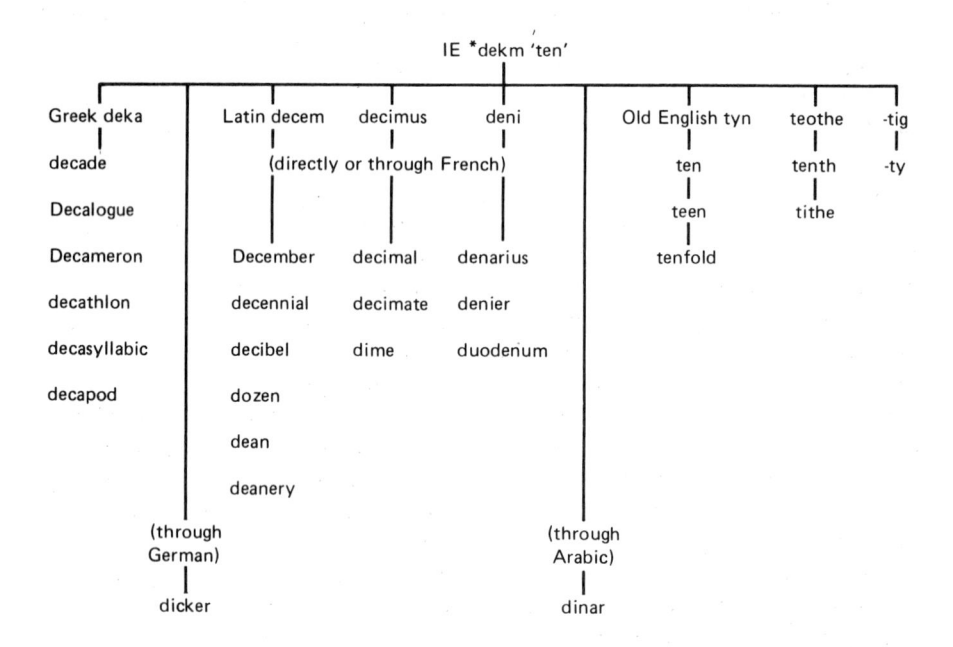

```
                              IE *dekm 'ten'
      ┌───────────┬──────────────────────────────┬──────────────┬──────────┬────────┐
  Greek deka   Latin decem    decimus    deni   Old English tyn  teothe    -tig
      │           │              │         │          │            │        │
   decade    (directly or through French)             ten         tenth    -ty
      │                                                │            │
  Decalogue                                           teen         tithe
      │        December    decimal    denarius         │
  Decameron                                         tenfold
      │      decennial    decimate    denier
  decathlon
      │      decibel      dime       duodenum
  decasyllabic
      │      dozen
  decapod
             dean

             deanery

          (through                          (through
           German)                           Arabic)
             │                                  │
           dicker                             dinar
```

The purpose of this chapter has been both to give you an overview of the history of our language and the sources of our words, *and* to show that the examination of this material is far from dry and academic. Words are the coins we use to exchange ideas with one another. They each carry an interesting history and a knapsack full of association.

EXERCISES

1. Look up *skirt* and *shirt* in a dictionary. Where do they come from? Does this reveal anything about the history of the language?
2. Examine the different versions of the Lord's Prayer. What can you ascertain about word-order change in English?
3. Watch some commercials on television and list the coinages like "superiffic" and "Big Mac." How is TV advertising changing our language?

FURTHER READINGS

BROOK, G. L. *A History of the English Language.* New York: W. W. Norton, 1964 (first published in 1958). An excellent history of the language.

JESPERSEN, O. *Growth and Structure of the English Language*, 4th ed. New York: D. Appleton, 1931 (reprinted frequently). Still the best survey of this material.

MCKNIGHT, G. H. *English Words and their Background.* New York: D. Appleton 1930. A valuable work on vocabulary.

PEI, M. *The Families of Words.* New York: Harper & Brothers, 1962. A fascinating work on word families.

Even when two persons share the same mother-tongue, neither speaks it in exactly the same way: what the speaker says in the light of his experience, the listener has to interpret in the light of his, and these are not the same. Every dialogue is a feat of translation.

—*W. H. Auden*

4 TEACHING ORAL COMMUNICATION SKILLS

This chapter includes a rationale for teaching oral communication skills, standards for establishing programs in listening and speaking, and suggestions for implementing effective instruction. Assessment and evaluation techniques are interwoven throughout the chapter. The oral communication skills, listening and speaking, are considered the primary language arts skills. Although all children who develop normally learn to speak and to listen, each of these skills is developed differently in each child. Some children have vast speaking vocabularies, while other children seem to be verbally impoverished; some children listen attentively and are able to reconstruct complex stories or texts they have heard; other children are unable to retell even the simplest stories. Are these differences simply the product of differences in attention? Yes, in part, but the differences are also a function of the instruction each child receives in oral language skills. Children *can* be taught how to listen attentively and how to express themselves clearly and effectively. Before we discuss the specifics of teaching oral language skills, we will examine the concept of oral communication.

ORAL COMMUNICATION PROGRAMS

In the past, oral communication programs consisted of training in speech; the emphasis of these programs was on the product, on speech itself. Children were taught elements of poise, articulation, gesticulation, and

The oral communication skills, listening and speaking, are considered the primary language arts skills. Although all children who develop normally learn to speak and to listen, each of these skills is developed differently in each child. (*Photo by Linda Lungren*)

modulation in order to produce a perfect product, with little emphasis on effective listening. In more recent, innovative programs, however, the emphasis of oral communication education has been placed on the communicative aspects of both speaking and listening. Children are taught the functions of communication, the reasons for communicating, and the ways in which communication is carried out most effectively.

In an attempt to make oral communication programs more effective, the American Speech-Language-Hearing Association and the Speech Communication Association have established standards for effective oral communication programs that emphasize the communicative aspects of oral language. These organizations make it clear that language is a vehicle of communication and not an end unto itself.

The focus of this chapter is on developing an effective oral communications program that builds on our most current and most thorough knowledge about listening instruction and speaking instruction. We begin by presenting some theories about the origins, essence, and development of listening skills.

LISTENING

When children come to elementary school, they can already speak and listen to some extent. However, preliminary to learning to read, they must learn to follow more complex information and instructions. The kinds of directions and instructions a child must learn to follow involve care and precision in listening; these are skills that can be taught.

In defining listening, Stammer (1977) speaks of a four-level hierarchical processing task:

1. Hearing
2. Attention and concentration
3. Listening
4. Auding

At the level of hearing, Stammer maintains that children must possess sensory and perceptual awareness and acuity to recognize different sounds in their environment. In order to progress to the level of attention and concentration, he states that children must possess the ability to focus on both the source of a message and the message itself. At the level of listening, children must be able to understand and comprehend what they have heard. At the highest level, auding, he maintains that real listening occurs when children are capable of processing oral language in a meaningful way.

Tiedt and Tiedt (1967) offer an interesting cyclical model of the processes involved in listening which they call the Listening Loop.

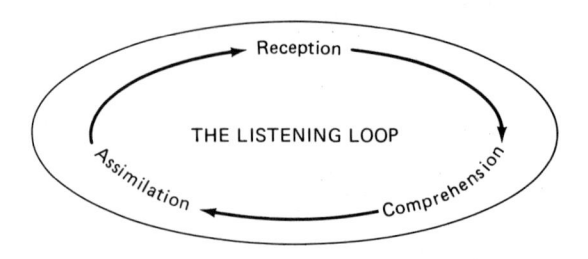

```
        ────► Reception ────
      ╱                      ╲
     │   THE LISTENING LOOP   │
      ╲                      ╱
       Assimilation ◄──── Comprehension
```

Reception includes hearing sounds, distinguishing among them, and deciding whether to listen. Comprehension consists of understanding single words and ideas and recognizing purposes for listening. Assimilation consists of reacting to what has been heard by agreeing, questioning, adding, deleting, and evaluating messages that are heard. In the Listening Loop, each step is important to the total listening experience because the three tasks are interdependent and self-generating.

The Massachusetts State Board of Education devised the following list of listening competencies:

A. Basic Listening Skills
   1. Recognize words and phrases used by the speaker
   2. Indicate why the speaker can or cannot be understood
B. Understanding What You Hear
   1. Understand spoken words and ideas
   2. Identify and understand main ideas
   3. Associate important details with main ideas
   4. Understand descriptions of events and experiences (follow oral directions)
   5. Understand speaker's purpose
C. Using What You Hear
   1. Understand and respond to survival words used in emergency situations (fire = get out)
   2. Summarize information and draw conclusions
   3. Recognize when words and phrases are used to convince or persuade (propaganda)
   4. Follow straightforward directions

CRITICAL LISTENING SKILLS

Many researchers and educators discuss the importance of developing critical listening skills, the highest level of such skills. Lundsteen (1979) lists what she considers the ten most important critical listening skills:

1. Distinguishing fact from fancy, according to criteria
2. Judging validity and adequacy of main ideas, arguments, and hypotheses
3. Distinguishing well-supported statements from opinion and judgment and evaluating them
4. Distinguishing well-supported statements from irrelevant ones and evaluating them
5. Inspecting, comparing, and contrasting ideas and arriving at a conclusion about statements, such as the appropriateness of one descriptive word over another
6. Evaluating the use of fallacies, such as (a) self-contradictions, (b) avoiding the question at issue, (c) hasty or false generalization, (d) false analogy, (e) failure to present all choices, (f) appealing to ignorance
7. Recognizing and judging the effects of various devices the speaker may use to influence the listener, such as (a) music, (b) "loaded" words, (c) voice intonation, (d) play on emotional and controversial issues, (e) propaganda and sales pressure
8. Detecting and evaluating the bias and prejudice of a speaker or of a point of view
9. Evaluating the qualifications of a speaker
10. Planning to evaluate the ways in which a speaker's ideas might be applied in a new situation

Throughout the second part of this chapter, we present a variety of teaching suggestions for instructing your children in each of the listening skills with emphasis on critical listening abilities.

FACTORS INFLUENCING LISTENING

Successful listening is affected by many factors; some external and some internal. External factors may include clarity of the speaker, dialect of the speaker, content of the material, mode of transmission (person, tape recorder, stereo), speed of transmission, and environmental noise. Klinzing's (1972) experiments show that there is no need to slow speech down to help young children comprehend what is said to them.

Internal factors that affect listening comprehension many include mental and physical health of the listener, intelligence of the listener, attention to the task, previous experience, and listener's attitude. A listener's attitude may reinforce or change a spoken message; a listener may "create" a message unintended by the speaker.

SPEAKING

The second language skill to be acquired by children is speaking. Early speech serves a variety of purposes and develops into a form of direct interpersonal communication. By the time children begin elementary school, they have been practicing spoken language for four or five years. They have developed extensive speaking vocabularies consisting of approximately twenty-five hundred words. They know aspects of the phonological, syntactic, semantic, and pragmatic systems of their language. Children begin to acquire proficient speech in their preschool years.

Widdowson (1979) describes proficient speech as grammatical and communicative competencies. He criticizes current methods of instruction for their failure to develop proficient speakers. A new emphasis on language as an instrument of communication has brought about new ways to characterize speech acts in terms of their use. In a modern curriculum, language instruction is organized by functional categories.

Brown and Allen (1976), arguing that speech education in the past has been based on the product of the act, the speech itself, have proposed an instructional model for an effective oral communication program. The following chart, constructed from Brown and Allen's work, illustrates their view of communication competence. They suggest that all communication must be viewed in terms of its functions. Their model describes five general functions of communication:

1. Control function
2. Feeling function
3. Informing function
4. Ritualizing function
5. Imagining function

Each function consists of several subcategories, which are listed for each communication function:

Model of Nature of Communication Competence
Functions of Communication
(Functions that competent people use)

CONTROLLING FUNCTION

1. *wanting:* "I want some more milk."
2. *offer:* "I'll help you fix it."
3. *command:* "Get my bike now!"
4. *suggestion:* "Let's read books."

5. *formulation:* "You're s'posed to pick up your toys before you go."
6. *permit:* "You can play with my boat."
7. *intend:* "I'm going to the store."
8. *query want:* "You wanna play cards?"
9. *query permission:* "May I use your scissors?"
10. *query intention:* "Are you playing or not?"
11. *promise:* "I'll always defend you."
12. *threat:* "I'm gonna tell your mom."
13. *warning:* "You're gonna fall."
14. *prohibition:* "Don't touch my doll."
15. *condition:* "If you help me (I'll play ball too)."
16. *contractual:* "I'll give you some candy if you let me have that car."
17. *command-verbalization:* "Tell her about it." *or* "Stop talking right now."
18. *assent:* "Sure, O.K."
19. *refuse:* "No, I won't."
20. *reject:* "I don't want to go."
21. *evasion:* "We'll see." *or* "I don't know."
22. *query justification:* "Why did you do it?"
23. *justification:* "Because my mom told me to." *or* "It's naughty to do." *or* "Children aren't allowed to do that."

FEELING FUNCTION

1. *exclamation:* "Wow!" *or* "Nuts!"
2. *expression of state/attitude:* "I feel just terrible today." *or* "I really don't like that program."
3. *query state/attitude:* "How do you feel now?" *or* "What do you think about 'Popeye'?"
4. *taunt:* "You're a real baby."
5. *challenge:* "I bet I can stay up later than you."
6. *approval:* "You had a nice idea."
7. *disapproval:* "You did a silly thing."
8. *cajole:* "You know how—come on."
9. *congratulate:* "Good for you!"
10. *commiseration:* "I'm sorry you were hurt."
11. *endearment:* "I'm your best friend."
12. *tale-telling:* "And then he hit me with the truck and. . . ."
13. *blaming:* "John broke the glass, not me."
14. *query blame:* "Who wrote on the wall?"
15. *command to apologize:* "Say you're sorry."

16. *apology:* "I'm sorry I broke your picture."
17. *agree:* "I hate him, too."
18. *disagree:* "I think you're wrong—he's nice."
19. *reject:* (same as control)
20. *evasion:* (same as control)
21. *condition:* "I'd like her if she was nice to me."
22. *query justification:* (same as control)
23. *justification:* (same as control)

INFORMING FUNCTION

1. *ostension:* "That's (*pointing*) the car I like."
2. *statement:* "I never hit other people."
3. *question—positive/negative:* "Is that your car?"
4. *content question:* "Who runs fastest in your neighborhood?"
5. *why question:* "Why does he always win?"
6. *query name:* "What's that thing called?"
7. *response:* "Bill runs the fastest."
8. *affirm:* "You're right."
9. *deny:* "No, you're mistaken."
10. *reject:* "No, it's not terrible."
11. *evasion:* (same as control)
12. *condition:* (same as control)
13. *justification:* (same as control, but wider in scope—includes all supporting material)

RITUALIZING FUNCTION

1. *greetings:* "Hi, how ya doing?"
2. *farewells:* "See you tomorrow."
3. *turn-taking:* "And what do you think?" *or* all nonverbal cues signaling the back and forth flow in conversation.
4. *call:* "Nancy..."
5. *availability response:* "Yea? You called me?"
6. *request to repeat:* "Say that again."
7. *repeat:* "I said, 'Give it to me.'"
   Other rituals include *introducing* someone, *welcoming* a person, *acknowledging* another's new status, and so on.

IMAGINING FUNCTION

1. *commentary:* "And then the old man put his can down..."
2. *expressive:* "Wow, you sure are a pretty doll!"

3. *heuristic:* "When the sun goes out, then it gets dark and then the moon appears."
Other imaginary sequences, as in role playing, follow the communication acts for all other functions.

From: K. Brown & R. Allen, eds., *Developing Communicative Competence in Children.* Skokie, Ill.: National Textbook Company, 1976.

Brown and Allen argue that the oral language curriculum should focus on the instruction of each function listed. Children should be given opportunities to try out, experience, and practice each function of communication.

There are different levels of competence for each function of communication, as shown in the following chart:

Level 1 *Repertoire of Experiences*
Passive repertoire

To be flexible communicators, children must be capable of performing the wide range of communication acts required by their social environment. As children grow in experience, they acquire a number of communication strategies that may be used to accomplish these various acts. An important function of communication instruction is to provide experiences that expand the repertoire of communication strategies available to children when dealing with everyday situations that are important to them.

Level 2 *Selecting Strategies*
Choosing from repertoire

Taking into consideration the relevant characteristics of the communication context—participants, topic, task, setting, and preceding events—children select from their repertoire of strategies those that they perceive to be the most appropriate for the specific situation at a given moment in time. Implicit in the selection process are criteria that help children decide how to act in communication situations. A second important function of communication instruction is to provide an opportunity for children to identify and sharpen the criteria they use in choosing communication strategies.

Level 3   *Implementing Strategies*
Performing

Having determined a strategy to use in a given communication context, children must be willing to carry that strategy into action. Through implementation, children experience themselves using verbal and nonverbal behaviors designed to accomplish a given intent. A third important function of communication instruction is to enable children to experience themselves in dynamic interaction as they give verbal and nonverbal expression to their strategic choices.

Level 4   *Evaluating Performances*
Assessing how good you were. Total performance, not just speech, as in the old way.

Having performed a communication act, children must evaluate their communication behavior in terms of its appropriateness to the communication context and its interpersonal effectiveness—satisfaction to the child and to others. As one grows in competence, one makes informed judgments about his or her own communication. These judgments influence the strategic choices that are made and the implementation that occurs in sustaining the communication act. Ultimately, they contribute to the repertoire of experiences that provide the broad base for future communication encounters. A final, important function of communication instruction is to provide opportunities for children to sharpen their critical awareness of self and others in moments of communication interaction.

SPEAKING SKILLS

The Massachusetts State Board of Education has developed guidelines for assessing competence in the area of speaking skills. Fourteen skills have been chosen as representing the basic skills for effective speaking programs:

    A. Basic Oral Communication Skills
        1. Use words and phrases appropriate to the situation
        2. Speak loudly enough to be heard by a listener or group

A variety of factors may affect successful speaking—the speaker's mental and physical health; his/her attitude toward the content of the message and the audience; the physical setting; audience size, composition, and response. This puppet theater provides a forum for speaking and listening. (*Photo by Linda Lungren*)

3. Speak at a rate the listener can understand
4. Say words distinctly
B. Planning, Developing, and Stating Spoken Messages
   1. Use words in an order that clearly expresses the thought
   2. Organize main ideas for presentation
   3. State main ideas clearly
   4. Support main ideas with important details
   5. Demonstrate knowledge of standard English usage
C. Common Uses of Spoken Messages
   1. Use survival words to cope with emergency situations
   2. Speak so listener understands purpose
   3. Ask for and give straightforward information
   4. Describe objects, events, and experiences
   5. Question others' viewpoints

FACTORS INFLUENCING SPEAKING

A variety of factors may affect successful speaking. Internal factors include the speaker's mental and physical health and his or her attitude toward the content of the message and toward the audience. External factors may include physical setting, audience size and composition, and audience response.

INTERRELATIONS OF LISTENING AND SPEAKING AND THE OTHER LANGUAGE ARTS

Most researchers agree that the four language arts—reading, writing, listening, and speaking—are interrelated in some way. Lundsteen models this relationship as follows:

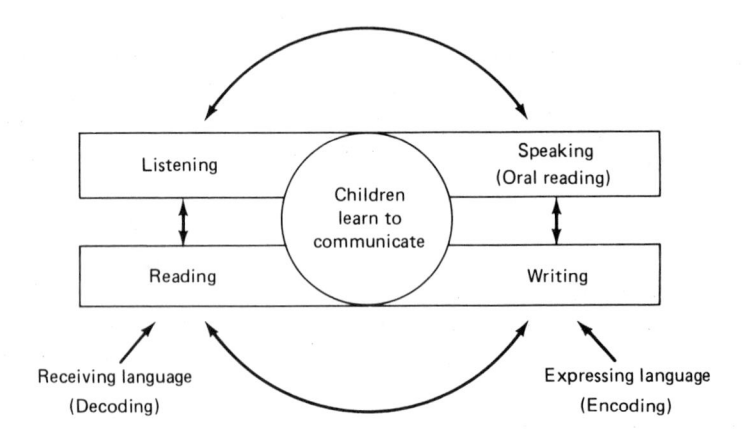

```
          Listening              Speaking
                                (Oral reading)
                   Children
                   learn to
                   communicate
          Reading                 Writing

   Receiving language       Expressing language
      (Decoding)                (Encoding)
```

The arrows denote the continuous interaction among the language arts; communication is at the core of the interaction.

In some cases, teachers have incorrectly assumed that the development of one language skill will help develop facility with all the others. Although it has frequently been suggested that high-achieving children tend to achieve in all the language arts, it has also been found that listening skills will not necessarily make students better readers; nor has it been found that reading automatically improves students' writing.

IMPLEMENTING A LISTENING/SPEAKING PROGRAM

As you use the information presented in the previous pages to develop your oral communications program, you will want to make provision for the following tasks:

1. Listening to tapes
2. Dictation
3. Following directions
4. Telephoning
5. Interviewing
6. Formal/informal speeches
7. Reader's theater
8. Role playing
9. Storytelling
10. Puppetry
11. Creative dramatics
12. Improvisation
13. Choral speaking

Listening to Tapes

While the debate still continues over the effects of simultaneously listening to and reading the same materials, there is no debate about the merit of listening to tapes as an activity that strengthens listening capacity and acuity. Major industries throughout the United States (for example, the Sperry Corporation) have instituted listening programs, based on listening to tapes, which enhance their employees' listening skills.

It is important for you to establish a listening center within your classroom. In a corner of your room, set up a quiet place where students can listen to tapes. You can guide their listening by preparing a question sheet that will assess their listening comprehension.

It is important for you to establish a listening center within your classroom. Listening to tapes and reading along benefits children's comprehension. (*Photo by Linda Lungren*)

While some educators are unsure about the benefits of simultaneously listening to and reading the same material, we believe that your children can profit from this kind of instruction. We believe that you can enhance your children's comprehensive instruction by asking them to listen to tapes and read along. (Many of the major children's books can be purchased on tape at the present time. Alternatively, you can make a tape of the stories or books that you will want your children to read.)

Dictation

Dictation is an excellent way to reinforce listening and writing skills. The task demands of dictation exercises are well-focused and important for the child's education. During dictation, children have an opportunity to practice all the following skills:

1. Listening attentively
2. Listening with concentration
3. Handwriting
4. Punctuation
5. Spelling

In addition to straightforward dictations such as the one listed in Sample 1, you may enjoy assessing your students' abilities to process ambiguous spoken information by orally emphasizing the italicized words in Sample 2.

Sample 1
On June 20, Jane Hern flew to Germany. She had to attend two business meetings within one week. One meeting was held on Monday, June 28, and the other was held on Friday, June 28. She flew to England on Tuesday, June 25, to attend the tennis matches at Wimbledon and flew back to Germany on Thursday, June 27, in time for her second meeting.

Sample 2

Hanna fed her dog, *Biscuits.*
or
Hanna fed her *dog* biscuits.
or
Hanna fed *her* dog biscuits.

Following Directions

Following directions is a critical listening skill. Before a child can read and follow directions, he or she should be able to listen to directions and follow them precisely. The following tasks may be helpful:

A. SENDER-RECEIVER

MATERIALS: Envelopes containing identical shapes

DIRECTIONS: Say the following—Listen carefully. I will only give the directions once. First, find a partner. I will give each of you an envelope containing identical shapes. Next, you should decide who will be the sender and who will be the receiver. Then sit back to back with your partner. The sender will give the directions to the receiver only once. The receiver cannot ask questions. The receiver must listen to the directions that are given by the sender. The listener has to draw the shapes that the sender mentions in the order in which the sender gives them. If the directions have been clear and precise, and if the receiver has listened attentively, both partners will have the same set of shapes in the same order.

B. **MARKING ILLUSTRATIONS**

MATERIALS: Worksheets, pencil, crayon, and/or pen

DIRECTIONS: Pass out a sheet containing a set of pictures or symbols. Then give specific directions such as the following:
Cross out the sun with a blue crayon.
Mark an "X" with a yellow crayon under the clown's right foot.
Make a purple star on the bottom of a specific object on the page.

C. **GUESS THE TITLE OF THE POEM**

MATERIALS: Poems and paper and pencil if children compose their own poems

DIRECTIONS: Read poems such as the ones that follow; do not read the titles. After reading the poem, ask the children to guess the title. Children could be encouraged to write poems of their own with a similar style and read them to the class, asking the class to guess the title.

The Toaster

A silver-scaled Dragon with jaws flaming red
Sits at my elbow and toasts my bread.
I hand him fat slices, and then one by one,
He hands them back when he sees they are done.

William Jay Smith

The Garden Hose

In the gray evening
I see a long green serpent
With its tail in the dahlias.
It lies in loops across the grass
And drinks softly at the faucet.
I can hear it swallow.

Beatrice Janosco

The Eagle

He clasps the crag with crooked hands
Close to the sun in lonely lands,
Ringed with the azure world, he stands
The wrinkled sea beneath him crawls;
He watches from his mountain walls,
And like a thunderbolt he falls.

Alfred Lord Tennyson

Telephoning

All children (and adults) find the telephone fascinating. Young children play with the telephone and adolescents use the telephone, for long periods of time, as a communication instrument. The skills of telephoning are important because they teach children how to listen carefully, how to communicate effectively, and how to practice turn-taking, an important element in oral communication. The telephone forces the child to use language effectively, because the contextual and visual (body language) cues, which are important at early stages of language development, are inaccessible through the telephone. The telephone is an

The skills of telephoning are important because they teach children how to listen carefully, how to communicate effectively, and how to practice turn-taking, an important element in oral communication. (*Photo by Linda Lungren*)

extremely useful tool in second-language instruction; you really do not understand a second language until you can process it through the telephone, until you can understand what other speakers are saying, and until you can communicate with a person across telephone lines without the help of gestures.

Interviewing

Interviewing techniques are extremely important skills to acquire. Although not every child needs to become a commercial success as an enormously overpaid television celebrity, children should learn the basic skills of interviewing because such skills integrate and develop the simultaneous processing of thinking and speaking skills. At an early age, children should be taught methods for conducting interviews. You can begin your program with prepared questions for the children. Then, move them on to the concepts of prepared, but flexible, questions that allow the speaker to wander freely and the interviewer to follow up each answer with as many questions as necessary for eliciting useful, interesting information. Needless to say, not every interview is a social encounter in which the speaker recounts feats, exploits, and conquests. Children should also be introduced to the elements of employment interviews and news interviews and they should have the opportunity to serve both as the interviewer and the interviewee. You may want to use the following guidelines:

Guidelines for Interviewing

1. Plan for the interview by learning something about the person to be interviewed.
2. Research the topics that are going to be discussed during the interview.
3. Stay on the topic of the interview.
4. Follow up interesting answers with appropriate questions that stick to the topic.
5. Don't let the interview drag on. End it when the interviewee is no longer giving useful information.
6. Make sure the interviewee knows that he or she is going to be interviewed so that he or she can come prepared.

As you begin to teach children how to interview, you may want to have them interview a cooperative adult, using the following questions as guidelines:

Who am I interviewing?   Name_____

                              Date_____

Questions: **Answers:**

What is your profession? _____
How long have you been doing
   this job? _____
Why did you choose this job? _____
Did you ever want to do any
   other job? _____
What job? _____
Why didn't you do the other
   job? _____
Do you think you'll ever have
   another job? _____
What training do you think
   you'll need? _____
                   Thank you.

It usually works to have children interview one another. If you decide to do this, you may want to structure the interview so that it won't "wander." The following is one example of a structured interview between students:

Do you have any hobbies? _____
   What are they? _____
How did you get this as your
   hobby? _____
Can you teach someone
   else how to do it? _____
If yes, give some suggestions. _____
Would you recommend that
   others take up this hobby? _____
                   Thank you.

Formal/Informal Speeches

Children should have many opportunities to give speeches and to listen to speeches throughout their school years. There are many books that will help you understand the types of speeches that children can prepare, for example, how-to speeches, expository speeches, and speeches of persuasion. It is important to reiterate that formal/informal speeches are excellent opportunities for developing your children's listening skills.

Children should be taught to have a purpose when they are listening to speeches. One good way to encourage children to listen effectively is to ask them to outline the speech or to paraphrase it after it has been delivered. For example, if it is a speech of persuasion, ask the children to follow this outline:

    A. What was the overall purpose of the speech?
    B. What was the main idea of the speech?
        1. Example 1 of a supporting detail
        2. Example 2 of a supporting detail
        3. Example 3 of a supporting detail
    C. What was the conclusion of the speech?

Reader's Theater

Reader's theater is a form of dramatic interpretation in which children are given the opportunity to read orally. No scenery, costumes, or actions are used in Reader's theater. The reader must project the storyline, or plot, through his or her reading; the reader must also convey mood, emotion, and tone through interpretation of the script.

Reader's theater helps students in the audience listen attentively because they do not have scripts in front of them. They have to listen critically to make sure that they are comprehending the story accurately. Reader's theater also helps the children who are doing the acting to speak effectively. They must read their lines with expression so that the audience can imagine the entire story.

As they read, all the players in reader's theater hold copies of the scripts they are performing. They do not attempt to become the character; rather, they give the audience an idea of the character. The audience, the listeners, must use imagination to complete the picture. No actions by the players are introduced; the audience must use its own creative resources to interpret action and to build an inclusive picture of the entire story.

Reader's theater works extremely well as a speaking and listening activity because it does not require that a student physically portray a character, which can be extremely threatening to children. Children who are acting in the play have the opportunity to practice oral skills in an unthreatening way; they have the script in front of them. Less able readers can participate in this activity fully because they can almost memorize their lines. Children who serve as the audience have an opportunity to hone their listening skills.

Reader's theater can integrate a wide range of activities within your language arts curriculum. For example, a group of students may research the life and legend of a historical character and write a Reader's theater script for presentation to the entire class. This type of format may be especially helpful in having your children interpret the information they find in reference materials. In one classroom, we saw one group of middle-school children write a reader's theater script using the writings of Martin Luther King, Jr., as the basis of drama; a second group used writings from historical accounts and plays about Abraham Lincoln as the source of their script.

The way in which you set up your stage is extremely important in Reader's theater. The following is an illustration of a successful Reader's theater presentation of *Poor Old Lady*:

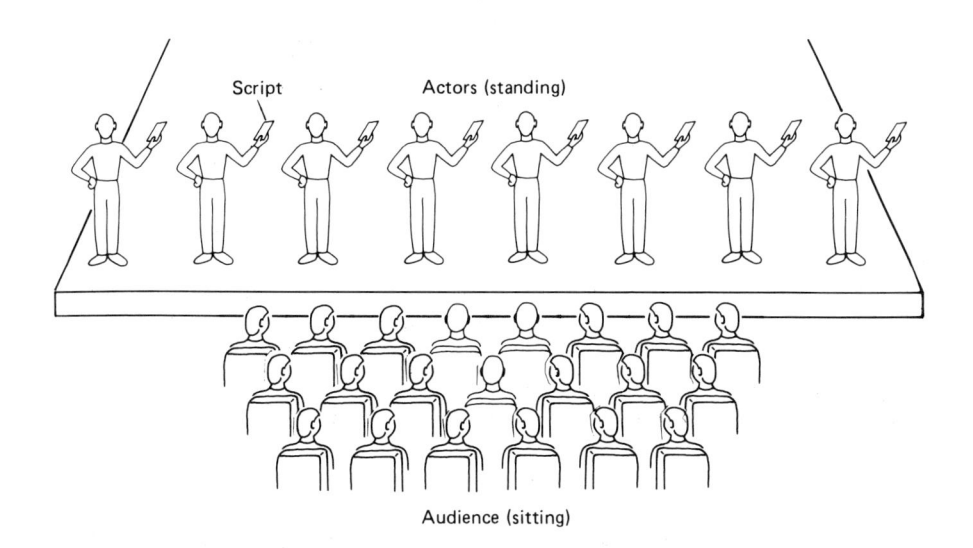

The script is included below:

POOR OLD LADY

1: Poor old lady, she swallowed a fly.
    I don't know why she swallowed a fly.
2: Poor old lady, I think she'll die.
3: Poor old lady, she swallowed a spider.
    It squirmed and wriggled and turned inside her.
1: She swallowed the spider to catch the fly.
    I don't know why she swallowed a fly.
2: Poor old lady, I think she'll die.
4: Poor old lady, she swallowed a bird.
    How absurd! She swallowed a bird.
3: She swallowed the bird to catch the spider.
1: She swallowed the spider to catch the fly,
    I don't know why she swallowed a fly.

2: Poor old lady, I think she'll die.
5: Poor old lady, she swallowed a cat.
   Think of that! She swallowed a cat.
4: She swallowed the cat to catch the bird.
3: She swallowed the bird to catch the spider,
1: She swallowed the spider to catch the fly,
   I don't know why she swallowed the fly.
2: Poor old lady, I think she'll die.
6: Poor old lady, she swallowed a dog.
   She went the whole hog when she swallowed the dog.
5: She swallowed the dog to catch the cat.
4: She swallowed the cat to catch the bird.
3: She swallowed the bird to catch the spider,
1: She swallowed the spider to catch the fly,
   I don't know why she swallowed the fly.
2: Poor old lady, I think she'll die.
7: Poor old lady, she swallowed a cow.
   I don't know how she swallowed the cow.
6: She swallowed the cow to catch the dog,
5: She swallowed the dog to catch the cat,
4: She swallowed the cat to catch the bird,
3: She swallowed the bird to catch the spider,
1: She swallowed the spider to catch the fly.
   I don't know why she swallowed a fly.
2: Poor old lady, I think she'll die.
8: Poor old lady, she swallowed a horse.
All: She died, of course.

The following books for children can serve as sources for effective Reader's theater scripts:

BISHOP, CLAIRE. *The Five Chinese Brothers.* New York: Harper & Row, 1975.
BURCH, ROBERT. *Queenie Peavy.* New York: Viking Press, 1966.
FENNER, CAROL. *Gorilla Gorilla.* New York: Random House, 1973.
FRITZ, JEAN. *Early Thunder.* New York: Coward-McCann, 1967.
GREENE, CONSTANCE. *The Unmaking of Rabbit.* New York: Viking Press, 1972.
HINTON, S. E. *The Outsiders.* New York: Dell, 1967.
HOBAN, RUSSELL. *A Bargain for Frances.* New York: Harper & Row, 1970.
HUNT, IRENE. *Across Five Aprils.* New York: Follett, 1964.

Role Playing

Role playing is important in helping children develop their skills in the following areas:

1. Listening skills
2. Attention/concentration skills
3. Speaking skills
4. Oral interpretation skills
5. Emotive skills
6. Empathy/sympathy skills

You can compose scripts for your children by creating a scene that ends at the point of conflict. The role-playing episode can explore alternative answers for the conflict that you have described. Role playing can be used as a motivating activity for a story or text you are reading with your children. It can also be used to start off a writing activity.

The following situation may be used for elementary-school-aged children:

Your older brother Frank has made it clear that he doesn't want you to ride his new 10-speed bike. One day, you take it out for a ride when he is away. You and your friend Philip decide to go biking to the beach. You don't have a lock for the bike, so you ask Phil to chain his bike with your brother's. Phil says, "Don't worry. I'm not going to chain my bike." You protest, but Phil has already taken to the shores. You run after him. When you return from the beach, you see your brother's bike has been hit by a car; one wheel is bent and its spokes are broken. At that moment, your brother turns the corner with a group of his friends. He sees you and the bike. You say:_____

The following procedures will help you "direct" your children's role-playing sessions:

1. Warm up. The audience needs to be warmed up to a situation that is similar to the situation to be enacted. Good beginnings might include, "Has anyone ever found themselves in a situation where...." or "Have you ever felt...."

2. Read the actual situation. The situation must have some dramatic sense. Give the characters names, include descriptions (limited), and include dialogue. Continue the story to a crisis point—a point at which a character must either say or do something.
3. Discuss the reading. Ask students what they would do and what they think about the situation. Ask a prospective player to delineate his or her character. Ask for characteristics and feelings beforehand.
4. Select players. Try to have students volunteer, but be selective. Choose someone who has a feeling for the character and a point of view.
5. Ask players to describe themselves alone and then in relation to one another. Ask them what they want to be doing, where they want to be standing, sitting, and so forth.
6. Have students who are not players observe a specific player. The net effect of this is involvement.
7. Play the scene. This is the point at which personal taste, choice, and objectives come into view. You may want to play the scene up to a crisis point or until it's played out.
8. Ask the players how they feel about what happened.
9. Ask the nonplayers to respond. If a student has another point of view (and you think it's worthwhile), ask the student to elaborate on the way he or she would have done it. Ask students to play the part and to reenact the scene.
10. Select new players. You may choose a combination of old and new players.
11. Play the scene.

Storytelling

All the world loves a story and a storyteller. You will want your children to share in this ancient activity both as listeners and as tellers of stories.

Storytelling is oral language. It is literature in oral tradition. Bower (1976) explains that story script is part of the cognitive structure that provides readers with schema that are used to comprehend what is read. Mandler and Johnson (1977) maintain that listening to stories helps children develop the following skills: sequencing of events, recognizing cause-and-effect relationships, and identifying beginnings and endings of stories. All these skills are critical for effective reading. It has been acknowledged that children who have participated in storytelling activities or in library story hours where stories have been read have made gains in reading comprehension, word knowledge, and vocabulary.

The following stories from all over the world lend themselves to successful storytelling:

AFRICA. *Anansi the Spider.* Adapted and illustrated by Gerald McDermott. New York: Holt, Rinehart & Winston, 1972.

GERMANY. *The Bremen-town Musicians* by the Brothers Grimm. Retold by Ruth Belov Gross. Illustrated by Jack Kent. New York: Scholastic Book Services, 1974.

ISRAEL. *It Could Always Be Worse.* Illustrated by Margot Zemach. New York: Farrar, Straus & Giroux, 1976.

NIGERIA. *Why the Sun and the Moon Live in the Sky* by Elphinstone Dayrell. Illustrated by Blair Lent. Boston: Houghton Mifflin, 1968.

Puppetry

Children love puppets. Puppetry is an activity in which all children can participate as speakers. If some of your children are very shy or uncomfortable in performing in front of other children, puppetry may be a way in which they can speak to the group through a persona without fear of ridicule or rejection. Puppets can be either very primitive or very elaborate in their construction; children can create their own puppets from simple brown paper bags. You may select or write (or ask the children to write) scripts for the puppet show. Note that puppetry is closely related to role playing.

If some of your children are very shy or uncomfortable in performing in front of other children, puppetry may be a way in which they can speak to the group without fear of ridicule or rejection by other children. (*Photo by Linda Lungren*)

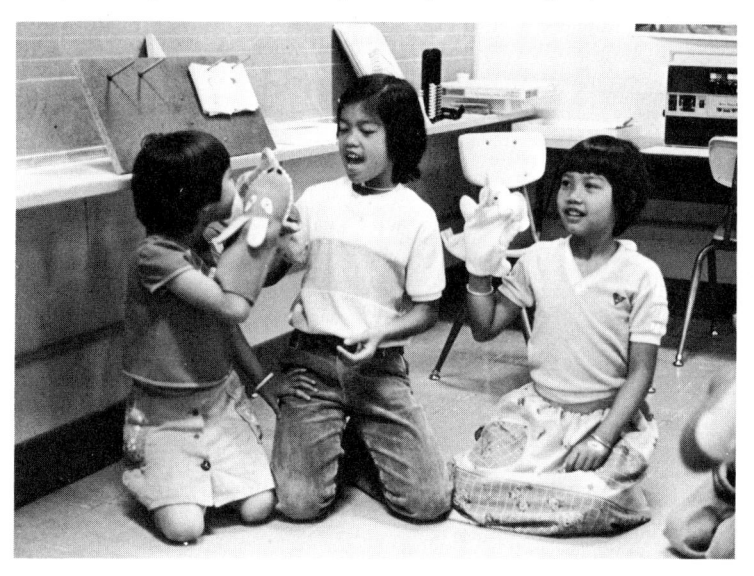

You and your children can easily make the following two kinds of puppets:

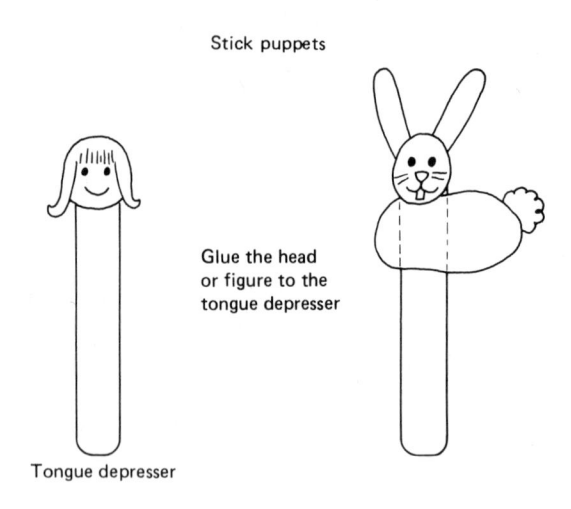

Stick puppets

Glue the head or figure to the tongue depresser

Tongue depresser

Paper bag puppets

The following books may be useful to you as you begin to prepare your puppetry curriculum:

BEVERFORD, M. *How to Make Puppets and Teach Puppetry.* New York: Taplinger Publishing Company. This book contains ideas for the primary-school-aged child.

CHARNOFF, G. *Puppet Party.* New York: Scholastic Book Services. This book is useful in working with preschoolers.

ENGLER, L., AND TYIAN, C. *Making Puppets Come Alive.* New York: Taplinger Publishing Company. This book contains activities that will be useful for working with toddlers.

LEWIS, S. *Making Easy Puppets.* New York: E. P. Dutton and Company. This book contains activities that will help elementary-school-aged children in making puppets.

Improvisation and Creative Dramatics

Creative dramatics has a place in every classroom. Children need opportunities for performing creative, spontaneous enactments of dramatic materials. You can write the materials yourself or you can select scripts that have been written for classroom acting. Children need to explore the range of their own voices as well as the range of their own ability to interpret and convey meaning to an audience. Creative dramatics is an excellent vehicle with which to accomplish this.

Before you begin creative dramatics activities, you may want to have the children do some warm-up exercises such as the following:

1. Facial expressions only: sad, happy, angry, annoyed, elated, frustrated.
2. Facial expressions with gestures: sad, happy, angry, annoyed, elated, frustrated
3. Pantomime a simple action: climbing a ladder, washing a window
4. Pantomime a complex action: scoring the winning point in the basketball game, changing the typewriter ribbon

Choral Speaking

Choral speaking is an excellent activity for helping children develop oral speaking skills and reading skills in a nonthreatening way. As children read along with the group, they learn the skills of syllabication, pronunciation, prosody (pitch, stress, tone), and interpretation. You (or one of your children) can direct this activity in the role of a conductor. Assign specific lines to individual children and ask them to do something special as they speak their solo line, for example, ask them to shout their line or to say the line softly or to say the line in a staccato manner. Your children may enjoy doing a choral reading of Carl Sandburg's "Jazz Fantasia."

Jazz Fantasia

Drum on your drums, batter on your banjoes,
sob on the long cool winding saxophones.
Go to it, O jazzmen.
Sling your knuckles on the bottom of the happy
tin pans, let your trombones ooze, and go husha-
husha-hush with the slippery sand-paper.
Moan like an autumn wind high in the lonesome tree-
tops, moan soft like you wanted somebody terrible,
cry like a racing car slipping away from a motorcycle
cop, bang-bang! you jazzmen, bang altogether drums,
traps, banjoes, horns, tin cans—make two people fight
on the top of stairway and scratch each other's eyes
in a clinch tumbling down the stairs.
Can the rough stuff . . . now a Mississippi steamboat
pushes up the night river with a hoo-hoo-hoo-oo . . .
and the green lanterns calling to the high soft stars
. . . a red moon rides on the humps of the low river
hills . . . go to it, O jazzmen.

ACTIVITIES FOR YOUR STUDENTS

Each of the following activities will help reinforce the importance of listening skills.

LISTENING

NAME OF ACTIVITY: Simon Says

SKILLS DEVELOPED: Practice naming parts of the body and following directions

MATERIALS NEEDED: None

PROCEDURES: Students follow direction only when teacher begins the sentence with "Simon Says." Otherwise, children disregard the command.

• • •

NAME OF ACTIVITY: Big Wind Blows

SKILLS DEVELOPED: Practice naming colors, objects (clothing)

MATERIALS NEEDED: None

PROCEDURES:
1. Teacher says, "Big Wind Blows."
2. Students say, "What does it blow?"

3. Teacher says, "It blows those who wear red socks."
4. Students wearing red socks must run.

. . .

NAME OF ACTIVITY: Opposites

SKILLS DEVELOPED: Interpretation of word meaning

MATERIALS NEEDED: None

PROCEDURES: Teacher says a word; students say the opposite of the word. Or: Teacher says a noun; student says its verb. (For example, "Put the book on the *stand*"; I can't *stand* there.")

. . .

NAME OF ACTIVITY: I Packed My Bag

SKILLS DEVELOPED: Memory

MATERIALS NEEDED: None

PROCEDURES: Teacher starts by saying "I packed my bag. In my bag I placed a _____." Students must repeat the previous sentence and add their own words. The final sentence will be built quite long depending on the number of students in your group.

. . .

NAME OF ACTIVITY: What Am I?

SKILLS DEVELOPED: Drawing conclusions from stated clues; creating definition

MATERIALS NEEDED: None

PROCEDURES: Teacher reads a four- or five-line description of an object. Students guess the object.

. . .

NAME OF ACTIVITY: Strip Story

SKILLS DEVELOPED: Logical sequencing and organizing abilities

MATERIALS NEEDED: Story cut up into sentences, which are written on strips of paper and distributed to students

PROCEDURES: Students have to organize the story. The child who thinks that he or she has the first part, reads it. Other students build on the story.

. . .

NAME OF ACTIVITY: Building Story

SKILLS DEVELOPED: Developing students' word phrases, sentences, and logical thinking

MATERIALS NEEDED: None

PROCEDURES: One student starts the story by offering an opening. A second student repeats the previous sentence and adds his or her own. Activity continues until everyone has contributed a part and ended a story.

• • •

NAME OF ACTIVITY: Gossip

SKILLS DEVELOPED: Ability to listen to and repeat a sentence without mistakes

MATERIALS NEEDED: None

PROCEDURES: Teacher may start the message by whispering to a player. The player whispers the message to the next player and the activity continues until all the players have had a chance to receive and give the message. The last one tells the group what he or she heard and compares it with the original message.

• • •

NAME OF ACTIVITY: Three Ideas

SKILLS DEVELOPED: Find main idea

MATERIALS NEEDED: None

PROCEDURES: One child is given three ideas such as (1) a trip (2) a happy day, and (3) a family. He or she is asked to tell a story to the class using these three main ideas. The other children are told to listen for them. As a variation, do not tell the ideas of the story to the children who are listening, but have them guess what they are.

• • •

NAME OF ACTIVITY: Predicting News

SKILLS DEVELOPED: Making inferences

MATERIALS NEEDED: Television; paper and pencil if desired

PROCEDURES: After listening to a newscast, the children are asked to predict the outcome of the event. They may also discuss what possible event led to the situation, using the facts supplied by the newscaster.

Teaching Oral Communication Skills   97

Each of the following activities will help reinforce your children's speaking skills.

• • •

NAME OF ACTIVITY: Newscast

SKILLS DEVELOPED: Speaking in the role of someone else

MATERIALS NEEDED: None

PROCEDURES: Children compose fictitious news stories and report them to the class.

• • •

NAME OF ACTIVITY: Tongue Twisters

SKILLS DEVELOPED: Articulation

MATERIALS NEEDED: None

PROCEDURES: Have students write tongue twisters, which are then put in a box. Each child chooses a twister and attempts to recite it.

• • •

NAME OF ACTIVITY: Train Game

SKILLS DEVELOPED: Initial sounds

MATERIALS NEEDED: None

PROCEDURES: One child is an engineer and gives an initial sound. The engineer calls on someone to give the same sound and if the sound is correct, the child joins the train.

• • •

NAME OF ACTIVITY: Listen and Remember

SKILLS DEVELOPED: Listening, remembering, and then restating what is heard.

MATERIALS NEEDED: None

PROCEDURES: One child says something. You write it down or record it. The next child then attempts to restate the utterance of the first child.

• • •

NAME OF ACTIVITY: Whose Voice Is It?

SKILLS DEVELOPED: Auditory acuity

MATERIALS NEEDED: None

PROCEDURES: Have five speakers ready to speak. The other children should all be ready to listen, with their heads turned around. Ask one of the five children to speak and ask the listeners to guess who spoke.

· · ·

NAME OF ACTIVITY: Context Game

SKILLS DEVELOPED: Exercising the ability to figure out context when a word in speech is missing or garbled

MATERIALS NEEDED: None

PROCEDURES: Replace a word in a sentence with a nonsense word. Students guess, through use of context, the meaning of the word. The guesser then creates another sentence.

· · ·

NAME OF ACTIVITY: Off the Cuff

SKILLS DEVELOPED: Learning to give oral speech on the spur of the moment

MATERIALS NEEDED: None

PROCEDURES: Ask students to define words such as: *adolescent, adult, education, knowledge, kindness, rudeness, fairness, love, honesty, peace, hate, war,* and *family*. Students thus give definitions without preparation.

EXERCISES

1. What are the counterparts of the four levels of listening for speaking skills?
2. List the ways in which listening and reading are alike and the ways in which they are different.
3. List the way in which speaking and writing are alike and the ways in which they are different.
4. Design an informal test of listening skills and an informal test of speaking skills.
5. Explain the ways in which a child may be inhibited from developing effective listening/speaking skills in a classroom where the product of learning is more important than the process of learning.

REFERENCES

Bower, G. "Experiments on Story Understanding and Recall." *Quarterly Journal of Experimental Psychology* 28 (1976):511-538

Brown, K., and Allen, R. *Developing Communication Competence in Children.* Skokie, Ill.: National Textbook Company, 1976.

Carroll, J. *Learning from Verbal Discourse in Educational Media: A Review of the Literature.* (ETS RB-71-61) Princeton, N. J.: Educational Testing Service, 1971

Devine, T. "Listening: What Do We Know After Fifty Years of Research and Theorizing?" *Journal of Reading* 21 (1978):269-304.

Mandler, J., and Johnson, N. "Remembrance of Things Passed." *Cognitive Psychology* 9 (1977):111-151.

Stammer, J. "Target: The Basics of Listening." *Language Arts* (1977):661-664.

Sticht, T. "Learning by Listening." In R. Freedle and J. Carroll, eds., *Language Comprehension and the Acquisition of Knowledge.* Washington, D. C.: V. H. Winston and Sons, 1972, pp. 285-313.

BIBLIOGRAPHY

Galvin, Kathleen M., and Book, Cassandra L. *Speech Communication: An Interpersonal Approach for Teachers.* Skokie, Ill.: National Textbook Co., 1973.

Klinzing, Dene G. "Listening Comprehension of Pre-School Age Children As a Function of Rate Presentation, Sex and Age." *Speech Teacher* 21 (1972): 17-26.

Lundsteen, Sara W. *Listening: Its Impact at All Levels on Reading and The Other Language Arts.* Urbana, Ill.: ERIC Clearinghouse on Reading and Communication Skills, National Institute of Education, 1979.

Tiedt, Iris M., and Tiedt, Sidney W. *Contemporary English in the Elementary School.* Englewood Cliffs, N. J.: Prentice-Hall, 1967.

Widdowson, H. G. *Explorations in Applied Linguistics.* Oxford: Oxford University Press, 1979.

FURTHER READINGS

Brown, K., and Allen, R. *Developing Communication Competence in Children.* Skokie, Ill.: National Textbook Company, 1976. Provides a logical framework for designing your oral communication programs.

Devine, T. "Listening: What Do We Know After Fifty Years of Research and Theorizing?" *Journal of Reading* 21 (1978):269-304. An excellent article, which synthesizes research in an attempt to answer the questions: What is listening? Can it be measured? Can it be taught? How is listening related to intelligence, reading, and thinking?

LUNDSTEEN, S. *Listening: Its Impact at All Levels on Reading and the Other Language Arts*. Urbana, Ill.: National Council of Teachers of English, 1979. A comprehensive review of listening research. The author includes a listening taxonomy and describes both commercially prepared and unpublished assessment instruments.

WOOD, B. *Development of Functional Communication Competencies: Pre-K–Grade 6*. Falls Church, Va.: Speech Communication Association, 1977. Provides comprehensive activities for children grades K–6 with follow-up questions that develop communication competence.

In semi-literate countries demagogues pay court to teen-agers.

—*W. H. Auden*

5 WRITING SYSTEMS

Before looking at the processes of writing, spelling, and grammar, we will examine the development of writing in human culture and the evolution of the alphabet in particular. The development of writing is one of the greatest achievements of humanity, and it is closely allied with art and culture.

READING AND WRITING

When we speak of the "language arts," we are talking about four things: speaking and listening and reading and writing. The first two employ the auditory modality—they require sound for transmission. The second two are visual.

Reading and writing—the use of the visual modality to transmit verbal information—are secondary to speaking and listening. Primitive man had no notion of writing, and even today there are many peoples who have no need for it. Prehistoric man and various aboriginal peoples today seldom venture beyond their tribal territory. Voice, gesture, drum, whistle, and horn suffice for communicative purposes.

Storytellers or "medicine men" were traditionally chosen by virtue of personality and memory. Without writing, it was encumbent upon the the wisemen (or wisewomen) of the tribe to remember the past, the rules, the rites, the herbs to be used for this or that, and the times of the year for sowing, herding from one pasture to another, and harvesting.

The development of humankind from the band to a larger group and from the hunter-gatherer to the agricultural stage meant that some kinds of information had to be recorded and that aids to memory had to be devised. The earliest records of attempts to preserve material appear in inventories and trade lists. If the local band was not self-sufficient, then the merchant, the caravan operator, and the purchaser had to know (for example) how many bronze tripods or bolts of cloth or clay jugs were being taken, transported, and delivered. The earliest precursors of writing are actual physical tokens of the things they represent.

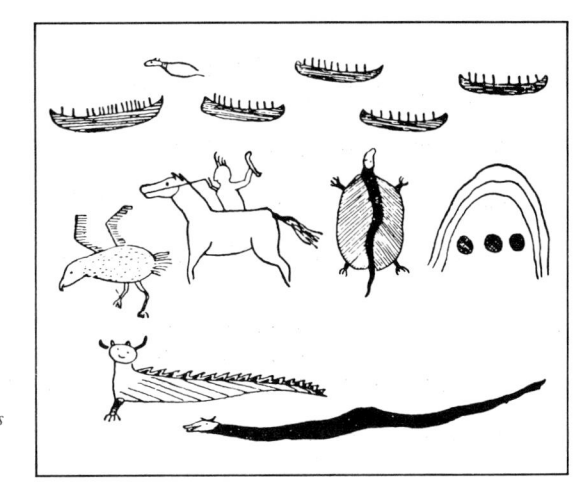

FIGURE 5-1. An Amerindian drawing from Michigan.
[*From:* H. R. Schoolcraft, *Historical . . . information . . . Respecting . . . Indian Tribes* (Philadelphia, 1851), plate 57B.]

FIGURE 5-2. A Cheyenne letter.
[*From:* G. Mallery, *Picture-Writing of the American Indians* (Washington, 1893), p. 364.]

It is apparent that such a system is both cumbersome and limited in the scope of things that can be represented. Even using a varied set of symbols, the nature of the message is quite constrained. It is said that the ancient Scythians (inhabitants of what is now southern Russia) once sent a message to the king of the Persians, which consisted of a bird, a mouse, a frog, and five arrows. Its import was: "Persians! Can you fly like a bird? Can you hide in the ground like a mouse? Can you bound through swamps like a frog? If not, do not go to war with us, for we will overwhelm you with arrows" (three animals, but five arrows).

104   Writing Systems

Many Amerindian tribes used the calumet, or "peace pipe," to signify peace or war; wampum among the Iroquois was color-coded for meaning: white for peace, red for war or anger, black for death or misfortune, and yellow for gold or tribute.

The Yebu in Nigeria use cowrie shells strung together to convey messages: Two shells back to back are a reproof for nonpayment of a debt; four shells, in face-to-face pairs, signify good will and a request for a personal interview.

Knotted cords and message sticks are other symbolic, nonverbal ways of sending messages. But all these are very limited. People had to develop the capability to send a more complex string of messages.

KINDS OF WRITING SYSTEMS

The writing system with which we are all familiar, the one you are reading at this moment, is an alphabetic system. That is, spoken sounds are represented by marks or symbols or "letters." However, humans did not begin writing with this kind of system, nor is it the only one that exists.

Iconography consists of drawing actual objects. A sequence of such fragmentary pictures gives a static impression. Humans began expressing their thoughts in picture-writing. Such pictures (for example, on cave walls primarily in southern France and in Spain) are a beautiful and long-lasting

FIGURE 5-3. Prehistoric drawings from three sites in Europe: Altamira, Spain; Lascaux, France; and Norway.

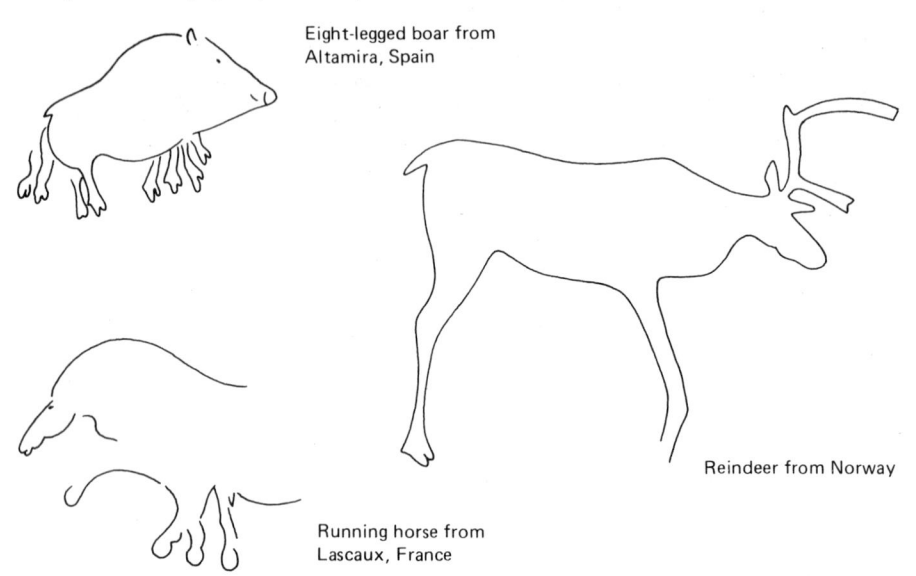

Eight-legged boar from Altamira, Spain

Reindeer from Norway

Running horse from Lascaux, France

attempt on the part of ancient peoples to express their innermost thoughts, to communicate inportant events. We do not know exactly what the ancients were trying to say, but it appears clear that the majority of the cave drawings had magical or totemic intent.

Synthetic, or ideographic, writing was a step forward from iconography. Here people attempted to put their pictures into a connected sequence, to "tell a story," to write songs or epic poems. But here, as in iconographic representation, there was no connection between the object pictured and what it was called. That is, there was no relationship between the graphic symbol and the phonological representation of the object.

Analytic, or transitional, writing was probably the beginning of systematic writing as we know it. Almost all the writing systems of the ancient world were of this type. Here, a particular picture, in simplified form, became the conventionally accepted symbol for its "name." The "name" of the picture, then, was closely identified with the object itself. Cuneiform ("wedge writing"), Egyptian hieroglyphics, and the Chinese, Mayan, and Aztec scripts all appear to have arisen in this manner.

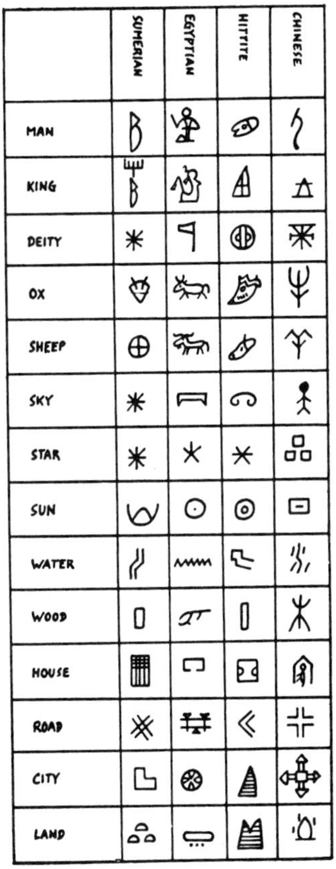

FIGURE 5-4. Some pictorial signs in Chinese, Hittite, Egyptian, and Sumerian.
[*From:* I. J. Gelb, *A Study of Writing* (Chicago: University of Chicago Press, © 1952), figure 54.]

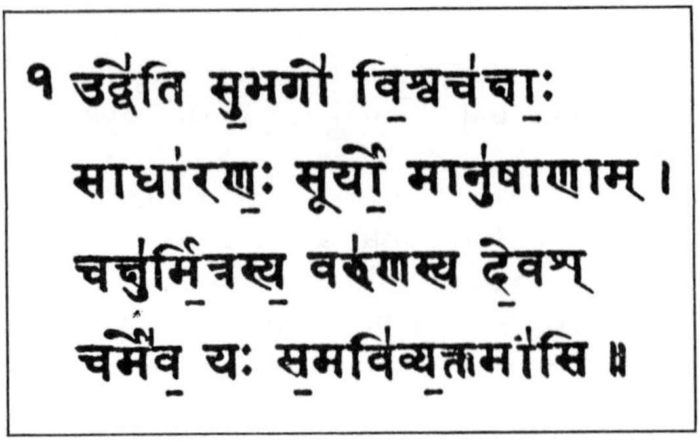

106 Writing Systems

FIGURE 5-5. An example of Sanskrit, in Devanagari script. The text is from the *Rig-Veda:* It reads: Up rises the genial all-seeing sun, /common to all men, the eye of Mitra/and Varuna, the God who rolled up the darkness/like a skin. [*From:* A. A. Macdonnell, *A Vedic Reader for Students* (Oxford, 1917), p. 125.]

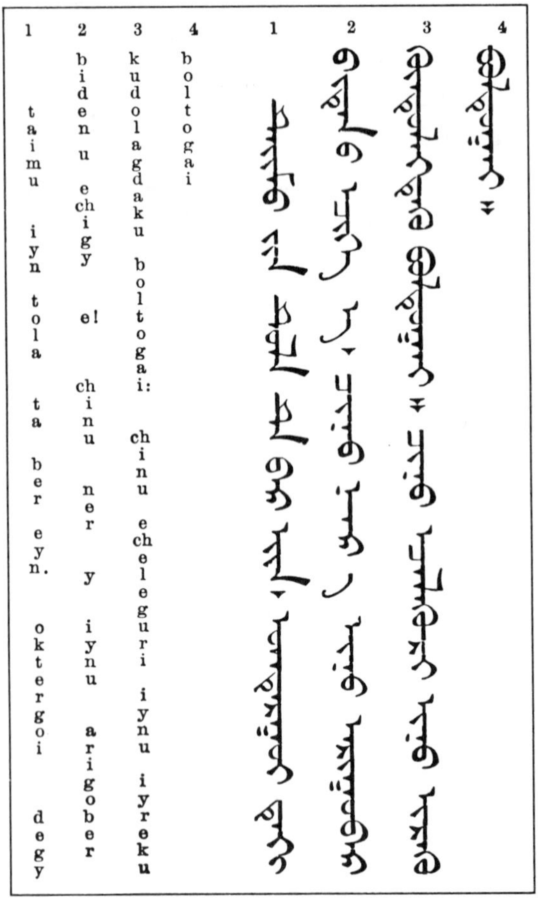

FIGURE 5-6. An example of Mongolian writing. This is Manchu script, used by the Buriats north of Lake Baikal. It is derived from Syriac, and visually is much like Arabic or modern Persian. The difference is the result of the change in the direction of writing. Rotate the book 90° clockwise and note the difference in the impression given; if you then rotate it 90° counterclockwise from upright, it will resemble the Devanagari. All three of these non-Roman scripts are derived from a common ancestor.
[*From:* Taylor, *The Alphabet,* p. 303.]

Phonetic systems are those in which the written symbols clearly represent sounds, either syllabic sequences or single alphabetic sounds. The Semitic scripts and their descendants are of this type; the Greek, Roman, and Slavic alphabets are probably familiar to you.

BEGINNINGS OF WRITING

The ancient cave paintings of southern France and northern Spain date from about 35,000 to 40,000 years ago. Since many of these vivid and beautiful drawings appear to have served religious or cult purposes and to have "communicated" messages, we might consider them to be the very beginnings of iconographic writing. However, it took people many millennia to make the "leap" to analytic writing.

The earliest Mesopotamian tablets date from about 5,500 years ago, from about 3500 B.C. The wedge-shaped, "cuneiform" script was executed by pressing a stylus into wet clay and then later chiseling the signs into stone or inscribing them into bronze, copper, gold, or silver. There are several hundred thousand cuneiform tablets of clay that have come down to us, preserving documents in a variety of languages: Sumerian, Akkadian and Babylonian, Hittite, and Old Persian were among the most important. Cuneiform writing flourished until about 600 B.C.

FIGURE 5-7. Part of the "Darius" Inscription, in Old Persian Cuneiform. From Behistan, 65 miles west of Ecbatana. The text begins: Says Darius the King: O thou who shalt be king in the future, whatever man shall be a deceiver, or whoever shall be a wrongdoer, be not a friend to these; punish them with severe punishment.
[*From:* H. C. Tolman, *Ancient Persian Lexicon and Texts* (Nashville, Tn., 1903), p. xii.]

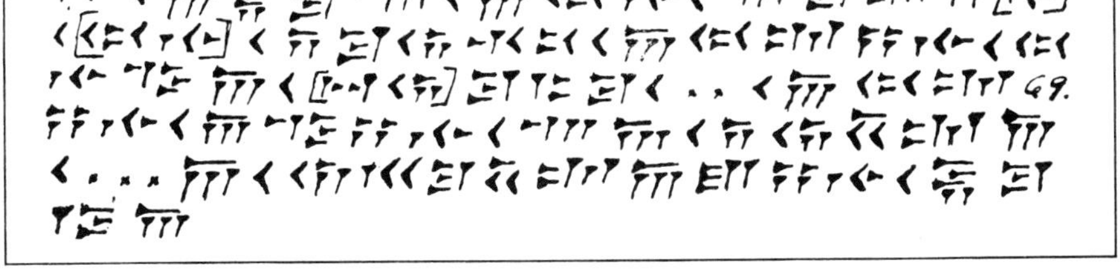

108   Writing Systems

Egyptian writing—hieroglyphic, hieratic, and demotic—is almost as old as Mesopotamian writing: Our oldest relics date from about 3000 B.C., although at the beginning of the third millennium B.C., hieroglyphic writing was already a fully developed system and must have been in use for some centuries. There is scholarly agreement, however, on the greater antiquity of the Mesopotamian system. True hieroglyphic writing was a "monumental" writing system. That is, it was used on stone monuments and on tombs, for the most part, although it was sometimes used on more perishable materials such as papyrus (the ancestor of our paper) and cloth.

Hieratic was the name given by the Greeks (in the first millennium B.C.) to the Egyptian writing used by priests for religious texts. It is a cursive form of hieroglyphic and was used parallel to it for nonmonumental purposes for 3,000 years. This resembles our use of cursive in writing, parallel to our use of block capitals and upper and lower case on signs, in books, and on monuments.

Demotic was a still more cursive derivative of hieratic, used from 600 B.C. through 500 A.D. In general, it would be fair to say that hieroglyphic was the monumental system, hieratic was the "neat" script, and demotic was the everyday "scrawl."

The Egyptian writing system had three kinds of signs: word signs, phonograms or phonetic complements, and category signs. The phono-

FIGURE 5-8.   Hieroglyphics: The Narmer Palette.
[*From:* J. E. Quibell, *Zeitschrift fuer aegyptische Sprache* 36 (1898), plates 12 and 13.]

AFFILIATION OF EGYPTIAN AND SEMITIC ALPHABETS.

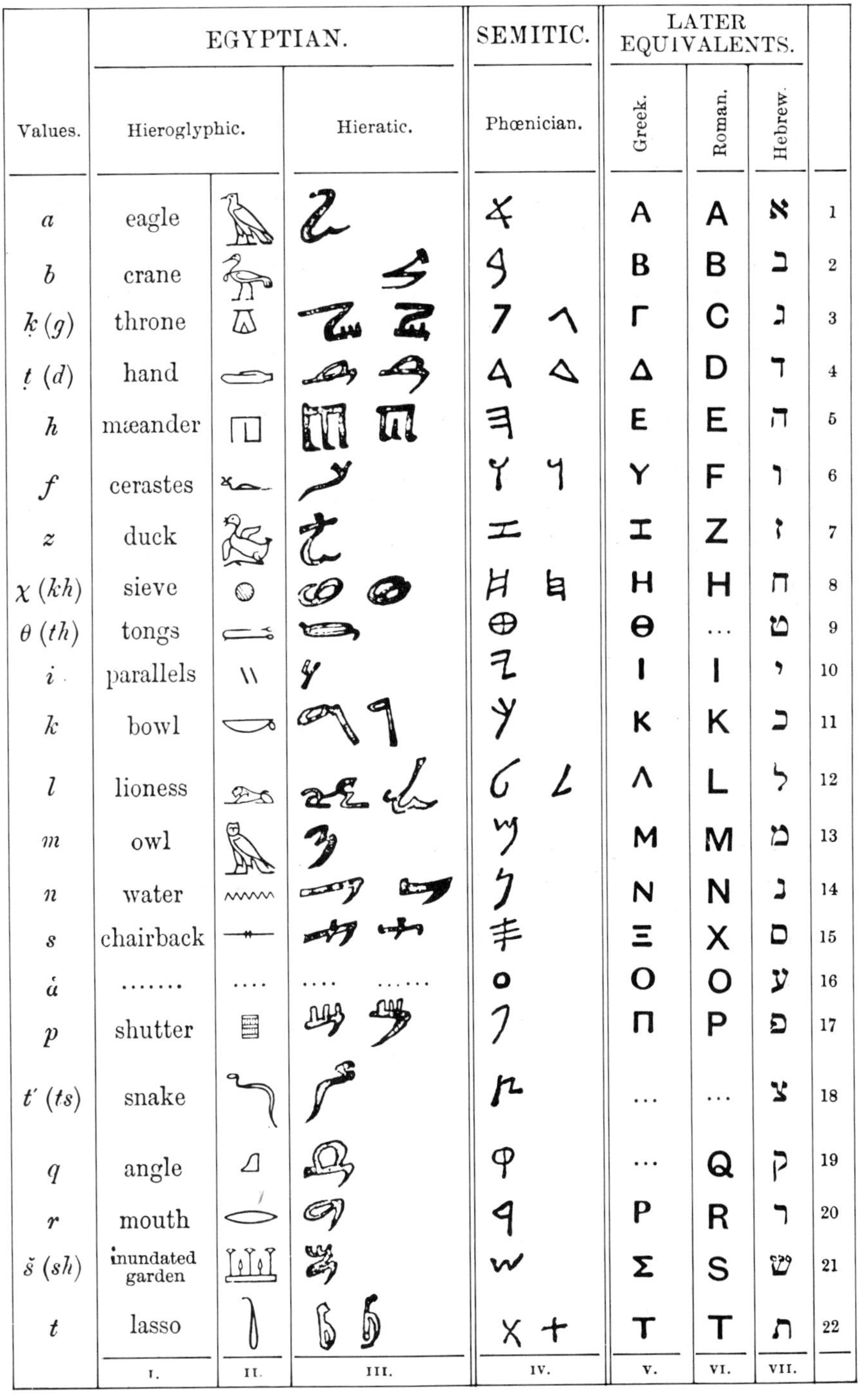

Values.	Egyptian Hieroglyphic.	Egyptian Hieratic.	Semitic Phœnician.	Greek.	Roman.	Hebrew.	
a	eagle		⩓	A	A	א	1
b	crane		⋀	B	B	ב	2
$k\ (g)$	throne		7 ⋀	Γ	C	ג	3
$t\ (d)$	hand		△ △	Δ	D	ד	4
h	mæander		∃	E	E	ה	5
f	cerastes		Y Y	Y	F	ו	6
z	duck		I	I	Z	ז	7
$\chi\ (kh)$	sieve		H h	H	H	ח	8
$\theta\ (th)$	tongs		⊕	Θ	...	ט	9
i	parallels		Z	I	I	י	10
k	bowl		⋎	K	K	כ	11
l	lioness		6 L	Λ	L	ל	12
m	owl		⋎	M	M	מ	13
n	water		⋎	N	N	נ	14
s	chairback		≢	Ξ	X	ס	15
$\dot{a}$	....		o	O	O	ע	16
p	shutter		⋎	Π	P	פ	17
$t'\ (ts)$	snake		⋎	...	...	צ	18
q	angle		Φ	...	Q	ק	19
r	mouth		⋎	P	R	ר	20
$š\ (sh)$	inundated garden		w	Σ	S	ש	21
t	lasso		✕ ✝	T	T	ת	22
	I.	II. III.	IV.	V.	VI.	VII.	

FIGURE 5-9. The Egyptian, Semitic, Greek, and Roman alphabets.
[*From:* I. Taylor, *The Alphabet,* vol. 1 (London, 1883).]

grams and phonetic complements were aids to pronunciation; for while a reader might know from the pictograph, or word sign, what something meant, he or she would not know how to pronounce it. Category signs were aids to word types, as though we indicated before or after *present* something like *gift* (noun) or *verb*.

In Europe, the pre-Greek civilization of Crete was the only one comparable to those of Egypt or Mesopotamia. This culture is usually known as Minoan or Aegean. It possessed a writing system that, unfortunately, has not yet been completely deciphered. It does appear, however, that one version of the script, known as Linear B, may well be related to the Greek of Homer. The pictographic scripts, dating from about 1700 B.C., have not yet been deciphered.

One important relic of this system is the Phaistos Disc, found in 1908. It is a circular clay tablet the size of a small salad plate, with sign groups printed on both sides in a spiral. The pictures appear to relate the disc to the Egyptian system, but it is unknown whether the object is indigenous to Crete or whether it originated in North Africa or Asia Minor.

Chinese writing first appeared in the Shang period (1400-1100 B.C.). By the ninth century B.C., most of the system as we know it today had come into being. Chinese pictographic script is the only one that has remained nonalphabetic over a 3,000-year history: this is unlike Egyptian, in which hieroglyphic-hieratic-demotic gave way to alphabetic script, and Hittite, in which hieroglyphic writing gave way to syllabic cuneiform. Although there has been an extensive simplification of the characters themselves over the past twenty years, the internal changes of the Chinese system have

FIGURE 5-10. The Phaistos Disc, the most striking Minoan inscription.
(Heraklion Museum)

FIGURE 5-11. A redrawing of the reverse of the Phaistos Disc.
[*From:* A. J. Evans, *Scripta Minoa* I (Oxford, 1909), plate 13.]

been nearly imperceptible over its history. Because there are a very large number of Chinese characters (well over 10,000 as compared with our 26 letters), and because there are large numbers of homonyms in Chinese, pictograms are frequently accompanied by "classifiers" that indicate the category within which the meaning of the word is situated. For example, a whole series of words with nearly the same sound can be written without confusion; *thung* ("with, together") can be combined as follows:

chin ("metal") + *thung* = *thung* ("copper, bronze")
mu ("wood") + *thung* = *thung* ("the tung-oil tree")
hsin ("heart") + *thung* = *thung* ("moaning, dissatisfied")
chu ("bamboo") + *thung* = *thung* ("flute")
hsing ("to go") + *thung* = *thung* ("side-street")
shui ("water") + *thung* = *thung* ("cave")

thung is nearly always a phonetic element, never a classifier or determiner. *shui* ("water") is nearly always a determiner, as in

shui + *mo* ("branches") = *mo* ("froth, foam")
shui + *lan* ("late, end") = *lan* ("waves")
shui + *chhi* ("the varnish tree") = *chhi* ("lacquer")
shui + *chha* ("fork") = *chha* ("branching streams")
shui + *mei* ("each, every") = *hai* ("the sea")

Finally, the two ancient scripts of Mexico, Mayan (from about 400 A.D.) and Aztec (about 1300 A.D.) must be mentioned. Except for a few calendar signs, the Mayan script is undeciphered; and Aztec script, which appears to be a derivative of the Mayan, is somewhat better known but is also largely undeciphered.

112 Writing Systems

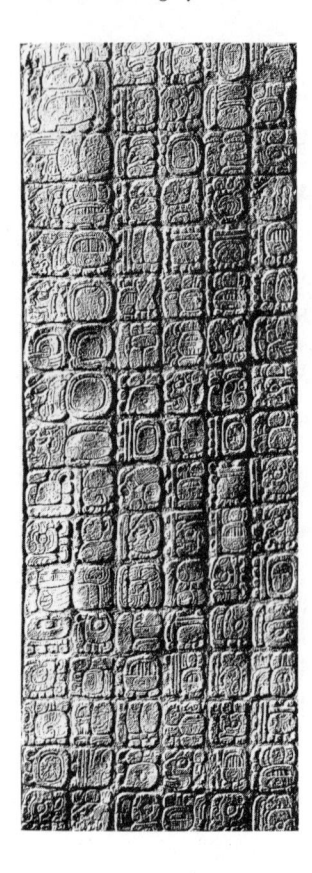

FIGURE 5-12. A Mayan inscription, from the left side of a cross at Palenque, now in the British Museum.

FIGURE 5-13. An Aztec inscription, from the "Codex Boturini".
[*From:* E. Seler, *Gesammelte Abhandlungen zur amerikanischen Sprach-und Altertumskunde* II (Berlin, 1904), p. 35.]

There are a few other nonalphabetic scripts, such as that on the fifteen wooden tablets found on Easter Island in the Pacific Ocean, twenty-five hundred miles west of Chile, and covered with pictures of humans, fishes, and birds. All the other scripts are quite minor, and they are both undeciphered and uninterpretable for the most part.

One of the important things you can give to your students is a greater awareness of language and of written language in particular. Suppose your students are working on a unit in social studies that concerns other cultures or the ancient world. Once they have seen the Egyptian tombs, or pyramids, and have been exposed to the notion of picture-writing, you can have them each devise a set of pictograms and write something using it. Ask each student to supply a key or glossary to his or her creation. Then have other members of the class "decipher" the new system. You might want to have them make up a system more like Chinese and then discuss ways in which concepts can be combined to make new concepts.

The international road signs are, in many ways, pictograms; they convey meanings without relation to the names of what they represent. Ask your students if they know what a red octagon means (STOP); an inverted triangle (YIELD); or any of the other nonverbal signs they have seen.

At this point, it may be important for you to point out the limitations of a nonphonetic system. For example, one could read signs and menus throughout China, even though there are a number of different dialects (some as different as English and German) spoken in that country. But you would not know how to pronounce those "words" in whatever the local dialect was. On the other hand, all of us can read the street signs all over Western Europe and North and South America, but we haven't any idea as to the meanings of the things we have said.

In a pictographic system, you may have some idea as to the meaning of a sequence of signs you have never seen before, but you have no clue as to pronunciation. In an alphabetic system, you know (more or less) how to pronounce a new word, but you may have no clue as to what it means.

Of course, if the new word is a long one in English, it is most likely made up of parts you already know: *un* plus *gentle* plus *man* plus *ly* equals *ungentlemanly;* or *disenfranchise* from *franchise* ("right to vote"), *enfranchise* ("to give the right to vote"), *disenfranchise* ("to deprive of the right to vote").

One of the advantages of "playing" with writing systems with your students is that it will make them more aware of the system they are learning and using.

PHONETIC SCRIPTS

Basically, there are two types of writing systems that represent sounds rather than ideas: syllabic systems and alphabetic systems. Ancient cuneiform was a syllabic system in which every symbol represented a syllable. Only modern Japanese still uses such a syllabic system, and this is facilitated by the fact that Japanese has no consonant clusters nor any syllables that end in a consonant other than *n*. In a syllabic system, it would be easy to write a word such as *family—fa-mi-ly*, but it would be both cumbersome and confusing to write something such as *sa-ta-re-nga-tha-sa* for *strengths* or *ta-wa-el-ef-tha-sa* for *twelfths*. For a language such as English, with many consonant clusters, an alphabetic system is more efficient.

THE ALPHABET

Our alphabet is a descendant of the North Semitic alphabet dating from about 1000 B.C. However, the original alphabet of this stock most likely arose about 500 years earlier than that. This script gave rise to several other scripts. One branch developed into the Hebrew and Arabic systems, another into the Brahmi system still in use in India and much of South Asia, while a third branch developed into the Greek alphabet. All the modern scripts of Europe and the Americas are derived from the wonderful invention of the Greeks, which probably was developed in the ninth century B.C.

The Greeks claim to have learned of the alphabet from the Phoenicians, and there is no reason to doubt this notion. Originally, the Greek script, like the Semitic, was written from right to left. This was superseded by the *boustrophedon* style, alternate lines written right-to-left and left-to-right. After 500 B.C., however, Greek was generally written left-to-right.

The Greek alphabet is unique in the history of the development of writing. While the Semitic system contained only consonants, with but a vague indication in later times of the vowels in words, the Greek alphabet transformed this system into a modern alphabet representing both consonant and vowel sounds. They also made the script more symmetrical and, in the opinion of many, more "artistic." The Roman adaptations of the Greek script, on the one hand, and the Slavonic adaptations on the other, have ensured the permanent influence of the Greek innovations on our thought.

We will not discuss non-Roman scripts here, but will merely mention the existence of the Russian (Cyrillic, named after St. Cyril, who Christianized the Slavs) alphabet and the early Irish (Ogham) and Scandinavian (Runic) varieties.

The earliest remnant we have of the Roman alphabet is from the sixth century. But it is only in the first century B.C. that we begin to find large numbers of inscriptions; and it was only with the great expansion of the Roman Empire from about 60 B.C. into the Christian era that writings became truly profuse.

Writing Systems 115

FIGURE 5-14. The Marsiliana Abecedarium. Read from right to left. This is an example of the later Etruscan alphabet.
[*From:* B. L. Ullman, *Ancient Writing and its Influence* (New York, 1932), plate lc.]

FIGURE 5-15. A church portal from Hellvi, Gotland, Sweden, about 1275. It reads: lafranz botui arsun maistera gerdi kirkiu bisa: ad uskilaim = L., the son of Master Botvid, from Eskelhem, built this church.

The Romans took twenty-one of the letters of the Etruscan alphabet: A, B, C (representing both *g* and *k*), I, H, I (representing both *i* and *j*), K, L, M, N, O, P, Q, P (representing *p* and *r*), S, T, V (representing both *u* and *v*), X, Y, Z, and F (the Greek 'digamma'); and added some Semitic characters to them. This was done to fill out the phonetic requirements of Latin. There was also some re-ordering.

This re-ordering is most apparent if we look at the last characters of the alphabet. Early on (probably before the third century B.C.) the last five letters were T, V, X, Φ, Ψ. In the first century B.C., we find V, X, Y, Z. V appears to have evolved quite early, perhaps in the 9th century B.C.; X appears to be as early as the 7th century; Y and Z were borrowed from Greek in the first century B.C. However, U and V were not differentiated until the tenth century A.D., and W only appears in the eleventh century A.D. It has taken nearly two millennia for us to "achieve" T, U, V, W, X, Y, Z.

It may be worth noting here that script (cursive writing) was a later invention, and that punctuation marks are a relatively recent invention.

FIGURE 5-16. A leaf from the Gospel According to St. John in uncial script. Seventh century English ms. (Stonyhurst College Library)

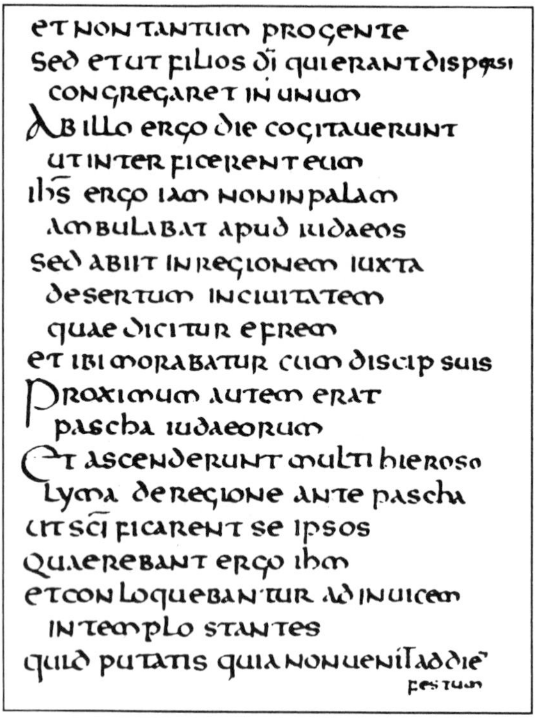
et non tantum pro gente
sed et ut filios di qui erant dispersi
congregaret in unum
Ab illo ergo die cogitauerunt
ut interficerent eum
ihs ergo iam non in palam
ambulabat apud iudaeos
sed abiit in regionem iuxta
desertum in ciuitatem
quae dicitur efrem
et ibi morabatur cum discip suis
Proximum autem erat
pascha iudaeorum
Et ascenderunt multi hieroso
lyma de regione ante pascha
ut sci ficarent se ipsos
Quaerebant ergo ihm
et conloquebantur ad inuicem
in templo stantes
quid putatis quia non uenit ad die
festum

After the achievement of language, writing may well be the most important invention of the human race, for it is through this medium that we have been able to transmit messages across space and across time. It is our ability to "restore and treasure" (Milton) the knowledge of the past that makes humans able to relate their achievements to future generations. Without it, as Joseph Addison wrote, "man is but a splendid slave. A reasoning savage."

EXERCISES

1. Invent a set of characters and compile a dictionary of twenty words, using these characters for the entry word and its definition.
2. Write out the characters of a different writing system (Greek or Russian alphabets are the best). Because there is no way to represent *sh* in Greek, or *w* in either Greek or Russian, decide the best way to represent these sounds in your system.
3. In one of his books, Alfred Bester has characters named "Wyg&" (Wygand) and "@kins" (Atkins). Ask your children to explain how they read these words.

FURTHER READINGS

There are a number of truly excellent books on writing systems. Perhaps the best and most accessible is

GELB, I. J.   *A Study of Writing.* Chicago: University of Chicago Press, 1952.

We also recommend

DIRINGER, D.   *Writing.* New York: Praeger, 1962.

Some writers confuse authenticity, which they ought always to aim at, with originality, which they should never bother about.

—*W. H. Auden*

6 THE PROCESSES OF WRITING

This chapter includes an overview of the processes of writing, approaches to the teaching of writing, and suggestions for developing a successful writing program. A structured approach to teaching writing to young children and measures for assessing children's writing are also discussed in this chapter.

Writing is a cognitive process. Vygotsky (1962) viewed written speech as a separate linguistic function,

> differing from oral speech in both structure and mode of functioning. (p. 98)

He noted that writing is difficult for the child because of its abstraction.

> Our studies show that it is the abstract quality of written language that is the main stumbling block, not the underdevelopment of small muscles or any other mechanical obstacles. (p. 99)

In discussing the relationship of writing to inner speech, Vygotsky maintained that written speech is more difficult than inner speech because it is condensed, abbreviated speech. He argued that writing is

> extremely detailed, suggesting, one might even say that the syntax of inner speech is the exact opposite of the syntax of written speech, with oral speech standing in the middle. (p. 99)

Children's egocentrism affects their writing; it makes it more difficult for them to write for an audience. Moffett explained that

> the majority of communication problems are caused by egocentricity, the writer's assumption that the reader thinks and feels as he does, has had the same experience, and hears in his head, when he is reading, the same voice the writer does when he is writing. (p. 83)

Writing is a cognitive process which can be difficult for the child because of its abstraction. (*Photo by Linda Lungren*)

In part, the writer who fails to communicate has failed to move from the syntax of inner speech to that of written speech. Emig (1971) maintains that it is erroneous to assume that writing and speaking are the same process because she found that a

> number of transdisciplinary sources suggest that talking and writing may emanate from different organic sources and represent quite different possibly distinct language functions. (p. 273)

Olson (1977) maintained that the relationship between the writer and oral languages has affected whole societies. As we noted in Chapter 5, the development of alphabetic written languages has had significant impact on the development of societies. Olson argued that the availability of a writing system within a society rendered explicitness of thought and logic a necessary part of the writing process. Before the invention of print,

> it was generally assumed that meaning could not be stated explicitly. (p. 263)

He further argues that written language is a formal system that guides the creator towards providing definitions, making all assumptions and premises explicit, and observing the formal rules of logic. (p. 268)

In order to understand the explicitness of thought and logic that Olson maintains is essential to writing, it is necessary to understand writing as a process. In recent years, educators have begun to analyze the thought processes that writers use as they create written texts. Formerly, writing curricula consisted of assigning students "compositions" or "themes," which they would hand in to the teacher in final form. The teacher would then correct the completed essay. This instructional approach emphasized the written product, rather than the processes that were used to complete the task. Educators tended to use a "write-correct-revise" approach that allowed for little teacher guidance before the important work had been done.

Most books on writing methods suggest that there are sequential steps involved in writing. This traditional approach is exemplified in Warriner's *Handbook:*

> The writing of a composition is best approached as a series of steps that can be taken one at a time . . . as a rule . . . you will find it helpful to take each of these steps separately and in order, solving the problems of one before moving on to the next; (p. 406)

and

> The completion of the topic outline marks the end of the planning stage. You have settled on what you want to say; it remains to find the right way of saying it. (p. 413)

The underlying assumption of this approach is that writing is a linear, isomorphic, sequential set of activities, passing through stages from prewriting to editing. A second assumption is that writers know what they want to write before they write. This assumption is faulty because it is based on the principle that writing is static; it is not a discovery process.

The most recent view of writing as including three stages—prewriting, writing, and revision—may also be problematic because it does not take into account the dynamic, idiosyncratic, recursive nature of writing. Emig (1971) contends that there are many processes of writing, rather than a single process. She suggests that the processes of writing can be changed, shortened, or lengthened by a number of factors. In her view, writing is recursive, a loop rather than straight line in which the writer can write, then plan; or revise, then write. Perl (1979) refers to the recursive nature of writing as "retrospective structuring," in which the writer reaches forward in order to clarify. She shares the view that writing does not divide itself neatly into a preliminary stage of thinking followed by writing.

MODELS OF THE WRITING PROCESS

Many educators have examined the components of the writing process and have generated models to describe it. Hayes and Flower (1980) propose a model that is divided into three parts: (1) the task environment; (2) the writer's long term memory; and (3) the writing process.

In their model, Hayes and Flower suggest that writing involves simultaneously acting upon many constraints and demands. Their model is interactive. Writers, they suggest, are serial processors, that is, they are able to process only a limited amount of information at one time. They argue that writers may have cognitive overload on their short-term memory unless they select the demands to which they can effectively attend. Hayes and Flower maintain that writers must acquire a repertoire of strategies: discarding a constraint, partitioning the problem, establishing priorities, calling upon well-learned and well-practiced procedures and planning. In their model, the process of writing is based on a cognitive-developmental viewpoint of processing and a psycholinguistic notion of writing. Writing is a sophisticated cognitive process in which the writer acquires, organizes, and produces information. The process is selective and active—the writer generates and processes information in a way that is compatible with previously acquired information, including rules of organization, syntax, and categorization.

In a new form of writing instruction (writing-as-process, rather than writing-as-product), writers are concerned not only with correctness of form, but also with learning, generating, and discovering through writing.

FIGURE 6-1. Hayes's and Flower's Model of the Writing Process.

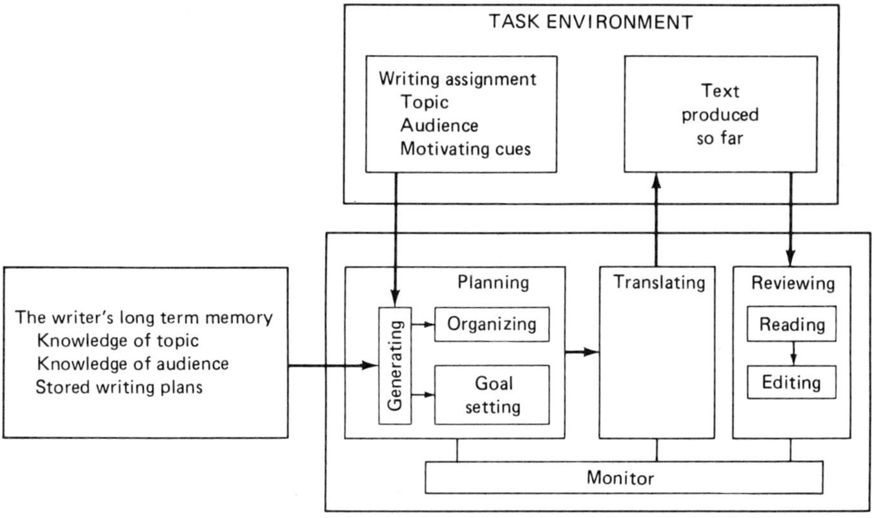

Teachers must stimulate all aspects of the process. Activities such as creative dramatics, role playing, and reader's theatre, as described in Chapter 4, can serve as excellent motivators for encouraging children to engage in all the processes of writing. Many other activities and instructional tools for stimulating a process-oriented instructional plan will be presented throughout this chapter.

MURRAY'S RECOMMENDATIONS FOR TEACHING WRITING

The following recommendations for teachers are in keeping with Murray's (1974) list of seven skills necessary for the successful teaching of writing. He suggests that teachers of writing must do the following:

1. *Listen,* because the content of writing belongs to the student. Some teachers are stern disciplinarians and some are lenient, but if they are effective, they establish communication with their students as speakers and themselves as listeners.

2. *Coach* by designing programs that work with the potential of each student.

3. *Diagnose,* because the teacher is a physician (not a judge) who can spot the critical problem in a student's writing. The teacher realizes that confused and complex syntax is usually an attempt to fit information where it does not belong. It may not be a grammar problem, but a thinking problem.

4. *Remain flexible.* One rule that the teacher must repeat in many different ways is, "Be Specific." Students need examples. Teachers should have extensive libraries of materials because no *one* device will be useful with every child. The teacher should use newspapers, classical literature, records (lyrics), or whatever materials are needed to help students develop their writing skills.

5. *Write* with their students to demonstrate that writing is a process. By writing with them, the teacher brings the students into the process by exposing his or her own struggle.

6. *Keep their distance.* The writing teacher cannot be a psychiatrist, parent, aunt, or uncle. The teacher has to be aware of the amount of emotional outpouring that he or she can accept. The writing teacher must have a sense of humor about the task.

FIVE APPROACHES TO THE TEACHING OF WRITING

As you begin to develop your instructional program, you may ask, "What *is* the best approach to the teaching of writing?" There is no single answer to this question. Miles Meyer (1978) has suggested that there are at least five successful approaches to such teaching that you may choose from as you attempt to meet your students' needs.

The Models Approach

This approach assumes that children can learn to imitate a writing style before they have the power of sustained thought. I. A. Richards has been quite successful in using this approach in writing instruction. Such teaching uses a direct dictation approach or variations, including asking students to paraphrase passages. These ideas have been used by teachers in many different ways. For example, young children may be taught to write their names by tracing letters or may learn what a story is by retelling the story to the teacher. The "Mix-Up Monster" approach has been used in the Circle Preschool in Oakland, California. The Mix-Up Monster confuses things such as "hello" and "goodbye," and he tells the children the story of "Goldilocks and the Three Pigs." The children must help the Mix-Up Monster and correct the story by telling the monster where and how he is mixed up.

Teachers who object to the models approach maintain that the emphasis of this approach is on the product of the task. Children are not informed of the necessary processes in which they must engage while the product is being prepared.

The Steps Approach

This approach, founded on the works of several researchers and educators, informs students about three assumed processes in writing: prewriting, composing, and editing. In prewriting, Rothman found that preparation time for writing was essential for exploring and discovering. In her research, Janet Emig (1971) found that most writing assignments in schools allow no time for prewriting. In composing, it may be useful to turn your classroom into an art workshop in which students write on brown paper draped over easels. They can either write about the same topic (object) or select their own topic. In the same way as art teachers consult with students during the composing process, you can consult with students as they write. The students should be free to roam around the room consulting with their colleagues. In editing, you can create groups of students in which one student serves as composer and two as editors. In this way, students consult with the author as they edit. Practice in editing is very important in developing analytic skills of precision in writing.

Objections to this approach center on a number of questions that remain unanswered: How are students selected for instructional groups? How are skills sharpened? How are students helped with their particular areas of difficulty?

The Sentence Combining Approach

This approach shares some features with the models approach, which assumes that children can learn skills through imitation of structures, and with the steps approach, which assumes that students can edit each others' work.

Here, the sentence is the entity focused on because it has discrete boundaries and is manageable due to its brevity. Proponents of this approach suggest that assigning a composition is tantamount to asking children to deal with all the complex problems of writing at once. Unlike the models approach, which has its roots in a literary tradition, the sentence combining approach has its roots in a linguistics tradition. It is based on Chomskian notions of tranformational grammar, in which the sentence is thought to have a deep structure (how the sentence began) and a surface structure (how the sentence appears on the printed page). For example, the surface structure sentence "Hanna and Emily knew Maggie had won the prize" began as "Hanna knew something, Emily knew something, and Maggie won the prize." Hunt (1965), following the rules of transformational grammar, invented a system of evaluating children's writing in which discrete elements were called T-units. His studies showed that children's T-units increased with age.

Early attempts at teaching the sentence combining approach to writing focused on requesting children to combine simple sentences into a single sentence, for example:

>Frank ate tomatoes.
>Scott ate tomatoes.

into

>Frank and Scott ate tomatoes

and changing sentence forms, for example:

>The dog chased the cat. *to* Did the dog chase the cat? (Question)
>The dog chased the cat. *to* The cat was chased by the dog. (Passive)

Critics of the sentence combining approach maintain that focusing on the single sentence does not allow children opportunities for writing whole texts.

The Relationships Approach

This approach emphasizes the relationships that exist between writers and their audiences and writers and their subjects. Young children often write for a very close audience on a very personal subject; this reflects their natural egocentrism. Extending the audience to include a community and the topic to encompass a more generalized notion requires maturity and a decrease in egocentrism. Piagetian notions of cognitive development from preoperation to concrete to formal stages parallel this development.

Myers points out that the sequence in classrooms looks something like this:

1. Improvisations, panels, trials—all organized by students: developing a sense of audience (the other students in the improvisation or trial)

2. Journals, diaries, letters, and autobiographical incidents: moving the audience from oneself to others and learning to act as spectator to one's own experiences

3. Interviews, reports, Socratic dialogues and arguments: moving to an anonymous audience in the world at large and acting as spectator to the experiences of others

Objections to this approach stem from the fact that educators find difficulty providing different audiences for children and helping children move from personal experience writing to idea writing. They argue that in schools, children are always writing for the teacher, school secretary, or principal. To do otherwise is "pretend writing."

The Theory-of-the-World Approach

This approach assumes that the child must have a theory of the world in order to write effectively. Instruction in this approach is based upon teaching predication and visual models. For example, Josephine Miles argues that "My Home Town" is not an appropriate topic for an essay, but "My Home Town Stinks" is appropriate because the child's noun has a predicate. She argues that the child who says, "I don't know what to say" is really saying, "I don't have a predicate for my noun or nouns." She maintains that it is the predicate that sharpens the essay or composition. Visual models play an important role in this teaching approach: One group of students draws a line, circles, and abstract designs; a second group draws a scene using the marks made on the paper; and a third group writes a story from the scene.

Critics of this approach point to the fact that young children need instruction to cultivate a theory of the world. It is developed, rather than intrinsic to the child.

Each of the approaches discussed above has obvious merits and limitations. As you plan your curriculum, you will want to include each approach. It is important to remember that the writing process is idiosyncratic. Given the varying levels of cognitive development and maturity of the children in a classroom, no single approach can successfully tap the potential for good writing within each child. As you come to know your students' strengths and weaknesses, you will be better able to judge which combination of approaches will best meet their needs.

SIX STEPS TO A SUCCESSFUL WRITING PROGRAM

Motivating Writing

In the language arts curriculum, there is almost no need to motivate a child to write: Children want to communicate, they want to leave their mark. Even just writing their names—"Chico"—is important to them. Showing children in the early grades how they can tell a story about themselves—what they did over the weekend, what they got for their birthdays, with whom they played—will, of course, result in products that are linear in form. They will concern events in strict chronological order. But only after mastering strict chronological order will children be able to vary chronology:

> We visited my grandmother over the weekend. My grandmother lives in Centertown and we drove there in our car. I played with Rex, my grandmother's dog. He is a poodle. I love playing with him. We had roast beef for dinner.

can be transformed after a period of time into

> I played with my grandmother's poodle, Rex, and ate roast beef when we visited her in Centertown this past weekend. We had driven there in our car....

with only a little effort.

Once the children have mastered personal narrative, you can have them invent narratives. After they have achieved this sort of fictionalization, they will be able to begin nonfictional prose.

Children want to communicate; they want to leave their mark. Even writing their names on an art project is important to them. (*Photo by Linda Lungren*)

One way to encourage prose composition of nonfiction is to have your class recommend something to others: a book, a TV program, a movie, or an activity. Having to present a recommendation for *A Baby Sister for Frances* or roller skating or *The Muppet Show* will constrain students to logical presentation and yet be somewhat personal, since such compositions will involve them in some favored activity.

Writing is expression. Children love to express themselves, as can be seen in their drawings. Getting children to express themselves in writing is not difficult if you "ease" them into it. You can encourage creativity through personal anecdote or by having children tell a story to accompany pictures.

The following suggestions may help motivate your children to write. The first sample should be used as an art activity.

Ask your children to draw a picture to accompany each of the following labels:

Smaller than a goldfish	Larger than your hand
Taller than a giraffe	Noisier than chicks
Harder than a rubber ball	Faster than an elephant

Illustrating Stories. The following exercise may encourage your children to write stories after they have generated artwork to stimulate their thinking:

Did you ever wish it was many years from now? _____

Where would you be? _____

What would you be doing? _____

Show it here:

Your children may enjoy drawing a picture to accompany their story. Children may find it helpful to draw their pictures before writing their stories or they may enjoy drawing pictures to accompany their stories after they have written them.

Sentence Starters. As you begin your writing program, you may want to ask children to complete some "sentence starters."

1. All of a sudden, right in front of me I saw _____
2. The small rabbits were _____
3. As I looked under my bed _____
4. At the birthday party we _____
5. A loud sound made us _____
6. In the moonlight I saw _____

Developing Thinking Through Sentence Writing. The following exercise, writing sentences that include three specified words, will develop your children's thinking, organizing, and composing skills, for example:

        nose   stars   bike

While Jasmile was gazing at the stars, she fell off her bike, hit her head on the ground, and cut her nose.

1. penny   boy   TV

2. candy   car   moon

3. book   sun   flower

Vocabulary Development

The second step in a successful writing program is to stimulate children to select and use words carefully.

Word Families. Point out that words can be divided into families, and ask your students to try to think of words in several categories. A bulletin board can be used to display the words.

Sensory words	Emotions	People	Holidays
Sour	Sad	Wrinkled	Reindeer
Roar	Worried	Pudgy	Harvest
Splash	Gleeful	Gangly	

Making a Class Thesaurus. To encourage word variety, ask your students to choose words that are overworked and then to think of synonyms for them. Their suggestions can be compiled in a class thesaurus, for example:

Happy: glad, joyous, gleeful, laughing, smiling, elated

Correct Forms

While correct language usage shouldn't be valued above creativity, the more writing your students do, the greater their need to know the correct language forms as aids to expression. The third step in your program is to provide your students with these forms and with opportunities to practice using them. You can design wall charts that illustrate forms of usage:

Punctuation

Primary Grades: I am so tired.   Intermediate Grades: Sara asked, "How
                 Look out!   old are you?"
                 Are you   Joan's cat,
                 ready?   Chester, is miss-
                                                               ing.
                                                               Dear Nathan:

Capital Letters

Sentences begin with capital letters.
   Let's go outside.
   Are you coming with us?
All proper names start with capital letters.
   Delaware, Katy, Thanksgiving, Grove Street

Writing Practice

A successful writing program provides students with the opportunity to practice writing. Motivating and writing-preparation techniques that stimulate the desire to write should be followed by adequate time to do so.

Children's competence as writers will vary. It is important that the teacher provide guidance and counsel during and following the writing process. Having the group compose different kinds of writing helps students establish a sense of confidence and gives the teacher the opportunity to identify and correct problems with language usage.

Sharing

The fifth important step in the writing process is sharing one's writing. Students should be made aware that they are writing for an audience. Their writing efforts will prove more successful if they are given ample opportunity to share them. Stories may be shared through a class book, bulletin board, daily readings, class or school newspaper, or folders sent to parents.

Extending Composition Skills

Children need to receive positive feedback about their writing. The sixth step in a successful writing program is to reward your students with lavish praise. Be specific, rather than general, in your comments: "Your ending is wonderful." "I like the way you used the word _____." "Excellent! Your beginning really caught my attention!" A child will accept constructive criticism only after he or she feels confident about writing.

Sager (1976) suggests a four-part program in "Reading, Writing, and Rating Stories," which encourages children to improve the clarity and style of their writing. Children are given criteria to rate stories according to vocabulary, elaboration, organization, and structure. They are taught the need for rewriting in order to achieve a good final product through the process of assigning values to the stories in their lessons. Sager found that children are then able to apply the same judgments they used in the lessons to their own compositions; they rework and rewrite their own stories.

DESIGNING YOUR PROGRAM

Too often, children view writing experiences as dull chores or as just another task at which they are unsuccessful. In many classrooms, students are not given proper preparation for writing assignments, and they write without adequate guidelines from their teachers.

As we begin to plan programs that will stimulate growth in children's writing skills, it is important to remember that we must maintain a balance between the emphasis placed on the *process* and the *product* of writing. We must capitalize on students' natural inclination to share their ideas, fantasies, expressions, and dreams through their writing. The teacher who values form above content is in danger of stopping the natural flow of ideas. This is not to say that form should be disregarded—for their expressions to be successfully shared, students must adhere to conventional forms of language use. It is important that the teacher make clear that content and form are inextricably interwoven. However, even experienced writers give priority to expressing their ideas; the teacher who examines his or her own writing process will find this to be true. Students need to understand that anything they write can later be rewritten, modified, and polished. Emig (1971) states that the successful teaching of writing involves "the proffering of freedoms and the establishment of constraints." Maintaining the delicate balance between process and product is no easy task. The following section discusses areas that require special attention.

Establish a Positive Classroom Environment

The child who does not feel secure and relaxed in the classroom will not feel free to express his or her feelings and ideas in writing. Nor will the child be apt to seek help in organizing feelings and thoughts while writing. The attitudes and actions of the teacher greatly influence a child's success in writing. The teacher who maintains an encouraging and supportive attitude toward students will meet with the greatest success in eliciting expressive writing from them. Every effort should be made to respect each child's personality and approach to the writing process. It should be reiterated that the writing process is idiosyncratic. The nature of the direction and guidance a teacher must give throughout the writing process will vary from child to child. Certainly there will be times when children prefer not to share what they have written. Teachers should respect the child's right to a certain amount of privacy.

As important as the rapport between teacher and student is the physical environment of the classroom. An attractive and interestingly decorated classroom can be the catalyst for stimulating effective and creative writing. The teacher should fill the classroom with exciting and colorful decorations and displays. Children must have access to materials they will need for writing: paper, pencils, books, magazines, dictionaries, encyclopedias. Their own writing and that of their classmates should be on display and readily available to them. Each child should feel that he or she has played an important part in creating the classroom environment.

Children whose initial writing experiences are positive, who have been provided every opportunity to express themselves imaginatively, and who have been given the tools they need to write will enjoy writing. As in any academic endeavor, success breeds success. The teacher of writing must understand the crucial role he or she plays in fostering successful writing in the classroom.

Teaching the Writing Process

Murray (1974) maintains that the effective writer must do the following:

1. Focus on a subject
2. Plan before writing
3. Document
4. Speak in the reader's language
5. Develop ideas into thoughts
6. Vary sentence structure
7. Search for the right word
8. Revise until the reader will understand

Writing is a thinking process that requires preplanning. Words, sentences, and paragraphs, and their combined effectiveness, depend on the thinking that underlies their arrangement. Perhaps the most difficult step for students is finding an appropriate topic and narrowing it sufficiently so that they can write concisely and effectively about it. Writing activities require preplanning that goes beyond creating a classroom environment conducive to creative thought. Writing involves making a series of choices from what must seem to many students a bewildering array of alternatives. Thus, student writing that is unorganized and that lacks a clearly defined purpose is frequently the result of too little direction and guidance from the teacher during the planning stages. Without help in focusing their topics, students may begin to write before they have a clear purpose.

Too often, topics for writing are simply assigned to students. However, if they are to write effectively and with feeling, students must have a personal interest in their subject matter. They must be guided toward discovering their own topics. There are many ways to develop topics for student writing. Class discussions enable students to consider new words and ideas. Discussions may be planned or may develop spontaneously. If the class suddenly hears a fire siren, the teacher might ask, "How do you feel when you hear a fire siren?" Such discussions may provide the catalyst that sparks a child's creative thinking. The child may then want to describe the time he or she witnessed a fire in the neighborhood. Then, drawing upon some of the words, emotions, and descriptions touched upon during the class discussion, the child can relate them to his or her own experience.

One method of generating writing is to create an idea box filled with possible topics. The box may contain a collection of magazine photographs mounted on cardboard. On the back of each photograph might be questions designed to stimulate writing ideas about the picture. Topics can also be kept in a card file or on charts displayed in the classroom. Graves (1978) suggests that a particularly effective approach is to ask children to bring in an object from home that has meaning for them: a worn toothbrush, an old photograph, an interesting seashell, and so on. Each student is then interviewed by classmates or by the teacher. For example, a student may be asked, "Where did you find the seashell?" "When did it happen?" "Why did you choose to keep it?" These and other questions stimulate the child's thinking; the student's train of thought will lead him or her to a topic for writing. Interview questions help focus the child's ideas. They can then be effectively expressed in an essay, story, or poem.

Similarly, a student may announce a desire to write about Egypt. Through interviews with classmates and teachers, a broad topic such as this can be honed to something more specific "What interests you about Egypt?" the teacher may ask. If the student answers "hieroglyphics," he or she is already on the road to developing a manageable topic for writing.

Once a student has decided upon a topic, it may be helpful to develop an outline. Even young children are capable of creating simple outlines to plan how a story is to be told or to list a sequence of steps to describe how something is done. It is important that outlining skills be taught in context; they are a means of planning what one wants to say about a particular subject. They may take either topical or sentence form. While it is important to teach outline format and to encourage children to be consistent in their use of it, it should be made clear to students that learning to use an outline is learning to use a tool. The purpose of the outline is to aid their writing. It is not an end in itself.

The outline may provide the confidence that the student may otherwise lack. For example, Samuel was a student at a local junior college. His reading and writing skills were barely at fourth-grade level when he began attending a university reading clinic. Years of failure in the language arts had made him doubt not only his competence as a writer, but also whether his ideas and emotions were even worth expressing. By providing an external framework on which to base his writing, an outline gave Samuel the confidence to begin. Samuel soon discovered that he had quite a lot to say and it remained only for him to fill in the details.

Initially, outlining may be taught as a group activity. The group effort builds confidence and provides a model for individual work.

Composing

Mickey Spillane, a detective-fiction writer, has been quoted as saying that he frequently writes the endings to his novels first. The message here is that all writing must be governed by a clear, controlling purpose. The writer must have an ultimate goal to work toward. This is not to suggest that the writer will always know what each intervening step will be when beginning to write. According to Murray, as a writer writes, he or she discovers what there is to say.

Too often, teachers are present only at the end of the writing process and then only to criticize and correct. Writing should be an interactive process. As students write, they may stop to reread what they have written and in doing so may discover that they need to talk through some of their plans and ideas or to consult resources before they can begin again. It is important that the teacher be attentive to students' behavior and available for consultation should a child show signs of needing help. Children should also be encouraged to consult with their classmates regarding their writing. One approach is to have some students act as teachers' helpers who circulate around the room as other students write, ready to listen to what a student has produced should that child say, "Tell me how this sounds so far."

You will probably discover that an effective writing activity cannot be completed in one day. You may want to spread the process over a period of days: one day to discuss and plan for writing, another to write, and a third to edit and rewrite. Writing activities should be enjoyable daily activities. One method of motivating students to write daily is to ask them to keep a journal.

Group writing activities are one particularly good way to build a child's confidence in writing and to give him/her a feel for the writing process. (*Photo by Linda Lungren*)

Group writing activities are a particularly good way to build a child's confidence in writing and to give the child a feel for the writing process. Class members volunteer suggestions, correct each other, plan, organize, consult sources to check spellings and meanings of words, provide detail and description, talk to themselves and to each other, and reread what they have written, all in order to produce a first draft. Thus, children are given a model to follow when they begin writing on their own. Children should understand that the creation of a first draft is only the first step in producing a polished final product. If they accept that anything that can be written can also be rewritten, they are closer to understanding that they may have to rewrite, modify, and polish their writing several times before it is ready to be shared with others. If enough thought has gone into the ideas and emotions that are expressed in the rough draft, the act of writing should generate even more ideas and move the composition or story to its conclusion.

Proofreading and Revising

While the very young child may not be ready to produce more than one draft, that child is capable of checking over his or her work to catch spelling and punctuation errors. At all levels, children should be given instruction in proofreading and revision and should be provided with standards by which to judge their writing. Just as group composition is a way of building students' confidence in their writing skills, so group editing is a useful tool for developing a set of standards and a model for applying them to written composition. You may want to begin by encouraging your class to list those things they think are important to check for when proofreading and revising. Their list might look like this:

Proofreading

1. Is my capitalization correct?
2. Is my punctuation correct?
3. Is my spelling correct?
4. Have I used words that say what I mean and have I used them correctly?
5. Can my teacher and classmates read what I have written?

Revising

1. Does my story or essay have a beginning, a middle, and an ending?
2. Does my story or essay follow a logical sequence?
3. Have I said what I meant to say and all that I meant to say?
4. Does the title describe my story or essay well?

You may wish to write sentences or paragraphs on the chalkboard that demonstrate to students how revision can be accomplished. You may ask your students to test the writing against the criteria they have established. Ask them questions to elicit suggestions. "Is this the best word to use here?" "Does this sentence belong here?" Once students have had opportunities to revise something as a group, they will be able to apply some of the same techniques to their own writing.

Another technique to teach revision is sentence combining, which is a way of encouraging syntactic sophistication in your students' writing. Students are asked to make one sentence out of two. For example:

1. Bill was cold.
2. Bill was hungry.

becomes

3. Bill was cold and hungry.

As students become adept at combining, the complexity of the possible combinations can be increased:

1. The boy realized something.
2. He would have to find a dog.
3. The dog would be courageous enough to battle the bear.

becomes

4. The boy realized that he would have to find a dog that would be courageous enough to battle the bear.

A BEGINNING METHOD FOR TEACHING WRITING TO YOUNG CHILDREN

Many children are ready and eager to write shortly after entering school. Sealey, Sealey, and Millmore (1979) proposed a structured language-experience approach to teaching young children to write. They discuss five stages of instruction:

Stage 1: Labeling and Captioning.
In the first stage, children draw pictures and label them. As they label their pictures,

| car | bird |

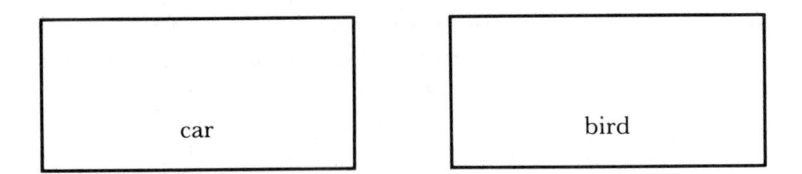

you may want to talk with them and discuss the ways in which they could "write" labels or captions.

Stage 2: Writing Complete Statements of One-Unit Length

As children progress from labeling a single object to writing complete sentences, you should ask them to watch you as you write their sentences. Point out to them that you are writing separate words, using capitals, and writing periods. As soon as your children are ready, have them write the statements themselves as the children have done in the following illustrations:

This is my house.

Stage 3: Writing Two Complete Statements

Children should be encouraged to compare two complete statements. As you write the sentences for your students, ask your children to observe sentence formation and punctuation. As soon as they are ready, ask them to do the writing themselves, for example:

| The car is red. | The bird flies. |
| My sister drives it to school. | It goes above the clouds. |

Stage 4: Writing Three or More Complete Statements

At first, children often compose three seemingly unrelated statements to accompany a picture of school, for example, "I play blocks," "I read books," "I paint." Children will need different levels of instruction to enable them to compose stories that are coherent and cohesive. Children should be encouraged to observe you as you write their sentences. As soon as they are ready, they should be encouraged to do their own writing.

Stage 5: Writing Thematically

Children should be encouraged to write thematically, that is, to compose several sentences that are related to each other in an orderly way: sequential, cause-effect, or ideational, for example:

| Sam always wanted to eat fish. So he went to the lake with his fishing pole. He put his line in the pond. He pulled out a beautiful trout. He went home and cooked the fish. It was good. | The car is red. My sister drives it to school. It goes fast. My sister drives it to work after school. Her car is clean. |
| Narrative | Non-narrative |

Sealey, Sealey and Millmore (1979) also recommended some practical suggestions for establishing effective writing programs for young children:

The writing area must be well-organized and attractive. It should contain:

1. Writing Instruments
   pencils

ball point pens
magic markers
crayons
chalk
erasers
typewriter
2. Pictorial Sources
magazines
pictures
3. Word Sources
dictionaries
Word cards
4. Post Office Box (Mail Box) for mailing letters

They have also suggested the following, useful ways to help children make books for their writings:

SOME WAYS TO MAKE BOOKS

Basic Materials

Papers and containers	Fasteners	Tools
heavy cardboard (boxes)	metal rings	scissors
oaktag	yarn, thread	glue
newspaper	ribbon, twine	1'' and 2'' tape
construction paper	staples	paper punch
newsprint	brass fasteners	paper cutter
manila paper	nuts, bolts, washers	needles
wallpaper sample books	shoe laces	stapler
flat boxes	elastic bands	
paper towel tubes		

Decorative Materials

crayons, paints, magic markers
contact paper scraps, used gift paper
cloth oddments—burlap, felt cottons

TYPES OF WRITING

Children need to be exposed to a variety of writing experiences and to practice writing in a variety of styles.

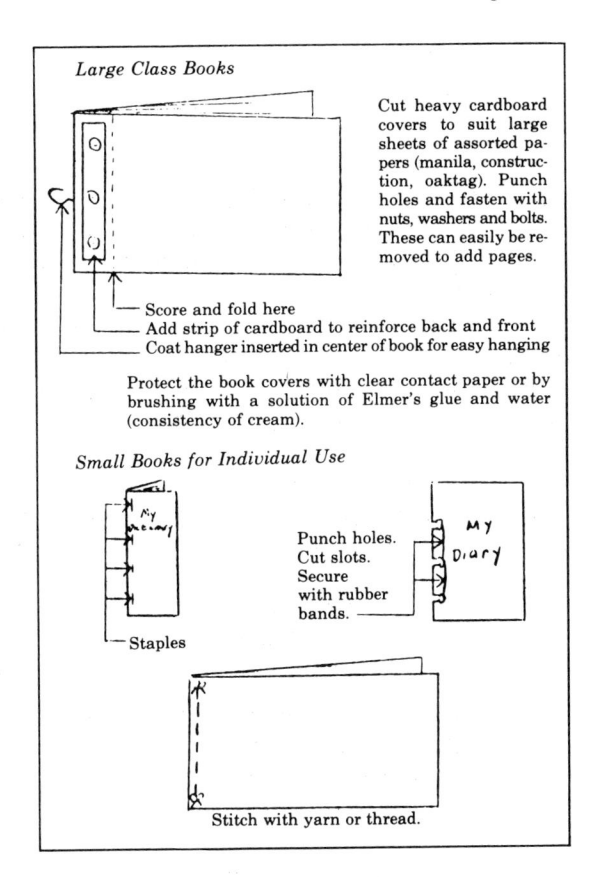

```
                                    Large Class Books
                                    ┌─────────────────┐    Cut heavy cardboard
                                    │                 │    covers to suit large
                                    │ O               │    sheets of assorted pa-
                                    │                 │    pers (manila, construc-
                                    │ O               │    tion, oaktag). Punch
                                    │                 │    holes and fasten with
                                    │ O               │    nuts, washers and bolts.
                                    │                 │    These can easily be re-
                                    └─────────────────┘    moved to add pages.

                                    — Score and fold here
                                    — Add strip of cardboard to reinforce back and front
                                    — Coat hanger inserted in center of book for easy hanging

                                    Protect the book covers with clear contact paper or by
                                    brushing with a solution of Elmer's glue and water
                                    (consistency of cream).
```

FIGURE 6-4.
(*From:* Sealey, L., Sealey, N., & Millmore, M. "Children's Writing, An Approach for the Primary Grades," Newark, Del.: International Reading Association, 1979, pp. 31-32.)

Small Books for Individual Use

Punch holes. Cut slots. Secure with rubber bands.

Staples

Stitch with yarn or thread.

Story Writing

Different types of writing develop different skills. As you remember from Chapter 4, a child's grasp of story grammar can be a key factor in the student's ability to comprehend stories and texts. One way to foster understanding of story grammar and to develop writing skills is to encourage students to write their own stories.

There are a number of ways to inspire story writing. Writing based on a child's personal experiences or on an experience the entire class has shared are often good starting points for stories. Children are naturally eager to relate their experiences in story form. They can be encouraged to present events in story form, including themselves as characters. A single word or an interesting object may motivate one child to write an entire story, while another may need a "story formula" as motivation to write. Such formulas require students to include a beginning, a problem, a climax, a following action or solution, and an appropriate ending. Students may want to consider some of the different ways that stories begin:

1. With an introductory description of the main characters
2. With a description of the setting of the story, including time, place, or circumstance
3. With a conversation to set the stage
4. With a question
5. With a summary of the point of the story
6. With the end of the story

Students must understand the importance of description to a story to bring characters and settings to life. Stories based on their personal experiences are often most effective with younger children because their knowledge of the world is limited and because they have an inherent interest in their own actions and desires.

Letter Writing

Letter writing is an important component of a good writing program. Letter writing activities are best taught as an outgrowth of real situations that call for correspondence. Children should learn how to write personal letters, thank you notes, requests, greetings, orders, sympathy letters, replies, invitations, orders. They need to understand that a letter can be divided into parts, with each part serving a specific purpose. Children should also be guided in conveying the appropriate tone in a letter.

It is vital that children be provided sample letters to model. The sample letter should show the date, salutation, body of the letter, and the closing. Bulletin board displays can be created to illustrate letter format. Samples of different kinds of letters can be collected in a "Letter Form" booklet. The booklet should include letter forms created by the students, as well as actual letters written by adults. You may want to establish a Letter Writing Center. The center should be equipped with paper, pens, pencils, perhaps even a typewriter. The Letter Form booklet can be stored in the center along with the names and addresses of people to whom the children might want to write: their classmates, penpals, senators and congressmen, local celebrities. Perhaps each class member can have his own mailbox to receive letters.

Children need to learn the purpose of writing different kinds of letters, and the differences those purposes dictate in content. Some occasions that warrant letters might be:

1. A thank-you note to the school band after the class has attended a concert
2. Friendly letters to children in another classroom in the school
3. A request that the cafeteria serve a special item on the menu
4. A get-well note to a sick classmate
5. An invitation to parents to visit the classroom

Poetry Writing

Poetry writing teaches children much about writing in general because it encourages them to express themselves vividly and economically. The ability to be both expressive and concise is important to all kinds of writing.

Often, poetry writing proves easier for children. They enjoy exercising their imaginations and expressing their emotions. Poetry writing allows a child more freedom to express himself or herself creatively. Certainly poetry writing can provide rewarding experiences for children. Before children begin writing poetry, they must be given the opportunity to read and to listen to poems with different characteristics, topics, and forms.

Children enjoy experimenting with various poetic forms. While the forms are useful for teaching children to work creatively, they must be used with certain constraints.

Cinquains. Cinquains are poems consisting of five lines. The first line of the following pattern of cinquain contains five words, with each succeeding line containing one less word.

Sunrise

Soft hues invaded the sky
Light entered my room
Darkness was broken
Sleep ended
Awake!

The second form of cinquain contains five lines, each of which has a purpose.

Skiing (state a one-word title; here the first line of
the poem is the title)

Slopes, snow (state two words that describe the title)
Jumping, Freezing, Racing (state three words that express action)
Shivers, Chills, Excitement, Joy, (state four words that express feeling)
Hotdogging (state one word for the title)

Limericks. Children enjoy writing limericks. A limerick is composed of a triplet and a couplet. The triplet includes lines 1, 2, and 5; the couplet includes lines 3 and 4.

As a beauty, I am not a star.
There are others more handsome by far.
But my face, I don't mind it,
For I am behind it.
It's the people in front get the jar.

146   The Processes of Writing

Haiku.   The Haiku is a classical Japanese poetic form. It consists of three lines and a total of seventeen syllables.

> Line 1: five syllables
> Line 2: seven syllables
> Line 3: five syllables

Catch

I like to play catch
A ball can come fast at you
It is hard to catch.

Other Forms.   Other forms of poetry include:

Couplets

All rooms have floors
But only some have doors.

Triplets

I skipped on the sand
I jumped on the land
The whole day was grand.

Shape Poems

[Hand-drawn illustration of a tree with a leaf, labeled "Shape Poems". Text on the leaf reads: "a leaf falls from an elm tree"]

Free Verse. Children need the chance to experiment with poetry. Most children are successful at writing free verse because it is a form without restrictions. It has no rhyme pattern, no set line length, and any topic can be treated.

What is hard?
Hardness is a baseball.
Hardness is doing homework.

Group composing is a good way to get children started writing poetry. Help your students develop vivid images before they actually attempt to compose a poem.

Writing Research Reports

Children should begin to write informational research reports as early as they can. Research reports can be elaborate projects or they can be brief papers on a subject that the child finds interesting. The beginning of the following research project was written by a fourth grader:

Louis Braille 1809–1852

Louis Braille was a blind Frenchman who invented the braille system and printing for the blind. He was born in Paris in 1809. He became blind in 1812 at the age of 3 in an accident. He made up his mind that he wanted to make a reading and writing system at the age of 12 at the National Institute for the Blind (N.I.B.). Louis learned to read using large books weighing many pounds. The pages were embossed with large capital letters which pupils read by passing their fingers over them to seek out their shape to put them into words. It was slow, but it was reading.

Louis wanted to read many books, not just a few. He decided he would someday invent a way to do this. One day in the spring of 1821 Captain Charles Barbier came to the Institute. The Captain had worked out a way for his soldiers to send messages . . . .

Writing reports provides children with skills they will need for much of the writing they do in the upper grades. It teaches them how to gather information and how to organize it. It also encourages them to discover what reference sources are available to them and how to use them.

Note-taking. Group activities provide a good way to show children how to take notes for a report.

> Ask the children to read a short selection about an interesting subject; then ask them to suggest statements describing what they learned.
>
> Give children a set of questions and ask them to find the answers by looking in the dictionary or in an encyclopedia: How far is it to the moon? What is a tornado? How large is the Sahara Desert?
>
> Show the children a film; ask them to record their impressions of the characters, the plot, and the setting.

Children need to understand that they should:

1. Take notes only on the subject
2. Take notes only on ideas that are important and interesting
3. Write the notes in their own words
4. Record the source of the notes

References. Children need to know how to use dictionaries, encyclopedias, almanacs, and atlases. At first, they should be encouraged to use only one source. From the beginning, they should be taught to record the sources of their information. A checklist helps students decide whether they have recorded everything they need to know about a source:

> Have I noted
> the author?
> the publisher?
> the place of publication?
> the copyright date?
> the appropriate page numbers?

Organizing the Report. Once children have gathered information on a topic through note-taking, they need to organize that information in logical order. As a group, the children should be encouraged to decide how many paragraphs their report will have, what information will be contained in each paragraph, and in what order the paragraphs will be arranged. After discussing these questions, the children should organize their material into an outline. For example:

>   Title
>   I.
>   A.
>   B.
>   C.

II.
    A.
    B.
    C.

Children should be taught the correct format for a report. Together, the teacher and the class can develop a set of standards for checking the form and neatness of a report:

1. Write the title of the report on the top line and in the center.
2. Capitalize the first word of the title. Capitalize other important words in the title.
3. Skip a line after the title, before beginning the report.
4. Leave margins on each side and at the top and bottom.
5. Write clearly.
6. Observe spelling and punctuation rules.
7. Be sure your name appears at the end of the report.

Forms

Throughout their lives, students will be required to complete forms. Therefore, instruction in the proper way to complete forms can be particularly useful. Children need to know that they must be accurate and neat when they fill out a form. They must follow directions carefully and be sure to provide all the information requested on the form.

There are many situations in which forms are used that you will want to discuss with your students:

1. Order forms: for books, subscriptions, free samples, and so on
2. Banking forms: deposit and withdrawal slips, applications, checks
3. Information blanks: library loans, headings for standardized tests, membership applications

Children can work as a group to complete sample forms. They can be encouraged to collect forms they find in the grocery store, in magazines, and so on. They may even want to create their own forms for use in the classroom.

EVALUATION

In evaluating students' writing, you will want to use two systems: a holistic scoring system and a checklist of specific skills.

A holistic scoring system is based on the assumption that more than one judge will give the same score to a piece of writing:

A Holistic Scoring System

	Poor	Below Average	Average	Above Average	Excellent
Organization	1	2	3	4	5
Clarity of expression	1	2	3	4	5
Mechanics of writing	1	2	3	4	5
Creativity	1	2	3	4	5
Holistic judgment	1	2	3	4	5

You may also need to develop or adapt checklists for specific kinds of writing. For example, in evaluating a letter, one might ask:

1. Is my letter concise and my purpose for writing clear?
2. Is my spelling correct?
3. Is my heading positioned correctly?
4. Is the inside address positioned correctly?
5. Is my greeting appropriate to the occasion?
6. Is my closing appropriate?
7. Have I signed my letter?

Evaluation should be an inherent, ongoing part of the writing process; it should not become an exercise in criticism or a way of accumulating a row of marks in a grade book. When you are evaluating your students' writing, keep in mind that your goal is to teach them to improve their writing. If you thoroughly discourage a child about his or her writing, that child will not want to write. Try to take a positive approach in your evaluation by emphasizing the strong points in the writing a child produces. Every piece of writing has something praiseworthy about it. Don't limit your comments to negative remarks. If you are giving letter grades or numerical scores, be sure to give the child an adequate explanation for the grade received. Always remember that evaluation permits you to diagnose difficulties a child is having. It should always be the basis for further teaching.

EXERCISES

1. Explain how the process approach to the teaching of writing can guide your writing curriculum.
2. Develop a writing program that flows from your definition of the writing process.
3. Design a classroom environment that would foster your students' growth in writing.

REFERENCES

ANDERSON, P., and LAPP, D.   *Language Skills in Elementary Education,* 3rd ed. New York: MacMillan Publishing Co., 1979.

BURNS, P., and BROMAN, B.   *The Language Arts in Childhood Education.* Chicago: Rand McNally College Publishing Co., 1979.

EMIG, J.   *The Composing Processes of Twelfth Graders.* Urbana, Ill.: NCTE, 1971.

FLOOD, J., and LAPP, D.   *Language/Reading Instruction for the Young Child.* New York: Macmillan Publishing Co., 1981.

GRAVES, D.   "Balance The Basics: Let Them Write." *Learning* 6 (1978): 30–33.

HAYES, J., and FLOWER, L.   "The Process of Writing." In L. Gregg, and E. Steinberg, eds. *Cognitive Processes In Writing.* Hillsdale, N.J.: Lawrence Erlbaum Associates, 1980.

HUNT, K.   "Recent Measures in Syntactic Development." *Elementary English,* 5, NCTE, 1966, 194–199.

MURRAY, D.   *A Writer Teaches Writing: A Practical Method of Teaching Composition.* Boston: Houghton Mifflin, 1968.

MEYERS, M.   Five Approaches to the Teaching of Writing." *Learning* 6 (1978): 38–41.

OLSON, D.   "From Utterance To Text: The Basics of Language in Speech and Writing." *Harvard Educational Review* 47 (1977): 257–282.

PETTY, W. T., and JENSEN, J. M.   *Developing Children's Language.* Boston: Allyn and Bacon, 1980.

RICHARDS, I. A.   *How To Read a Page.* Norton and Co., 1942.

ROTHMAN, G.   "Pre-Writing: The Stage of Discovery in the Composing Process." *College Composition and Communication.* Urbana, Ill.: NCTE, 1965.

RUBIN, D.   *Teaching Elementary Language Arts,* 2nd ed. New York: Holt, Rinehart and Winston, 1975.

SAGER, C. *Improving the Quality of Written Composition Through Pupil Use of Rating Scale.* Unpublished dissertation: Boston. Boston University School of Education, 1972.

SEALEY L., SEALEY, N., and MILLMORE, M. *Children's Writing: An Approach for the Primary Grades.* Newark, Del.: International Reading Association, 1979.

TIEDT, S. W., and TIEDT, I. M. *Language Arts Activities for the Classroom.* Boston: Allyn and Bacon, 1978.

VYGOTSKY, L. S. *Language and Thought.* Cambridge, Mass.: The MIT Press, 1962.

WARRINER, J. *English Grammar and Composition: II,* rev. ed. New York: Harcourt Brace and World, 1965.

FURTHER READINGS

EMIG, JANET. *The Composing Processes of Twelfth Graders.* Urbana, Ill.: NCTE, 1971. The original case study on writing. Emig found that the traditional "rules" for writing are not practiced by good writers.

FINN, PATRICK, and PETTY, WALTER. *The Writing Processes of Students.* Buffalo: The State University of New York, 1975. A series of papers delivered at a conference on the language arts. Includes essays by Squire, Emig, Graves, and Cooper.

GREGG, LEE, and STEINBERG, ERWIN, eds. *Cognitive Processes In Writing.* Hillsdale, N.J.: Lawrence Erlbaum Associates, 1980. An excellent series of papers on the processes writers must engage in while composing.

SEALEY, L., SEALEY, N., and MILLMORE, M. *Children's Writing: An Approach for the Primary Grades.* Newark, Del.: International Reading Association, 1979. One of the best collections on the subject.

Much as I loathe the typewriter, I must admit that it is a help in self-criticism. Typescript is so impersonal and hideous to look at that, if I type out a poem, I immediately see defects which I missed when I looked through it in manuscript. When it comes to a poem by somebody else, the severest test I know of is to write it out in longhand. The physical tedium of doing this ensures that the slightest defect will reveal itself; the hand is constantly looking for an excuse to stop.

—*W. H. Auden*

7 HANDWRITING

This chapter contains a brief sketch of the origins and development of writing in young children, a rationale for teaching handwriting, a list of handwriting skills, and suggestions for developing an instructional program. Evaluation procedures have been included for assessing the effectiveness of your program.

Earlier in the book, in Chapter 5, we discussed the development of writing. You may have noted the way block writing developed into script. This process did not occur only in our system but also in both the Egyptian system (where hieroglyphics gave way to demotic) and the Chinese system (where "grass" or "running" characters are in regular use). Our handwriting has developed from the Italian writing of the Renaissance and has continued in use for over four hundred years because of its ease, clarity, and lack of ambiguity.

THE ORIGINS AND DEVELOPMENT OF WRITING

Children differentiate between pictures (figures) and print very early in their development. They attend to "line" in relation to the surface in which it appears, for example, line versus background and figure versus background (Gibson and Yonas, 1968). Such discrimination may be a prerequisite for distinguishing between print and nonprint (pictures).

Graves (1978) found that two- or three-year-old children do not distinguish between the use of lines for writing or for drawing. At this age, their picture scribbles and their writing scribbles are not distinguishable. Later, children make distinctions, that is, their writing scribbles have characteristics of print; they are vertical, divorced from drawings, and are called writing. This development has been documented by de Ajuriaguerra and Auzias (1975).

Hildreth (1936) claims that by age three, children's productions or lines contain specific features of print: vertical strokes and horizontal lines.

Two- or three-year-old children do not distinguish between the use of line for writing or for drawing. At this age, their picture scribbles and their writing scribbles are quite similar. (*Photo by Linda Lungren*)

Gibson and Levin (1975) maintain that this occurs as a result of children's interactions with print. By age three, children know two important things about writing: (1) that scribbles must go up and down; and (2) that these scribbles are called writing, while pictures (figures) are not called writing.

Shortly after this time, children learn that print has distinctive features (Gibson and Levin, 1975), but variations in handwriting style do not alter the symbolic value of the scribble (letter) (Eden, 1960). Children learn that letters can be represented in many ways, for example, AND, and, *and* without changing their meaning (Bullock, 1975).

Clay (1975) has discerned a series of steps in the acquisition and development of writing:

> Out of primitive drawing skill emerges a letter such as "O", a form found in the scribble of two- to three-year-olds. When "O" is joined roughly this may produce an overshoot, an undershoot, and a spiralling effect.
>
> Accidental discoveries like these might bring a child close to new letters like d or a or e, forms like c, and forms like b or 6. (pp. 15)

Clay (1975) suggests that this is followed by the omission of letter-like forms and the production of conventional letters solely. She suggests that children's rules become more specific, for example, they use letters to write names: one five-year-old girl, in writing the names of her dolls, wrote "AUUDO," announcing: "This say Katrina." A next stage in the development of writing is evident in the following strategy used by one child. She used the correct number of letters for writing the word *mother* and generalized according to Clay's rule, "If you end with what you started with this may be the cue to the whole pattern." For example:

$$M@e\mathcal{f}\supset M$$

The rules that children seem to generate actually enable the children to "play" with print, to produce it, judge its worth, and correct it. This metalinguistic awareness is extremely valuable in the development of writing.

Instructionally, Clay (1975) notes that the writing of one's own name seems to be significant in learning what words are. She notes:

> As the child records his name the repetition of this familiar word may establish some very important concepts, namely, the invariant set of letters and order of letters that make up a remembered word. . . . But of any word in his mother tongue his name is likely to be the most highly motivating word to want to write. (p. 46)

Children learn the invariant sequence of letters within their own names. The information leads them to the notion of invariance of letter strings in other words; this is very valuable for future reading/writing development.

As children enter your classroom, they will be ready for handwriting instruction. The goal of all handwriting instruction should be legibility for the sake of effective communication. Just as children need to learn the necessity for clarity in expressing themselves in oral language, so too children need to learn that they must write down messages clearly enough to be understood by their audiences. You, as the teacher, need to develop your own handwriting so that you can demonstrate appropriate forms for your students.

GUIDELINES FOR ESTABLISHING OBJECTIVES FOR YOUR PROGRAM

The objectives of your handwriting program should take into account the grade level of each child. The following guidelines may be helpful:

1. Instruct your children in the concept of legibility for communication.
2. Teach your children that good handwriting helps develop expression of ideas and feelings.
3. Explain to your students that penmanship is related to speed. A mid-

point between speed and clarity needs to be found in which penmanship aids the writer in expressing thoughts. If too much attention is given to penmanship, the writer may slow down to such a degree that penmanship intrudes upon expression.
4. Set aside instructional time for introducing, teaching, and practicing penmanship.
5. Diagnose the handwriting problems of each of your students and provide appropriate instruction that will develop each child's handwriting.
6. Establish reasonable standards of acceptable penmanship for your students. Try to avoid capricious and ever-changing criteria for acceptable penmanship.

HANDWRITING SKILLS

Before discussing the "how" of handwriting instruction, it might be helpful to talk about the "what." The following questions may occur to you:

1. What are the skills that I will want children to acquire from their handwriting instruction?
2. What is the order in which children acquire these skills?
3. How can I teach these skills?

Each child will acquire handwriting skills at different times; some can write their own names by 3 years of age, while others may not master this skill until 6 years of age. This girl is tracing the letters in her name. (*Photo by Linda Lungren*)

The first two questions, dealing with the array of skills and the instructional sequence, will be addressed below. The third question, concerning teaching of these skills, will be discussed throughout the remainder of this chapter.

Each child will acquire handwriting skills at different times, some young children can write their own names by the time they are three years of age, while others may not master this skill until they are six years of age.

READINESS FOR HANDWRITING

Handwriting instruction, like all other areas of the language arts, demands readiness for the task. Young children must show an interest in handwriting through their curiosity about the task, their attempts at performing it, and their eagerness for an assessment of their attempts. Fine motor coordination skills are necessary requisites for the development of handwriting. Children need to explore their environment to discover all the written symbols in their world. They need to prepare for the task of handwriting by gaining experience with the following:

Directionality
Crayons
Scissors
Paint brushes
Pencils
Magic markers

Before learning handwriting, children need to have established hand dominance, an ability for copying simple shapes and forms, and a demonstrated interest in writing. Children will manifest their interest in several different ways and each child will exhibit a unique readiness for the task. You, as the teacher, must be prepared to deal with the readiness skills of your children at many different levels, for example, some children may want to begin their handwriting program with unlined paper, some may want to begin with heavy pencils, and some may want fine pens. The materials with which the child begins are not necessarily the most important factors in a beginning handwriting program.

WHY BEGIN WITH MANUSCRIPT WRITING?

Almost all teachers begin their handwriting program with instruction in manuscript writing. This may confuse you, and you may ask, "Why teach children manuscript writing when they will have to learn cursive eventually? Why not begin instruction with cursive and eliminate manuscript writing?" There are several answers to these questions:

1. There are only two movements in manuscript writing: straight lines and curved lines. These two movements are the underlying distinctive features of all printed letters in English. As you teach your children how to make these movements, you will be helping them with their beginning reading skills.
2. Manuscript writing is simpler in form than cursive writing. It is easier to correct errors in manuscript writing than in cursive writing because errors are more immediately visible, for example:

    e.g. Manuscript: *taken*
    Cursive: *taken*

3. Because each letter is formed separately in manuscript, the child has time to pause between letters. This pause may help children to see and correct errors and enable the children to prepare for the production of the succeeding letter.

However, it should be noted that controversy surrounds the issue of beginning with manuscript and moving to cursive. There are some educators who believe that the switch to cursive writing may intrude upon the child's development in the writing process; they argue that the switch to cursive writing involves focusing attention on a new set of symbols and that this new focus may interrupt the child's attention to the composing aspects of the writing process. They suggest either that children be taught cursive writing only, or that there be a more logical transition from manuscript to cursive writing in which attention is not totally focused on the production of a new set of symbols. One such method is the DeNealion method, in which manuscript and cursive writing are combined logically into one system. On page 160f, we have suggested how to accomplish a smooth transition from manuscript to cursive writing.

TEACHING MANUSCRIPT WRITING

Beginning lessons in manuscript writing should include instruction in using free, grand strokes. This can be accomplished by allowing the children time to practice at the chalkboard or at a large easel. After children have mastered this skill, they should be asked to complete their writing tasks on one-inch lined paper. By second grade, children should be using half-inch lined paper.

Children should begin by using chalk or crayons. When they move to

160　Handwriting

pencils while working on their lined paper, they should use medium-thick pencils with lead that is soft and wide.

During this early stage, children need models for creating letters and numerals. In addition to having the models in front of the room, the children should have the models before them at their work area. The models should demonstrate the order and direction of the movements that are necessary for producing each letter or numeral.

The following are samples of appropriate models:

a b c d e f g h i j k l m
n o p q r s t u v w x y z
1 2 3 4 5 6 7 8 9 0 ? !
A B C D E F G H I
J K L M N O P Q R
S T U V W X Y Z

Observe that the block capitals are true Capitalis Quadrata, as explained in Chapter 5; this system has been retained for over two thousand years.

MOVING FROM MANUSCRIPT TO CURSIVE WRITING

In teaching children how to produce cursive writing, it is important to remember that all children are unique. Individual differences should not be ignored. Some children imitate the writing of adults in their environment and need little direct instruction. On the other hand, children who are manifesting difficulty in learning to read should not be burdened with the difficult task of changing their writing form.

Children who indicate a need for direct instruction should be taught to move from manuscript to cursive writing with the lower-case letters first. The following chart will help students make the transfer.

[cursive alphabet chart: lower-case manuscript to cursive transitions a–z]

Capital letters should follow the lower-case letters. An effective way to begin instruction in the cursive writing of capital letters is to ask the children to write their own names and the names of all the children in your class. Naturally, you will have to provide direct instruction in the letters that do not appear as the beginning letters of the names of the children in your class: for example, if no child in your class has a name beginning with Q or X, you will have to teach these capital letters directly.

The following model contains the entire cursive alphabet:

[cursive alphabet model: Aa Bb Cc Dd Ee Ff Gg Hh Ii Jj Kk Ll Mm Nn Oo Pp Qq Rr Ss Tt Uu Vv Ww Xx Yy Zz]

TEACHING CURSIVE WRITING

It is important to remember that the goal of handwriting instruction is legibility for communication. No one handwriting is perfect—there is no evidence supporting the theory that one model of handwriting is superior to any other. Different handwritings offer variety to your class and manifest interesting aspects of children's personalities.

PHYSICAL FACTORS RELATED TO CURSIVE HANDWRITING INSTRUCTION

The most important physical factors associated with handwriting are the materials on which children write and children's posture during writing. It is generally accepted among educators that the following guidelines should be used during writing periods.

1. Children should sit in a comfortable position with both feet touching the floor.
2. Children's arms should be relaxed.
3. Children's wrists should be perpendicular to their writing line.
4. Children should hold the pen/pencil lightly.
5. Children's forefingers should be at least one inch from the tip, and they should be nearer to the point than the thumb.
6. Children's movement in writing should be a smooth coordinated effort of the whole arm, forearm, wrist, and fingers.

THE LEFT-HANDED CHILD

Approximately, 10 percent of the population is left-handed. Famous left-handed people include Albert Einstein, Leonardo da Vinci, Harry S Truman, and Judy Garland.

Although most infants are neither exclusively left-handed or right-handed, most children have demonstrated a hand preference by the time they reach school. Your left-handed children may be sensitive during handwriting instruction because they are different from everyone else—usually including their teachers. Be sensitive to them and provide opportunities for them to practice their skills. If there is more than one left-handed child in your class, group these children together for handwriting instruction.

Your left-handed children will learn to write well when they are given ample opportunity to practice, to edit, and to control their own efforts. Drummond's twenty-year-old principles for handwriting instruction of the left-handed child are still applicable today:

> Provide lots of writing on the chalkboard. It is practically impossible to use the upside-down style at the board.
>
> Make sure the paper is properly placed on the desk. For manuscript, paper should be square with the desk. For cursive, the bottom right corner should be pointed at the body. It is hard to write in the upside-down position if paper is placed properly. Also, less hand smearing occurs.
>
> Permit lefties to continue manuscript writing indefinitely. Their writing is almost always more legible before they learn to write cursive than afterwards. As the left-handed children begin to change to cursive, though, watch the placement of the paper like a hawk.

Encourage children to hold pencils or pens so that the top of the writing instrument is pointing over the shoulder of the same arm.

Encourage lefties to develop a writing slant which feels natural and good. The slant will, undoubtedly be a bit backhanded compared to generally accepted handwriting styles because it is natural that way. A *consistent* slant makes writing legible, and a lefty is not likely to be consistent using a slant which is natural for right handers.

Furnish lefties with pencils which have slightly harder lead than that used by right handers. Harder lead will not smear as easily, thus providing less reason for twisting the wrist so that the hand is in the upside-down position.

When ink is used, be sure that all lefties have a good non-skip ballpoint pen which has a high quality non-smear cartridge.

Encourage lefties to learn to type. Most classrooms should have typewriters to encourage children to write creatively.

The following diagram illustrates the model positions for left-handed writers. The "don'ts" of positioning during handwriting tasks are also pointed out:

FIGURE 7-3.

Paper and arm positions for the left-handed writers[a]

A
Reverse of right-handed position. Arm axis is 90° with paper ruling. Slant strokes are directed downward and outward (leftward). Slant is generally forward and uniform.

B
Paper is turned more to the right (clockwise) than the reverse of right-handed placement. Arm axis angle with paper ruling is greater than 90°. Slant motion is a sideward (leftward) push of the writing arm. Slant is uniformly forward.

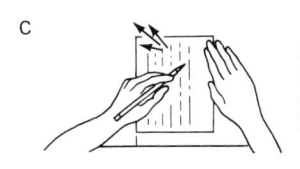

C
Extreme turning of the paper. Paper ruling is 90° (plus or minus 5°) with the front edge of the desk. Slant motion is a sideward (leftward and upward) push of the writing arm. Slant is generally forward and uniform.

The positions for writing with the left hand shown above are reported in the study as the most efficient adjustments to take into account (1) quality, (2) rate, (3) freedom from smearing, and (4) posture. Of these three, B was rated the most desirable, A the second most desirable, and C the third, among some fifteen positions found being used by left-handed writers.

[a] E. A. Enstromm. "The Relative Efficiency of the Various Approaches to Writing with the Left Hand," *Journal of Educational Research* 55 (August 1962), 573-77.

EVALUATING PROGRESS IN HANDWRITING

In evaluating your children's handwriting progress, it is important to clarify your own objectives for this instruction. As we mentioned earlier in the chapter, quality of handwriting has to be measured in relation to speed. No single handwriting is a perfect model for all children. Legibility for communication should be the goal of your program.

In assessing children's progress in handwriting, it is important to use the following guides:

1. Samples of appropriate handwriting of children at different age/grade levels
2. A general assessment instrument
3. A pupil self-analysis sheet
4. Assessment of rate

Appropriate Handwriting at Various Age/Grade Levels

The following are examples of acceptable handwriting specimens for various age/grade levels. You will need to establish objective criteria for evaluating your children's progress and these charts will enable you to establish your standards. As you will notice, several specimens from each level have been included to underscore our belief that there is no one best form of handwriting. Rather, several different styles of handwriting can be evaluated as acceptable:

I am a second grader at Valencia Park Elementary School. My favorite class is Math.

Sheryll

Handwriting

I am a second grader at Valencia Park Elementcia School. My favorite class is reading. Roslynn

Doug M. Sept 26, 1980
It is a very cloudy day. Maybe tomorrow the sun will come out.

I am fourth grader at Valencia Park Elementary School. My favorite classes are motor lab, reading and math.

Signed Shauneeg

I am a fourth grader at Valencial park Elementary School. My favorite class ih math.

I am a sixth grader at Valencia Park Elementary School.

My favorite classes are Math and Reading.

Jasmine

8th grade
Left-handed girl

If you were face to face with the guy and girl as they are shown on this page, you might feel threatened. Knowing that they are on stage performing for your entertainment causes you to react to them differently.

8th grade
Right Hand — Boy

Words and phrases take on different meanings in different situations. If you were face to face with the boy and girl as they are shown on this page, you might feel threatened. Knowing that they are on stage performing for your entertainment causes you to react to them differently.

Left-handed Girl   8th grade

Words and phrases take on different situations. If you were face to face with the boy and girl as they are shown on this page, you might feel theatened. Knowing that they are on stage preforming for your entertainment causes you to react to them differently.

General Assessment Instrument

The following may be used to assess children's writing:

General Assessment Sheet

Category	Assessment	Yes	No
Formation:	Is the letter/numeral appropriately formed? Does it look like the letter/numeral it is supposed to represent?	—	—
Slant:	Is the letter/numeral slanted in the right direction?	—	—
	Does the child know how to make the appropriate slant?	—	—
Size:	Are the letters/numerals too large, too small?	—	—
Alignment:	Are the letters/numerals within the specified space?	—	—
	Do they go above or below the lines?	—	—
	Is the paper positioned correctly?	—	—
Spacing:	Does the child provide adequate space between letters/numerals?	—	—

Pupil Self-Analysis Sheet

Children often need an opportunity to evaluate their own work. The following instrument, Sheaffer Pen's *Pupil Self-Analysis Sheet,* serves this purpose. Children have the opportunity to judge and improve their own handwriting.

Pupil Self-Analysis Sheet[1]

A. Here is how I write when I am in a hurry:
(Write: "This is a sample of my writing")

_____

_____

B. Here is how I write when I do my best writing:
(Write: "This is a sample of my best writing")

_____

_____

C. I would mark my fast writing: (circle one grade)   Excellent   Good   Fair   Poor
   I would mark my best writing: Excellent   Good   Fair   Poor
D. Here is my analysis of my handwriting: Excellent   Good   Fair   Poor

    1. Slant.............................
       Do all my letters lean the same way?   _____ ____ ____ ____
    2. Spacing...........................
       Are the spaces between letters and words even?   _____ ____ ____ ____
    3. Size..............................
       Are all small letters evenly small and tall letters evenly tall?   _____ ____ ____ ____
    4. Alignment.........................
       Do all my letters touch the line?   _____ ____ ____ ____
    5. Loops.............................
       Are *l, f, h, g, y, k, b* well formed?   _____ ____ ____ ____
    6. Stems.............................
       Are all my downstrokes really straight?   _____ ____ ____ ____
    7. Closings..........................
       Are *a, d, g, o, p, s* closed?   _____ ____ ____ ____
    8. Roundness.........................
       Are *m, n, h, u, v, w, y* rounded?   _____ ____ ____ ____
    9. Retraces..........................
       Are *t, i, d, p, m, n* retraced?   _____ ____ ____ ____
   10. Endings............................
       Do my words have good ending strokes without fancy swinging strokes?   _____ ____ ____ ____

[1] *From:* My Handwriting Quotient. Madison, Wis.: A. Sheaffer Pen Company, 1960.

Let us look at the writing specimen of a fourth grader. When asked to use the pupil self-analysis sheet, she recorded her self-analysis in the following way:

I am a fourth grader at Valencia Park Elementary School. My favorite class is Math.

Pupil Self-Analysis Sheet[1]

		Excellent	Good	Fair	Poor
D.	Here is my analysis of my handwriting:				
1.	Slant — Do all my letters lean the same way?		X		
2.	Spacing — Are the spaces between letters and words even?	X			
3.	Size — Are all small letters evenly small and tall letters evenly tall?		X		
4.	Alignment — Do all my letters touch the line?	X			
5.	Loops — Are *l, f, h, g, y, k, b* well formed?		X		
6.	Stems — Are all my downstrokes really straight?		X		
7.	Closings — Are *a, d, g, o, p, s* closed?	X			
8.	Roundness — Are *m, n, h, u, v, w, y* rounded?	X			
9.	Retraces — Are *t, i, d, p, m, n* retraced?		X		
10.	Endings — Do my words have good ending strokes without fancy swinging strokes?	X			

[1] *From:* My Handwriting Quotient. Madison, Wis.: W. A. Sheaffer Pen Company, 1960.

We would be inclined to agree with her assessment. Her handwriting is progressing very well; all she needs is refinement in slanting letters to the right.

Assessment of Rate

The Guiding Growth in Handwriting Scale provides you with normal speeds for children at different age levels. In the instruction for using this instrument, you are directed to ask children to practice writing samples (several times) that you have written on the chalkboard. Children are then timed to assess their speed. The following norms demonstrate the number of words children should have completed within two minutes: for example, to score a grade level 3, children must complete forty-five words in acceptable handwriting:

Grade	1	2	3	4	5	6	7
Rate (no. of words completed)	25	30	45	50	60	67	74

IMPROVING PERFORMANCE

If children are unhappy with their performance, you can help them in many different ways. The major area in which children have difficulty is in the writing of lower-case letters.

The following chart will help your students improve the legibility of their lower-case letters. Ask your children to read the following rules and to put each into practice:

FIGURE 7-14. Guiding Rules for Cursive Writing of the Small Alphabet*

1. In the lowercase alphabet, every letter, except *c* and *o*, must have a *straight* down-stroke, slanting from right to left.

    The downstrokes are straight.   *straight*

    The downstrokes are not straight.   *not straight*

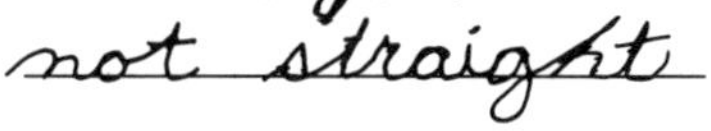

2. The *space* between two letters should be wide enough to hold an *n* without the upstroke:

    "n spaces" between letters   *space*

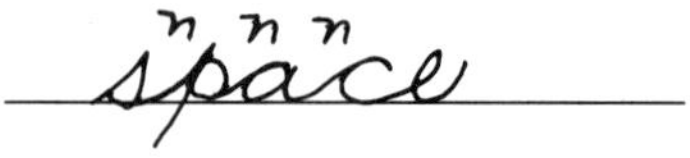

Spaces are too narrow.   *space*

Spaces are too wide.   *space*

3. All downstrokes must be parallel.

Downstrokes are parallel.   *parallel*

Downstrokes are not parallel.   *not parallel*

4. All letters must rest on the line.

Letters rest on the line.   *on the line*

Letters do not rest on the line.   *not on the line*

5. Letters must be of uniform and proportionate size.

acegijmnoqrsuvwxyz | dpt | bfhkl

6. The *total* slant of the writing should be parallel to the diagonal of the paper, whether by right-handed or left-handed writers.

---

* From: Max Rosenhaus, "You Can Teach Handwriting with Only Six Rules," *The Instructor* (March 1957), 60. Used by permission.

EXERCISES

1. Assess your own handwriting by using the Pupil Self-Assessment Sheet on page 169. List your strongest and weakest areas and suggest methods for improvement.
2. Assess the handwriting of one member of your class by using the same form you used for self-assessment. Explain why you think their handwriting is similar or dissimilar to your handwriting.
3. List the ways in which manuscript writing helps children in reading texts.
4. Examine samples of poor handwriting and explain why it is hard to read.

REFERENCES

Bullock, A. *A Language for Life.* London: H.M.S.O., 1975.

Clay, M. *What Did I Write?* Auckland: Heinemann Educational Books, 1975.

Creative Growth With Handwriting. Columbus, Ohio: Zaner - Bloser Co., 1979.

de Ajuriaguerra and Auzias. "Preconditions for the Development of Writing in the Child." In E. Lenneberg and E. Lenneberg, eds. *Foundations of Language Development: A Multidisciplinary Approach,* Vol. 2. New York: Academic Press, 1975. 68–77.

Drummond, H. "Suggestions for the Lefties." *The National Elementary Principal* 38 (February 1959). 18–25.

Eden, M. "On the Formalization of Handwriting." In R. Jakobson, ed. *Structure of Language in its Mathematical Aspect.* Providence: American Mathematical Society, 1960, 118–129.

Enstrom, E. "The Relative Efficiency of the Various Approaches to Writing With the Left Hand." *Journal of Educational Research* (August 1962):573–577.

Gibson, E., and Levin, H. *The Psychology of Reading.* Cambridge, Mass. The MIT Press, 1975.

Gibson, J., and Yonas, P. "A New Theory of Scribbling and Drawing in Children." In *The Analysis of Reading,* ERIC Document ED 034 663.

Graves, D. "Reasearch Update: Handwriting is for Writing." *Language Arts* 55 (1978):393–399.

FURTHER READINGS

Andersen, D. *What Research Has To Say To The Teacher: Teaching Handwriting.* Washington, D.C.: National Education Association, 1968. An excellent source surveying handwriting research.

Forester, L. M. "Sinistral Power! Help for the Left-Handed Children." *Elementary English* (February 1975): 213–215. Provides methodology for working with left-handed children.

Myers, E. *The Whys and Hows of Teaching Handwriting.* Columbus, Ohio: Zaner-Bloser Co., 1963. Provides an enlightened rationale for teaching handwriting.

Naiman, N. *A Blitz Handwriting Program.* San Diego, Calif.: Oak Park School, 1960. A solid instructional program in handwriting.

"Do you spell it with a 'v' or a 'w'?" inquired the judge. *"That depends upon the taste and fancy of the speller, my Lord,"* replied Sam.

Charles Dickens, The Pickwick Papers

8 LOOKING AT SPELLING

This chapter includes background information on spelling rules in English as well as lists of words to use in your spelling program and several activities for helping students develop spelling skills.

THE ACQUISITION AND DEVELOPMENT OF SPELLING IN YOUNG CHILDREN

As we explained previously, children learn the rules of writing by learning that words consist of letters in invariant forms. For example, we pointed out that children learn that their own names are always spelled the same way (at least by their parents and teachers). This knowledge then leads children to the conclusion that there is a standard, invariant spelling for every word of our language. However, the route to this discovery is rather complex.

Henderson (1981) describes the following stages of word knowledge:

1. Scribbling
2. Precise drawings
3. Drawings accompanied by scribblings which children describe as "writing"
4. Inquisitiveness about letters
5. Writing individual letters
6. Writing strings of letters, invented letters, numerals in a jumble or in any direction
7. Prosodic unit spelling (writing two words that sound like one word)
8. Spelling by a single letter
9. A letter-name strategy (phonemic spelling)
10. Vowel-transition spelling
11. Functional-relational spelling
12. Syntactic, semantic, and derivational spelling

Children learn the rules of writing by learning that words consist of letters in invariant forms; their own name is always spelled the same way. Labeling personal cubicles helps reinforce this. (*Photo by Linda Lungren*)

In this pattern, Henderson suggests that spelling is a developmental ability. Not every child passes through each of these stages, but most children who become competent readers and writers do follow this pattern.

Carol Chomsky (1976) cites evidence showing that children pass through an invented-spelling phase; she contends that this is very useful for children because they have the opportunity to try out spellings, to judge their suitability (matching to standard orthography, communication), and to correct them. She claims that "in children's development the ability to write actually preceded the ability to read." The ability of children to spell phonetically, using the letters of their own name or other letters for which they have corresponding sounds, enables them to write messages. Chomsky holds that this invented-writing system should be exploited by teachers as a prereading activity because it serves as personalized initial instruction.

Chomsky further explains that different children independently arrive at the same spelling system. Working with only twenty-six letters, children's spelling, which at first appears idiosyncratic, is amazingly similar; for example, almost all young children using invented spelling write *was* as *wuz* and *boat* as *bot*.

It has been suggested by many researchers that invented spelling should be encouraged because it provides practice in phonetics, in dealing with phonological abstractions, and with the principles of alphabetic writing systems. However, there are many educators who fear that children will thus learn bad spelling habits that will inhibit their reading and writing success. Chomsky (1976), however, found just the opposite. She found that the inventive speller is generally the successful reader; reading is facilitated because children have had to figure out the system. Piaget stated: "Children have real understanding only of that which they invent themselves, and each time we try to teach them something too quickly, we keep them from reinventing it themselves."

The following are examples of Henderson's developmental theory and Chomsky's invented-spelling theory:

FIGURE 8-1.
Single Letter Spelling.

FIGURE 8-2.
Phonetic Spelling.

THE ENGLISH WRITING SYSTEM

The advantage of a writing system such as ours is that it employs a small number of symbols to represent a large number of sounds and a vast number of words. It is difficult for the learner, however, because it is not regular. There are several reasons for this irregularity:

   1. The system really has too few symbols. While twenty-one consonant symbols represent twenty-four consonant sounds, *c, q,* and *x* really have no reliable or individual values (compare *cent* and *cup,* or the beginning and end of *Xerox,* for example). There is also variability in representation (compare the / š / of <u>sh</u>ore, <u>ch</u>ef, <u>su</u>gar, emo<u>ti</u>on, ten<u>si</u>on, and commer<u>ci</u>al, for example).
   2. There are very large numbers of loan words from a variety of languages, and in many cases we have retained the "native" spelling, even as we have adapted the phonology. For example, *ch* (as in *choose* or *chip*) was rendered more ambiguous when English borrowed words such as *chauffeur, chef,* and *charade.*
   3. English has retained orthographic differences where pronunciations have merged. In the seventeenth century, *meat* and *meet* were still distinct in London, although not as different as they must have been to, say, Chaucer before 1400. The vowels have since merged, but we have retained the spelling, which thus reflects an earlier stage of the history of English.
   4. Finally, English frequently represents morphological, rather than phonological information. As a result, *electric/electricity* and *critic/criticize* don't change the *-c-* to an *-s-.* This aids in recognition of morphemes in reading, but it causes trouble in pronunciation. On the other hand, words like *decide/decision* show the change in pronunciation. This does not merely happen with consonants, as can be illustrated by *pronounce/pronunciation; repeat/repetition.*

Though there have been a vast number of proposals for the reform of English spelling over the centuries, they all have been doomed to failure. The result of this is that we must resign ourselves to actually teaching English spelling.

SOME SPELLING RULES

In general, none of the rules we teach children is correct. However, they are valid for most of the words children encounter in primary school. It may well be, that for all the words young children encounter, the traditional rules suffice. For example, the "*i* before *e,* except after *c,* or pronounced as *a* in *neighbor* or *weigh*," is fine for words like *eight* or *receive*. It is not as satisfactory for items like *weird* and *specie*; but then, we do not expect elementary school children to encounter *specie* or *weird* as often as *receive* or *weigh*.

Other spelling rules have to do with the distribution of letters in English. Thus, while there are thirteen items in the unabridged dictionary that end in *j*, even the most familiar of them (*taj* and *raj*) occur so rarely that one can cheerfully tell a class that words do not end in *j*, and words that sound as though they do are written with *ge* (*wage*, *sage*) or with *dge* (*wedge*). We can treat *v* the same way, for while there are thirty items ending in *v* in the dictionary, only *Slav* and *leitmotiv* are among those one is likely to come across. Even simple words that sound as though they end in *v* are written with *ve* (*leave*) or *f* (*of*).

Outside of the Australian airline (*Qantas*) and some Middle Eastern place names (*Iraq*, the *Gulf of Aqaba*) English never writes *q* without a following *u*.

Finally, we can make the generalization that the following letters rarely are written double: *a, h, i, j, k, q, u, v, w, x, y*. The generalization is false, as you can tell from words such as *bazaar, radii, vacuum,* and *flivver*. But again, these are not words we expect primary school children to have contact with, and they can be pointed out as exceptions.

Following are some further generalizations about English spelling that work most of the time:

1. Proper nouns and most adjectives formed from proper nouns begin with capital letters:
    Puerto Rico
    Puerto Rican
    Chinese pastry

2. Words ending in a silent *e* usually drop the *e* before adding a suffix beginning with a vowel; however, they keep the *e* before a suffix beginning with a consonant:
    take - taking
    pile - piling
    time - timely

3. Words that end in a *y* that is preceded by a consonant change the *y* to *i* before adding a suffix, unless the suffix begins with *i*:
    lobby - lobbies - lobbying

4. Words of one syllable or words accented on the last syllable, which end in a single consonant preceded by a single vowel, double the final consonant when adding a suffix beginning with a vowel:
    get - getting
    drip - dripped - dripping
    commit - committed - committing - commitment

5. Rules for using possession:
   (1) The possessive of a singular noun (including those ending in *s, z, ss, or x*) is formed by adding '*s*:
   Tina's car
   James's desk
   Sox's stadium
   (2) The possessive of a plural noun ending in *s* is formed by adding an apostrophe.
   girls' dog
   (3) The possessive of a plural noun not ending in *s* is formed by adding an '*s*.
   children's books
6. Words ending in a *y* preceded by a vowel do not change the *y* to *i* when adding a suffix:
   stay - stayed - staying

BASIC (SPELLING-SOUND) RELATIONS

Despite the irregularities of English spelling, there are a number of basic regularities other than those included in the initial list that can be used in teaching children. These regularities are, in fact, handier for teaching reading than for teaching spelling, since they enable the child to know how a word is pronounced from the way it is printed or written. It is also quite clear that the orthography of English is such that it enables the reader to "see" relationships among words and between words and their derivatives.

One of the most important regularities relates vowel length to whether or not there is a following *e*. It is this regularity that yields

fat	fate
mop	mope
back	bake
fad	fade
lob	lobe

and many other pairs. This pattern also occurs with other vowels, so that we can set up pairs such as

Hal	halo
hug	Hugo
vet	veto

and even

(inter)com   coma

Another reliable regularity is that of doubling letters before suffixes. This convention enables us to differentiate between words such as the following:

wining	winning
lobed	lobbed
cuter	cutter
caped	capped

There are also regularities in the pronunciation/spelling of words when a variety of suffixes are added:

a	angel	angelic
	fable	fabulous
	humane	humanity
	sane	sanity
	state	static
e	convene	convention
	discreet	discretion
	meter	metric
	serene	serenity
i/y	cycle	cyclic
	decide	decision
	reside	residual
	rise	risen
	sign	signal
	type	typical
	wild	wilderness
o	dispose	disposition
	holy	holiday
	psychosis	psychotic
	tone	tonic
u	consume	consumption
	deduce	deduction
	presume	presumption
	reduce	reduction
ea	clean	cleanse
	deal	dealt
	heal	health/healthy
	mean	meant
	please	pleasure
	weal	wealth
	zeal	zealous

The spelling program you use in your classroom should be based on the recognized relationships between orthography and pronunciation. However, since each of you will be teaching not only spelling but also reading, it is of great importance to teach children about sound relationships, which will help children read real words.

It is important to recognize that English spelling is not chaotic but is the product of a long history and of borrowing a large number of words from other languages with other orthographic conventions and diverse phonologies. The material in the preceding chapters should make this clear.

HISTORY OF SPELLING INSTRUCTION

For centuries, there have been difficulties in teaching children to spell; and worldwide instructional practices have remained unchanged for many years. In the United States, several approaches to spelling instruction have been used. Some date back to colonial times with the alphabetic approach. The major objective of this approach was to have children learn letters by configuration discrimination; that is, students were drilled in letters horizontally, vertically, backward, forward, and crisscross until they could differentiate among all the letters presented to them.

The alphabetic approach was followed by the use of a syllabarium, as it was dubbed by Newberry in his 1776 edition of *A Spelling Diction of the English Language Syllabarium*. In this approach, the alphabet was taught first, followed by instruction in correct combinations of letters that make up words. It was believed that knowledge of syllable formation was a prerequisite to spelling. The word method of spelling was introduced into schools around 1850. The emphasis of this method was on knowing the meaning, rather than the structure, of the word. Spelling was considered a purely visual skill; it was therefore impossible for a student to spell a word he or she had never seen.

In 1861, Worchester's *A Pronouncing Spelling Book* shifted the emphasis of spelling instruction from a visual to an auditory approach that emphasized the oral spelling of a word as it was presented in italicized print within a sentence. This method was called the phonics method of spelling; it required that words be spelled by the sounds of letters. Noah Webster's *American Spelling Book* and McGuffey's *Spellers* were both based on the principles of this method. In the mid-1960s, educators such as Hanna and Hanna (1965) forwarded the notion that the spelling of English patterns was regular approximately 80 percent of the time; and further, that these patterns revealed a high level of predictability. These educators pointed out that the numbers of "spelling demons" amounted to only 3 percent of the seventeen thousand words analyzed. As a result of this study, it was assumed that traditional approaches to spelling would give way to methods based on linguistic principles.

In schools today, most spelling programs revolve around a spelling basal and instruction is often limited to the teaching suggestions offered by the textbook writers. Although supplementary instruction by the teacher is sometimes offered, it is infrequent. As a result, instruction in spelling is frequently inadequate.

This lack of effective instruction may result from the fact that most teachers really do not understand what should be taught, why it should be taught, or how it should be taught.

OBJECTIVES OF YOUR SPELLING PROGRAM

1. The first objective of your program should be to teach students the correct spelling of the words they must write. This aspect of the program should stress the introduction and memorization of a large number of high-frequency/high-utility words. Systematic instruction is necessary in teaching these words because incidental (accidental) learning has proven to be an inadequate teaching technique.
2. The second objective of your spelling program should be to incorporate spelling into a variety of areas of the curriculum.
3. The third objective of your spelling program should be to provide effective instruction in the use of common spelling rules.
4. The fourth objective of your spelling program should be to provide your students with the tools necessary for developing more than one strategy for spelling unfamiliar words.
5. The fifth objective of your spelling program should be to use an effective diagnostic evaluation procedure. Each student's strengths and needs must be recognized in order to maximize the effectiveness of the program.
6. A sixth and final objective of your program should be immediate and positive feedback for each child on a regular basis. The development of a positive student attitude toward spelling is essential in an educationally sound and effective spelling program.

ASSESSING STUDENTS' STRENGTHS AND NEEDS

Before you begin, it is important to evaluate the current level of skills your students possess. The following tools will assist you in this process:

1. The first technique may be used when placing students in appropriate instructional levels. Since it is not productive to teach words that students already know, you should select words for initial instruction that are both challenging and new for each student. To accomplish this goal, select twenty words at random from graded spelling lists, for example:

Before you begin work on your spelling instruction, it is important to evaluate the current level of skills that your students possess. (*Photo by Linda Lungren*)

Grade 2	Grade 3	Grade 4
wet	week	dream
win	name	drove
block	Friday	eight
top	these	base
game	sent	penny
boat	cent	cook
stay	keep	paid
nest	then	all right
friend	add	everywhere
fall	bread	careful
band	where	country
dinner	fight	church
dress	asked	comb
there	tall	coal
when	use	bow
thanks	with	busy
call	stopped	ocean
our	nuts	master
calling	snowball	lucky
something	throw	popcorn

Administer each list to your students. Children who score 75 percent or higher on one level should be quizzed on the next level until a score of less than 75 percent is obtained. It is at this level that instruction should begin.

2. A second method of assessment, a more formal method, is the use of standardized tests to assess spelling ability. One such test, the Gates-Russell Spelling Diagnostic Test, assesses a variety of spelling subskills: oral spelling, word pronunciation, word reversals, spelling of one- and two-syllable words, spelling attack methods, and auditory discrimination of words.

3. A final form of assessment is the informal technique. This method is essential for remedial spelling programs because it helps you evaluate each child's spelling in relation to your expectations, goals, and objectives. Attitude, motivation, and interest in spelling may be explored through these informal observations.

CURRICULUM DECISIONS

In developing your spelling program, you should follow your assessment with decisions about the following issues:

1. Number of words to be taught each week
2. Amount of time to be spent each day instructing your students
3. Number of minutes students will spend independently on spelling each week
4. Individual spelling study method that will be used
5. Words that should be studied
6. Ways in which spelling rules should be introduced and taught
7. Words that require particular attention
8. Frequency and type of review that you will use in your program

In deciding how many words should be taught during a spelling lesson, a number of factors should be considered: the number of words students can learn at a specific grade level, the amount of time spent on spelling in other subject areas, and the number of words included in the classroom textbook. It is only after carefully considering these factors that you can decide how many words can be added to or deleted from your weekly word list.

Some educators suggest accumulating words on a daily basis. For example, one or two words a day might be presented in grade 1, two or three words a day in grades two and three, and four to eight words in grades four and five. In the upper elementary grades (sixth, seventh, and eighth), you may not feel that you have the time to introduce new words every day. If this is the case, an alternate systematic approach is necessary; you must plan lessons with self-evaluation. Spelling lessons should be short and concentrated (approximately fifteen minutes daily) and periodic review lessons in the form of games or contests should be used to test maintenance of spelling words.

Once the instructional approach has been decided, you must decide what words your students should master. *The American Heritage Word Frequency Book* may serve as an effective initial spelling list because these words are the most frequently printed words in English. Knowing how to spell these words should help your children in reading and writing.

Word Frequency

English has a distinctive word frequency distribution.

10 percent of all the words written and printed in books, magazines, and newspapers for children and for adults are: *the* and *of*.

20 percent of all words that are written and read are: *the, of, and, to, a, is,* and *in*.

Basis for Heritage Listing

The Heritage Dictionary used a computer to find the relative frequency of 86,761 words in 5,088,721 running words carefully selected from 1,045 textbooks most commonly used in grades 3–9.

Pupil Use

Knowledge of the most frequently used and common words will allow a student to read any data with increased accuracy.

The following lists give the words ranked for frequency by each 5 percentage points through 75 percent as listed in the Heritage list. We have derived the percentages from the data in J. B. Carroll et al., *The American Heritage Word Frequency Book* (Boston: Houghton-Mifflin, and New York: The American Heritage Publishing Co., 1971), pp. 565–567).

HERITAGE LIST

the		is	20%	was	they		have
of	10%	you		on	at	30%	or
and		that		are	be		by
a		it		as	this		one
to		he		with	from		had
in		for		his	I		not

Looking at Spelling

but 35%	been	look	home	keep
what	its	think	big	children
all	who	also	give	feet
were	new	around	air	land
when	people	another	line	side
we	my	came	set 55%	without
there	made	come	own	boy
can	over	work	under	once
an	did	three	read	animals
your	down	word	last	life
which	only	must	never	enough
their	way	because	us	took
said	find	does	left	sometimes
if	use	part	end	four
do	may	even	along	head
will	water	place	while	above
each	long	well	might	kind
about 40%	little	such	next	began
how	very	here	sound	almost
up	after	take	below	live
out	words	why	saw	page
them	called	things	something	got
then	just	help	thought	earth
she	where	put	both	need
many	most	years	few	far
some	know	different	those	hand
so	get	away	always	high
these	through	again	looked	year
would	back	off	show	mother
other	much	went	large	light
into	before	old	often	parts
has	go	number	together	country
more	good	great	asked	father
her	new 50%	tell	house	let
two	write	men	don't	night
like	our	say	world	following
him	used	small	going	2
see	me	every	want	picture
time	man	found	school	being
could	too	still	important	study
no 45%	any	between	until	second
make	day	name	1	eyes
than	same	should	form	soon
first	right	Mr.	food	times

story	play	lines	4	probably
boys	toward	cold	A	needed
since	five	really	letters	<u>birds 65%</u>
white	using	table	comes	area
days	himself	remember	able	horse
ever	usually	tree	dog	Indians
paper	money	100	shown	sounds
hard	seen	course	mean	matter
near	didn't	front	English	stand
sentence	car	known	rest	box
better	morning	American	perhaps	start
best	given	space	certain	that's
across	trees	inside	six	class
during	I'm	ago	feel	piece
today	body	making	fire	slowly
others	upon	Mrs.	ready	surface
<u>however 60%</u>	family	early	green	river
sure	later	I'll	yes	numbers
means	turn	learned	built	common
knew	move	brought	special	stop
it's	face	close	ran	am
try	door	nothing	full	talk
told	cut	though	town	quickly
young	done	started	complete	whether
miles	group	idea	oh	fine
sun	true	call	person	5
ways	half	lived	hot	round
thing	sentences	makes	anything	dark
whole	red	became	hold	girls
hear	fish	looking	state	past
example	plants	add	list	ball
heard	living	become	stood	girl
several	wanted	grow	hundred	tried
change	black	draw	shows	road
answer	eat	yet	ten	questions
room	short	hands	fast	blue
sea	United States	less	seemed	meaning
against	run	John	felt	coming
top	kinds	wind	kept	instead
turned	book	places	America	either
3	gave	behind	notice	held
learn	order	cannot	can't	friends
point	open	letter	strong	already
city	ground	among	voice	warm

taken	third	building	mark	decided
gone	quite	question	ideas	seem
finally	carry	wide	heat	thus
summer	goes	let's	grew	legs
understand	distance	least	listen	nearly
moon	although	problems	ask	square
animal	added	followed	changes	England
mind	doing	books	single	moment
outside	sat	tiny	French	North
power	pictures	hour	clear	teacher
says	possible	B	Tom	happy
problem	names	happened	energy	changed
longer	heart	foot	week	products
winter	having	plant	explain	C
Indian	writing	moving	passed	bright
deep	real	care	lost	sent
mountains	simple	low	spring	present
heavy	snow	else	travel	plan
carefully	getting	gold	wrote	rather
follow	rain	build	cities	length
beautiful	suddenly	glass	farm	looks
beginning	easy	rock	circle	speed
moved	leaves	tall	cried	machine
everyone	lay	covered	whose	information
leave	size	alone	correct	except
everything	wild	reached	bed	figure
game	weather	bottom	working	you're
system	Mother	walk	measure	minutes
bring	Miss	forms	straight	free
watch	carried	takes	base	fell
shall	pattern	check	mountain	suppose
dry	sky	reading	caught	natural
hours	walked	fall	hair	ocean
written	6	poor	bird	government
10	main	map	per	lives
stopped	someone	scientists	wood	trying
within	ones	friend	running	horses
floor	center	c	color	The
Bill	named	language	South	s
ice	field	job	groups	baby
ship	stay	points	war	taking
themselves	itself	music	members	grass
begin	worked	buy	fly	plane
fact	boat	window	yourself	<u>pieces 70%</u>

Looking at Spelling

sides	iron	forest	examples	hit
pulled	trouble	River	guess	wife
8	store	months	begins	played
inches	beside	especially	forward	island
street	oil	dogs	huge	standing
George	modern	necessary	needs	there's
couldn't	filled	lower	closed	we'll
reason	fun	smaller	ride	opposite
difference	catch	he's	region	born
tells	growing	unit	largest	sense
maybe	business	flat	answers	cattle
larger	countries	7	nor	million
history	helped	direction	period	anyone
mouth	gives	south	finished	rule
middle	exactly	subject	blood	science
step	Jim	skin	rich	helps
thousands	King	wasn't	team	farmers
steps	reach	I've	waves	afraid
cars	lot	Europe	corner	women
child	won't	New York	Mary	produce
opened	answered	yellow	cat	pull
thinking	case	ships	amount	son
strange	speak	arms	liked	meant
eggs	shape	party	garden	broken
wish	eight	force	led	interest
soil	edge	test	note	ends
human	seems	bad	various	woods
trip	soft	temperature	race	Henry
woman	interesting	pair	developed	chance
eye	watched	ahead	bit	homes
milk	formed	wrong	clothes	thick
choose	stories	practice	uses	sight
north	village	sand	result	pretty
discovered	object	tail	greater	12
houses	stars	wait	fields	train
seven	placed	difficult	New	sets
easily	Joe	general	brother	fresh
famous	age	cover	addition	faster
pages	minute	areas	doesn't	Washington
late	wall	material	states	drive
rocks	b	talking	dead	lead
flowers	meet	isn't	weight	break
pay	record	thousand	thin	sit
sleep	copy	sign	stone	bought

hundreds	Jack	cause	walls	fit
radio	stick	man's	Africa	students
method	afternoon	stands	showed	turns
gets	silver	feeling	safe	clouds
king	nose	facts	grown	equal
similar	century	please	cost	War
return	saying	meat	wear	value
corn	therefore	lady	act	yards
decide	flying	west	wings	Americans
position	level	glad	Paul	beat
bear	you'll	British	hat	inch
hope	death	action	arm	walking
song	hole	divided	believe	sugar
engine	coast	greatest	major	key
missing	directions	happens	becomes	product
France	cross	pass	gray	desert
board	sharp	20	died	bank
playing	fight	returned	bones	farther
control	capital	adding	sitting	won
spread	Old	ears	wonder	total
knows	fill	soldiers	include	sell
evening	deal	type	interested	wire
brown	patterns	attention	describe	rose
picked	works	shouted	electric	cotton
clean	busy	gas	sold	moves
wouldn't	pounds	World	visit	spoke
section	beyond	actually	15	rope
spent	seeds	kitchen	sheep	rules
Dan	Bob	alike	I'd	fear
ring	produced	pick	waiting	shore
higher	fingers	scale	shoes	throughout
raised	send	basic	30	compare
9	100	West	office	Sam
weeks	love	President	contains	dollars 75%
teeth	materials	Uncle	row	
quiet	cool	Johnny	contain	
ancient	laughed	happen	objects	

SPELLING DEMONS

Words that can be used in every program are the words that all children misspell; these are Jones's (1913) one hundred spelling demons of the English language. These words often cause children difficulty because they violate expected orthographic patterns.

One Hundred Spelling Demons of the English Language

which	can't	guess	they
their	sure	says	half
there	loose	having	break
separate	lose	just	buy
don't	Wednesday	doctor	again
meant	country	whether	very
business	February	believe	none
many	know	knew	week
friend	could	laid	often
some	seems	tear	whole
been	Tuesday	choose	won't
since	wear	tired	cough
used	answer	grammar	piece
always	two	minute	raise
where	too	any	ache
women	ready	much	read
done	forty	beginning	said
hear	hour	blue	hoarse
here	trouble	though	shoes
write	among	coming	tonight
writing	busy	early	wrote
heard	built	instead	enough
does	color	easy	truly
once	making	through	sugar
would	dear	every	straight

Another popular list is Fitzgerald's (1951), which includes fifty spelling demons based on the misspellings of students in grades two through six:

am	going	pretty	time
and	goodby	received	to
because	guess	Saturday	today
coming	Halloween	some	tomorrow
cousin	have	sometimes	too
didn't	here	Sunday	two
don't	I'm	teacher	very
everybody	January	teacher's	we
February	know	thanksgiving	write
for	Mrs.	that's	writing
friend	name	their	you
from	now	there	your
getting	our		

Homophones also cause spelling problems for students. The following are some homophone demons:

affect—effect	one—won
air—heir	pane—pain
bear—bare	passed—past
coarse—course	peace—piece
die—dye	plain—plane
do—due—dew	principle—principal
fair—fare	ring—wring
gate—gait	so—sew
heel—heal	soar—sore
hole—whole	tale—tail
hour—our	threw—through
knot—not	too—to—two
led—lead	way—weigh
meet—meat	wood—would
	write—right

GROUPING FOR INSTRUCTION

Spelling can be taught in groups differentiated by ability. There may be three or four groups in an average classroom and the groups can meet independently or as part of reading or language lessons. You may discover that your children's skills overlap in the areas of reading, language, and spelling, and the groups that have been created will be appropriate for instruction in all of these areas.

INSTRUCTIONAL METHODS

Spelling can be taught by using either the corrected test method or the self-study method. The corrected test method uses a pretest before instruction, and the self-study method uses a progress test after some initial instruction. Hillerich (1977) found that the use of a pretest, followed by immediate self-correction, accounted for more than 90 percent of all the learning that occurs in spelling.

The procedure for using the pretest is as follows: Administer the test to the students and follow it up with an immediate self-correcting procedure by each student. All students should have their own spelling lists. After correcting each word, students must write the corrected version of each word next to the wrong word. You should collect each pretest, review it, and return it to the student. The pretest correction procedure should be monitored closely to ensure that the corrected version of each word is actually correct.

COMMON ERRORS AND CORRECTIVE MEASURES

Students will often make the same spelling errors again and again. The following list from Rubin (1980) might help you in correcting your children's errors:

Causes	Typical Errors	Corrective Procedures
Incorrect visual image	docter for doctor nitting for knitting familar for familiar	Make pupils conscious of the need to see each letter in the word. Break the words into syllables. Have pupils visualize the words. Look at the word for strong visual image.
Inaccurate pronunciation and inaccurate auditory memory	lighting for lightning pospone for postpone erl for oil chimley for chimney choclet for chocolate	Pronounce each word accurately on initial presentation. Pronounce words in concert with class. Listen for inaccurate pronunciation. Choose individual pupils for doubtful enunciation. Repeat several times the part of the word that is difficult to enunciate.
Insertion and omission of silent letters	lite for light lineing for lining no for know ofen for often tabl for table gost for ghost stedy for steady lisen for listen	Silent letters cause many difficulties in spelling. Since these letters do not appear in an auditory image, special stress must be placed on the visual image. Observe each part of the word and have pupils practice writing the part most likely to cause trouble. Provide practice exercises to fix habits of dealing with silent letters.

194 Looking at Spelling

Confusion of consonant sounds	acke for ache parck for park gudge for judge visinity for vicinity sertain for certain	Practice for correct image of the word. Children need to know that some letters have more than one sound: *s* may sound like *s* or *z*. *c* may sound like *s* or *k*. *g* may sound like *g* or *j*.
Confusion of vowel sounds	holaday for holiday turm for term oder for odor salery for salary rejoyce for rejoice	Have pupils break word into syllables and look at its parts. Practice for correct visual image of the word. Practice writing the word to develop kinesthetic feel of the letters.
Confusion of double vowels	reel for real quear for queer	Explain that Double vowels often take the sound of the single letter or another vowel combination.
Inaccurate formation of derivatives	stoped for stopped haveing for having flys for flies sinserely for sincerely omited for omitted	Work for more vivid image of word endings. Emphasize auditory image of endings. Break words into syllables. Have children observe the word in its parts. Call attention to generalizations concerning regular ways of adding endings. Stress closer understanding of adding suffixes. Provide practice exercises on word endings.
Reversals or transposition of letters	gose for goes form for from bread for beard	Pronounce the word distinctly. Have pupils listen for sequence of each sound in the word. Practice for correct visual image.

Looking at Spelling 195

Incorrect meaning —homonyms	dew for due our for hour sum for some	Illustrate use of the word with most common meaning. Use pairs of words in sentence to distinguish what each means. Provide practice on homonyms and stress word meanings at all times.
Phonetic spelling applied to non-phonetic words	bin for been gon for gone sum for some	While spelling embraces phonetics, pupils must be taught to look for numerous exceptions in our unphonetic language. They cannot rely on sound alone. They must realize that their visual memory must be their guide in many new words and word parts.
Confusion of words that are similar in sound	an for and were for where merry for marry effect for affect cents for sense	This error is often due to faulty auditory acuity. Care should be given to enunciation of these words. Pronounce the words in pairs and give the meaning of each.
Poor handwriting	stors for stars temt for tent	Provide practice on letter forms that cause special difficulty. Guide pupils in size, shape, slant, and spacing among letters and words.
Nervousness	Inaccuracies due to lack of control in deliberate thinking	Check child's health. Be sure vision and hearing are not defective. Remove all possible tensions.

| Carelessness | Errors due to poor concentration and careless habits of word study | Stimulate pride in work well done. Praise all improvement. |

ACTIVITIES FOR YOUR STUDENTS

1. There are twenty-six entries in the dictionary with *uu* in them. A few are personal and place names, many are medical or technical terms. Only four are in "real" use: *continuum, individuum, residuum,* and *vacuum.* Have your class look them up in the dictionary.

2. There are many words with double letters in them: 46,667 with one pair (like *keep* or *tree* or *shall*); 3,959 with two pairs of double letters (like *cottonseed* and *dripproof* and *tattoo*); 166 with three pairs of double letters (like *bookkeeper* and *committee* and *whippoorwill*); and only 4 with four pairs of double letters:

killeekillee

possessionlessness

subbookkeeper

successlessness

It is interesting to note that *bookkeeper* and its derivatives (to *bookkeep* and *bookkeeping*) are the only words with three double letters in a row, and that *subbookkeeper* is the only word with four double letters in a row. Have your students look up all the words with three and four pairs of double letters.

3. The longest "word" in the dictionary is

formaldehydesulphoxylate

which contains twenty-four characters. Ask your children to look up as many words as they can find that contain more than twenty letters.

4. There are only five three-letter words ending in *ly*. How many can the class think of? (*aly, cly, fly, ply, sly*)

5. There are twenty-three four-letter words ending in *ly*. How many can the class think of? (*ably, ally, bely, coly, duly, eely, holy, idly, illy, inly, July, lily, moly, oily, only, owly, paly, pily, poly, puly, rely, ugly, uily*)

6. It is frequently said that all the "long" English words ending in *ly* are adverbs (such as *calmly* and *totally*). There are, in fact, quite a few six-, seven-, and eight-letter words ending in *ly* that are not adverbs. Can your class think of any? (*barfly, botfly, brolly, comply, family, gadfly, anomaly, blowfly, duopoly, enjelly, firefly, panoply, reapply, reimply, shoofly, upgully,* and *monopoly*)

Looking at Spelling 197

7. Many English words begin or end with consonant clusters. The longest initial clusters are three characters long (as in *sclerosis, street, scream, spleen, spring*); the longest final clusters are five characters (although only three or four phonemes) long (as in *twelfths* and *lengths*). Ask your class to think of words with clusters at both the beginning and the end. The longest appears to be *strengths*, with three at the beginning and five at the end. Ask them to write as many words as they can that contain three-letter initial clusters and final clusters with three or more letters.

8. There are many words with a number of vowels (for example, *Hawaiian, obsequious, queue, ubiquitous*). There are even a few words that contain all five vowel symbols: *Rousseauian* and *exsanguious*, for example. You might discuss some of these with your class: While the consonant clusters appear to occur in "genuine" words, the large numbers of vowels appear to occur only in loan words and as the result of prefixation and suffixation. Ask your children to research the way in which words like *aqueousness, blandiloquious, cypraeoid, onomatopoeial, palaeoatavistic, radioautography, tonneaued,* and *visuoauditory* came about in English.

GAMES FOR YOUR STUDENTS

In these games, all words should be written on scrap paper to provide opportunities for visual cues and all words should be checked for accuracy.

GAME: Homerun Alley

SKILL DEVELOPED: Learning to spell various spelling "demons"

MATERIALS NEEDED: Heavy sheet of cardboard; four paper cups; construction paper; spelling demons word list; magic marker

PROCEDURE: On a heavy sheet of cardboard or thin piece of wood, paste four cups for the bases. Draw lines to show the base paths. Paste another cup in the pitcher's mound for "outs." Label as on a regular baseball field.
 For markers, cut squares approximately one inch in diameter from various colors of construction paper. Each team should have twenty markers of one color.
 The pitcher throws a word to the first batter (individual spelling demons are ideal for the word source). If the batter can spell the word correctly, he or she puts the first marker in the first-base cup; if the batter misspells it, the marker goes into the outs cup at the pitcher's mound. Two words spelled correctly put players on first and second; three words, bases loaded; four words,

bases loaded and one home run; and so on. After three outs, the second team comes to bat.

Both teams should keep score. The game ends after one to three complete innings or after a predetermined number of minutes.

GAME: Antonym Alley

SKILL DEVELOPED: Learning the antonyms of simple nouns

MATERIALS NEEDED: Any word list of nouns

PROCEDURE: Distribute to players a list of words plus their antonyms. In one turn they may add, change, or drop one letter at a time to change the original word into its antonym. The player who can arrive at the antonym with the fewest number of changes is the winner: For example, *tall* to short—*tall, stall, shall, shale, share, shore, short*—six changes.

GAME: Can you Fix it?

SKILL DEVELOPED: Strengthening use of prefixes, suffixes, and root words

MATERIALS NEEDED: Dictionary; paper

PROCEDURE: List prefixes, suffixes, and roots in three columns. Tell pupils to string together as many word parts as possible. Allow one point for each legitimate word correctly spelled. High score wins. The dictionary can be used.

GAME: Find Out

SKILL DEVELOPED: Vowel improvement

MATERIALS NEEDED: Paper; reference books on proverbs

PROCEDURE: Players write one or more proverbs, such as "A stitch in time saves nine," leaving out all vowels. Players then exchange papers and try to complete the proverbs. The first pupil to complete his or her paper correctly is the winner. This provides a good opportunity to acquaint students with the many excellent reference books on proverbs found in the library. You might want to limit the number of words in the proverb until the students become more proficient.

GAME: Name-Game

SKILL DEVELOPED: Categorization

MATERIALS NEEDED: Paper; dictionaries, reference books

PROCEDURE: Pick a word and write the letters horizontally across the top of your paper. Each player then names a category such as trees, birds, fish, countries, or oceans. Each category is written in the first column. The object of the game is to write a word in every category that begins with the letter at the top of each column. Chart your progress at the end of the game; the first player to have five items for each category is the winner. (See chart.)

Name-Game Answer Sheet

	S	P	E	L	L
trees					
birds					
fish					
countries					
ocean					

EXERCISES

1. Explain the issues involved in standardizing an orthography. Could we get along without a standardized orthography?
2. Describe three spelling rules; list exceptions to these rules and explain the origin of each of these exceptional words.
3. What is the developmental scheme under which most children learn to spell?
4. Discuss the merits and limitations of allowing young children to be involved in an invented-spelling curriculum.
5. How can you diagnose spelling problems? What instructional suggestions can you offer for diagnosed problems?

REFERENCES

Chomsky, C. "Creativity and Innovation in Child Language." *Journal of Education* 158 (1976):12-24.

Fitzerald, J. *A Basic Life Vocabulary*. Milwaukee, Wis.: Bruce Publishing Company, 1951.

Gates, A., and Russell, D. *Gates-Russell Spelling Diagnostic Test*. New York: Teachers College Press, 1940.

Hanna, Paul R., and Hanna, Jean S. "Applications of Linguistics and Psychological Cues to the Spelling Course of Study." *Elementary English* 42 (1965):753-759.

Henderson, E. "Developmental Concepts of Word." In E. Henderson, and J. Beers, eds. *Developmental and Cognitive Aspects of Learning to Spell*. Newark, Del.: International Reading Association, 1981, pp. 1-14.

Hillerick, Robert L. "Let's Teach Spelling—Not Phonetic Misspelling." *Language Arts* 54 (1977): 301-307.

Jones, W. F. *Concrete Investigation of the Material of English Spelling*. Vermillion, S.D.: University of South Dakota, 1913, p.24.

Rubin, D. *Teaching Elementary Language Arts,* 2nd ed. New York: Holt, Rinehart and Winston, 1980.

FURTHER READING

Henderson, E., and Beers, J. *Developmental and Cognitive Aspects of Learning to Spell*. Newark, Del.: International Reading Association, 1981. A highly useful set of essays on the developmental aspects of spelling.

A writer, or, at least, a poet, is always being asked by people who should know better: "Whom do you write for?" The question is, of course, a silly one, but I can give it a silly answer. Occasionally I come across a book which I feel has been written especially for me and me only. Like a jealous lover, I don't want anyone else to hear of it. To have a million such readers, unaware of each other's existence, to be read with passion and never talked about, is the daydream, surely, of every author.

—*W. H. Auden*

9 WRITING AND GRAMMAR

This chapter concerns the mechanics of writing and the teaching of grammar within the language arts curriculum.

TEACHING GRAMMAR

At the earliest stages, it is foolish to talk of "teaching grammar." As you read in Chapter 1, children acquire language at a regular rate and acquire language that is "ambient;" that is, they acquire the language around them. Toward the end of this book, we will discuss the child whose ambient language differs from the language discussed here: the child from a home where English is not spoken or the child from an area where the English dialect of the home is vastly different from that of the school environment.

Children, for the most part, arrive at school already speaking; and what they say is, as long as we comprehend the notions of dialect and development, "grammatical." In general, when we speak of teaching grammar, we are talking of teaching the child the formal conventions used in putting words and thoughts on paper.

In addition to these mechanical conventions, there are a few notions that must be introduced to the child in order to make his or her written communication effective.

REFERENCE

Perhaps the most important of these concepts is the notion of referentiality. Children generally assume that the person with whom they are conversing is as well acquainted with the situation being described as are the children themselves. They do the same thing in writing. As a result, much of children's writing is full of "he" and "she" and "they" without the necessary antecedent nouns. For example, in narrating the story of Meyer's *Frog, Where are You?*, one child began, "He's lookin' in the jar. An' he's in there. An' he goes to bed. An' while he's asleep the frog gets out an' in the mornin' he can't find him."

All of this is correct, for *Frog, Where are You?* begins with a boy and his dog looking at a frog in a jar. During the night, while the boy and his dog are asleep, the frog escapes, and the boy and his dog look for the missing frog.

The child's narrative leaves the listener at a total loss as to whom the "he" and "him" refer to. The job of the teacher in such cases is to make clear to the child narrator/writer the necessity of rendering the pronouns unambiguous: The listener/reader has to know just what's going on and just who the participants are or the story is a total loss.

AGREEMENT

Subject - verb agreement is the next most important grammatical fact for the child to learn. In many homes, forms such as

> The man walk to the corner

are tolerated, rather than

> The man walks to the corner.
> The man is walking to the corner.

or

> The man walked to the corner.

In other words, the agreement of number in the noun and verb, and the necessity of specifying present, present progressive, and past is not found in the regional and social dialects spoken in the homes and areas in which these children live. The children must be taught that the written language requires that they use these forms.

FORMAL GRAMMAR

It must be noted, however, that it is not necessary to burden the elementary-school child with formal grammar and require sentence diagramming in order to teach the child correct usage and how to write. It may be, in fact, that the dislike of grammar among the populace results from educators' insistence on using sentence diagrams as a way of teaching grammar.

Whether we are concerned with an essay, a story, or a letter, the purely mechanical aspect of writing must be differentiated from the creative aspect of writing. (*Photo by Linda Lungren*)

The important thing for the child to comprehend is that the written word is intended to convey information. If what the child writes is unclear or ambiguous, the reader cannot comprehend what is meant to be conveyed.

Formal grammar is a system for describing what the relationships are among the elements of a sentence; the elementary-school child would do better by writing than by attempting to understand the underlying relationships within the writing.

Whether we are concerned with an essay, a story, or a letter, the purely mechanical aspects of writing must be differentiated from the creative aspects of writing. Although we can view writing as a means of self-expression, it is also a means of communication. If we view the language arts as including listening, speaking, reading, and writing, the last is certainly one of the expressive modes. As we have said, reading and writing are secondary to speaking and listening, and so we have concerned ourselves with oral language before written language and with handwriting and spelling before composition.

MECHANICS

The basic mechanics of composition include organization (and paragraphing) and punctuation.

Organization

For most children, events occur linearly in time and thus direct cause and effect sequencing is exactly what they produce. In the primary grades, one of the problems is that your children will assume that their reader is as knowledgeable as they are, that you know as much about the situation (and the characters) as they do. The result is a sequence of sentences and sentence fragments that lack spatial, temporal, and personal reference. Some of the things your children will have to learn is how to supply the reader with enough information, and to have sentences and paragraphs which link up with one another, rather than having a helter-skelter arrangement of "and then" or "next" or "and she."

One of your chores will be to explain to your children how to organize the events they wish to express in writing, and their thoughts about those events, in a way that will be comprehensible to others.

At later stages in organizational instruction, you will have to explain the notion of non-linearity, of beginning at one point, having a "flashback," and then proceeding with the narrative. But the art of constructing a paragraph or an essay that is not strictly linear is far beyond most elementary school children. Perhaps the piece of basic mechanics you want to begin with is the fact that paragraphs are indented and that they are the building blocks of prose work. The actual structure of the paragraph is not at all easy to describe, but a few generalizations can be made:

1. The opening paragraph of a composition should attract the reader's attention, make the reader want to read further, give information about what is to follow, and set the stage for the remainder of the composition.
2. The beginning of a composition should reflect the mood or attitude of the author.
3. The opening paragraph should have a topic sentence that prepares the reader for the rest of the composition.
4. The later paragraphs of a composition should have topic sentences with small range and more limited focus, preparing the reader for that particular paragraph.
5. The final paragraph of a composition is something special. It should draw together whatever the essay is about and leave the reader with the impression that the main thought of the composition has been fully dealt with.

You can encourage your students to improve their paragraphing skills by having them read opening paragraphs in books and articles and by discussing.

1. What the author is trying to do
2. Why the paragraph is interesting
3. Whether the paragraph makes you want to read further

Another good topic for discussion is the difference between the opening paragraphs of a story or a novel and of a factual article or book. The best way to learn how to write well is to read works by good authors and to practice writing.

Of course, you must always be aware of the children's conceptual level. You cannot expect a group of second graders to write coherent, multiparagraph compositions about anything. In the lowest grades, you are much more likely to elicit a single paragraph, only a few sentences long, about "My Pet" or "Baseball," or about the traditional "Trip" or "How I Spent my Summer Vacation." It is only in the middle elementary grades that children become truly capable of extended narration concerning a single, coherent topic. While you must engage your children's minds in their tasks, you must be careful not to overtax them; for the frustrated child, incapable of achieving what is perceived as the teacher's goal, is more likely to abandon the task than to persist at it.

Punctuation

Some of the most important mechanics of writing a composition involve punctuation of a paragraph, which tells the reader where sentences begin and end, where clauses occur, and whether sequences of words are statements or questions. There are two types of punctuation in English: terminal and nonterminal.

Terminal Punctuation. Terminal punctuation occurs at the end of utterances. Since there are only three major sentence types in English, there are only three types of terminal punctuation: the period (.), which occurs at the end of declarative sentences; the question mark (?), which occurs at the end of interrogative sentences; and the exclamation point (!), which may occur at the end of imperatives and after interjections and exclamations.

THE PERIOD (.) The period is used after statements:

      Andrew saw a giraffe.
      He claimed that Warren was in Idaho.
      "Rainy Mondays occur infrequently," he said.

It is also used after indirect questions:

> He asked me when I had last seen the White House.
> They wanted to know why they had to buy a thermometer.

In general, requests phrased as questions are followed by (.), rather than (?):

> Will you please return this book as soon as possible.
> May I receive your apology by return mail.

The (.) is also used in abbreviations and as a decimal point.

THE QUESTION MARK (?) The question mark is used after direct questions:

> Why did the dog bark?
> Who is Linda Lu?
> Really?

as well as after questions embedded within other sentences:

> Someone once said (was it Groucho?) that there was no Sanity Clause.
> "Is today Monday?" she asked.

Question marks are also used in conjoined sentences that begin as declaratives but end as interrogatives:

> This is a bad meal, but could you do better?

and for "tag-questions":

> Elephants don't fly, do they?

Finally, the question mark is used to indicate doubt:

> The author of the *Canterbury Tales,* Geoffrey Chaucer (1300?-1400), also wrote A *Tale of Two Cities,* he claimed.
> The preceding is an innocent (?) error.

THE EXCLAMATION POINT (!) The exclamation point (or exclamation mark) is used after interjections and statements that are genuinely exclamatory:

> Help!
> Stop thief!
> Fire!

The (!) may also be used in writing for emphasis, but it should be used sparingly. Double or triple usage (!!, !!!) is the sign of a poor writer with little to say.

Non Terminal Punctuation. There are nearly a dozen nonterminal symbols used in standard writing: the semicolon (;), the comma (,), the colon (:), the dash (—), parentheses (()), brackets ([]), quotation marks (""), apostrophe ('), hyphen (-), and ellipsis (. . .). Though your children in elementary grades will not use all of them, secondary students should be acquainted with their use.

THE SEMICOLON (;) A semicolon may be used as a linking connective:

> Rhode Island is on the east coast; Oregon on the west.
> Piaget died in 1980; Luria in 1977.

Here the semicolon takes the place of a coordinating conjunction. The semicolon may also take the place of the comma in enumerating some sequences:

> Some (scholarly) journals are: *Language,* published by the Linguistic Society of America; *IJAL,* published by Indiana University; and *JAOS,* the quarterly of the American Oriental Society.

and:

> Among the more profilic novelists, one might name Trollope, who wrote over 50 novels; Powell, with 16 novels so far; and Dickens, Thackeray, and Meredith with over 15 each.

THE COMMA (,) The comma seems to be the bugbear of most students. Strangely enough, most comma faults seem to be the result of overusing this punctuation mark, rather than omitting it. The comma should be used before a coordinating conjunction that joins two independent clauses:

> I took a plane to Tashkent, but Mike traveled by camel.
> I could eat oysters all year, but they're hard to get in July.

Commas should be used after subordinate clauses that begin sentences, especially if the subordinate clause is long or if you feel that omitting the comma might make your sentence ambiguous:

> With the advent of warm weather, shoes vanish and sandals appear.

> After chasing outlaws all morning, Trigger grazed in his paddock.

Commas are used to set off appositives:

> William Blake, the poet and mystic, was also a graphic artist.
> Mohammed Ali, formerly known as Cassius Clay, was a better boxer than he was a poet.

Dates and addresses are punctuated with commas:

> On June 6, 1944, while I was living at 1306 West 11 Street, New York City, the Allied Forces landed at Normandy.

Elements in a series are customarily set off by commas:

> Aristotle, Augustine, Proclus, and Philo were his favorite philosophers.
> The dogs barked, jumped, wagged their tails, and tried to lick Kevin's face and hands.

THE COLON (:) The colon signals the reader that the material following it amplifies, explains, or completes that which has preceded it:

> The retriever had two duties: to find the ducks and to bring them to his master.
> He felt that there were only two worthwhile novelists: Hemingway and Eliot.

THE DASH (—) [Note: in typing always use two hyphens (--) to indicate a dash.]

The dash may be used to indicate an interruption of the chain of thought and the insertion of some parenthetical material:

> Despite all her words—and she said less than she spoke—I was in favor of Norman Mailer.
> The red-winged blackbird—not to be confused with the crested nuthatch—is a vivid creature.

PARENTHESES / () / Except in bibliographies, parentheses are used to enclose unimportant material:

> In 1971, Anthony Powell (pronounced *pole)* published the tenth novel in his *Music of Time* Series.
> After a seven hour flight we landed at the Geneva airport (Cointrin).

BRACKETS ([]) Within parentheses, brackets are used to set off material otherwise enclosed within parentheses:

> Chomsky made an impact upon linguistics with his first book
> *(Syntactic Structures* [1957])

In the event that recurring parentheses are required, alternate parentheses and brackets, for example, ([([])]).

QUOTATION MARKS (" ") Quotation marks are used to enclose a speaker's exact words:

> "Why in the world," he asked, "are you following me?"
> What did Milton mean by "man's first disobedience"?

(Note that commas and periods always go within the quotation marks; question marks may fall within or outside, depending on whether the words of the quotation are a question or not; semicolons and colons are always placed outside quotation marks.)
Quotation marks may also enclose slang expressions:

> In *Go West,* Groucho is the "low man on the totem pole."
> Television is sometimes called the "boob tube."

Titles of short stories, poems, essays, and articles are enclosed within quotation marks (titles of plays, magazines, newspapers, and novels are underlined).

> Sometimes I think that Auden's "Musée des beaux Arts"
> is my favorite poem.
> "Araby" is one of Joyce's best stories; it's in <u>Dubliners.</u>
> <u>The New York Times</u> publishes "All the News That's Fit to Print."
> We saw <u>Hamlet</u> last week.

Quotation marks may also be used to set off words or phrases that are in a different level of language from the main body of the text.

> All such statements are, one might say, "corny."

THE APOSTROPHE (') The apostrophe is used to indicate contractions and possessives:

> Doesn't Mississippi have a lot of *s*'s?
> That's Bob's typewriter.
> I live next door to Harry's sister.

(Note: The possessive of *it* is formed without an apostrophe [*its*] to avoid confusion with *it's* [it is]; the possessive of names ending in *s* adds an apostrophe and an s: James's hat, Jones's car; *except* some Biblical names: Moses' leadership, Jesus' nativity.)

THE HYPHEN (-) The hyphen is used between elements of compound numerals:

>ninety-three, seventy-five, eighty-six

The hyphen is also used at the end of a line to indicate that a word is incomplete:

>A dictionary is the best advisor as to where syl-
>labification occurs.

ELLIPSIS (...) An ellipsis is used to indicate that a statement is incomplete, or that a word or phrase has been omitted:

>"Get out of here," I said, "or I'll . . . ."
>The opening sentence of *Paradise Lost* ("Of man's first disobedience . . . in Prose or Rhyme") is sixteen lines long.

This concludes our itemization of punctuation marks and their use, as found in English. Let us now glance back at this section and, referring to the material in Chapter 2, attempt to explain these uses.

Commas are used to separate the remnants of whole sentences that have undergone various deletion transformations and that have then been conjoined to whole sentences or subordinated to other whole sentences. The use of the comma seems "to be the bugbear of most students." Let us examine the places in which commas occur.

In

>Todd took a plane to Paris, but Alex traveled by boat (S_1).

we have a conjoining of

>Todd took a plane to Paris (S_2).

and

>Alex traveled to Paris by boat (S_3).

The structure of the sentence is thus

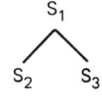

$$S_1$$
$$\diagup\diagdown$$
$$S_2 \quad S_3$$

In the process of conjoining these sentences, *to Paris* has been deleted from S_2. The comma in S_1 indicates that something has been deleted without a pronoun or conjunction being substituted. In a sentence such as

            I went to Paris while Alex was there.

with the structure

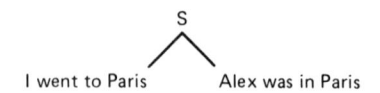

```
                    S
                   / \
          I went to Paris   Alex was in Paris
```

there is no comma, for the deleted *in Paris* here has left the locative pronoun *there* in its place. A locative pronoun is here required because *in Paris* is a place or location.

Describing the structure of

After chasing outlaws all morning, Trigger grazed in his paddock

is more difficult. The underlying structure is

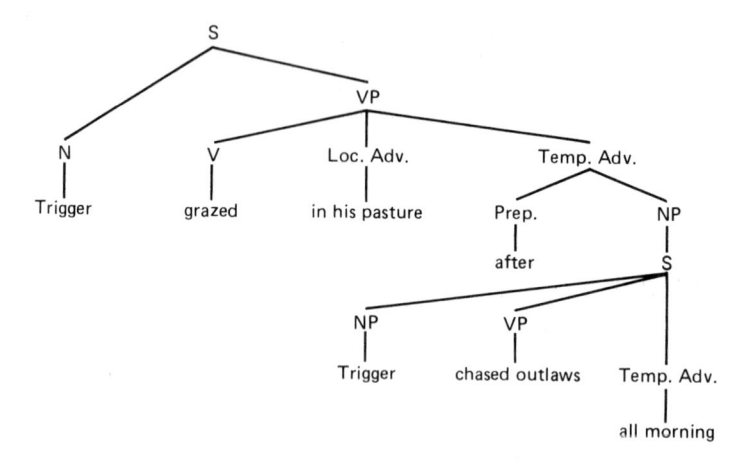

```
                    S
                   / \
                  /   VP
                 /   /    \        \
                N   V    Loc. Adv.  Temp. Adv.
                |   |       |         /    \
             Trigger grazed in his pasture Prep.  NP
                                            |     |
                                          after   S
                                                /  |  \
                                              NP   VP  Temp. Adv.
                                              |    |       |
                                           Trigger chased outlaws all morning
```

Successive transformations acting upon the deep structure of this sentence delete *Trigger* from the lowest S and then transfer the higher temporal adverb construction *(after chasing outlaws all morning)* to the beginning of the main sentence. The comma is now required after morning because of the displacement of the temporal adverb to primary position and the existence of an initial clause without a topic because of the deletion constrained by the identical topic in a higher sentence.

If we look at nouns (or NPs) in a series, the reasons for the commas and semicolons are fairly clear. In

> Robin, Maggie, Frank, and Sharon ate at the Peking Restaurant.

for example, we might postulate structures like

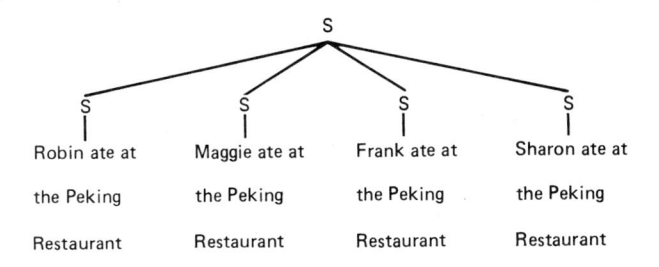

```
                            S
          ┌─────────┬───────┴───────┬─────────┐
          S         S               S         S
          │         │               │         │
     Robin ate at  Maggie ate at  Frank ate at  Sharon ate at
     the Peking    the Peking     the Peking    the Peking
     Restaurant    Restaurant     Restaurant    Restaurant
```

Here the commas are the vestiges of the VPs of the sentences

> Robin (Maggie . . . , Frank . . . , Sharon . . . ,) ate at the Peking Restaurant.

In

> The dogs barked, jumped, wagged their tails, and tried to lick Kevin's face and hands.

the commas replace the deleted NPs from a structure like

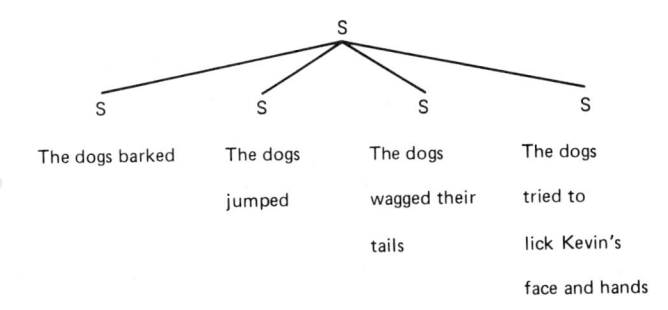

```
                         S
          ┌──────────┬───┴────┬──────────┐
          S          S        S          S
    The dogs barked  The dogs  The dogs   The dogs
                     jumped    wagged their  tried to
                               tails         lick Kevin's
                                             face and hands
```

From these examples it must be clear that commas are used to show just where portions of sentences have been deleted when the remnants of these sentences are subsequently conjoined with other whole sentences, are subordinated to other whole sentences, or when the order of the conjoining has been altered. Furthermore, this same explanation may be applied to parenthetic insertion (whether of nouns in apposition or of material tangential to the main chain of thought). For example

All their ice cream (31 flavors) is delicious.

may be derived from

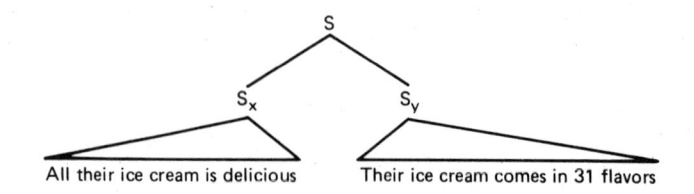

```
                    S
                   / \
                 Sₓ   Sᵧ
               /    \  /    \
All their ice cream is delicious   Their ice cream comes in 31 flavors
```

All their ice cream is delicious. Their ice cream comes in 31 flavors

where the object NP of the Prepositional phrase has been neither coordinated with nor subordinated to the primary sentence, but has been inserted between the NP and VP of the primary sentence.

We have tried in a few pages to demonstrate just how some of the aspects of English punctuation may be explained in terms of the grammatical descriptions discussed in Chapter 2.

Our purpose has not been to insist that you use syntactic trees in your classroom but rather to give you an understanding of how the English punctuation system looks and what functions are served by the symbols we use.

Abbreviations

The final topic to be discussed under the heading of mechanics is that of abbreviation.

Abbreviations are both useful and economical. They are used extensively in business and legal documents and in learned or scholarly prose. They are inappropriate, however, in most general or formal writing. The only true exceptions to the last statement are the titles *Mr., Messrs., Mrs., Ms., Mmes., Dr., St. (saint,* not *street);* the designations *Jr.* and *Sr.;* the time designations A.M. and P.M.; and the date markers A.D. and B.C. These aside, all other words should be written out fully in formal written English.

Titles. When a title such as *doctor* does not precede a name, it must be written out in full:

The doctor was late for the appointment.

However, note

> Dr. Jones was late for his appointment.

Similarly, military and academic titles, although usually written out, may be abbreviated, *but only immediately before the person's name:*

> General William Westmoreland reported to the President.
> General Westmoreland reported to the President.
> Gen. William Westmoreland reported to the President.
> The general reported to the President.
> Professor Jones berated Dean Wilson.
> Prof. Tom Jones berated Dean Wilson.
> The professor berated the dean.
> The Reverend Stephen Daedalus officiated.
> The Reverend Mr. Daedalus officiated.
> Rev. S. Daedalus officiated.

Given (or Christian) names should never be abbreviated in formal prose. Avoid *Geo., Thos., Chas.,* or *Wm.* in writing.

Agencies and Organizations. If a government agency of some other organization is known primarily by its initials, use these in writing, rather than the full name. Generally, such abbreviations appear without periods:

> FBI   TVA   AFL—CIO   NBC   DAR
> CIA   GOP   SPCA   MGM   UN
> FHA   ROTC   4—H CLUB   AT&T   AMA

Sometimes, words are produced by taking the first letters of words in titles. The resulting words are called *acronyms.* Some examples are

> UNESCO   SEATO
> CARE   VISTA
> NATO   NASA

Place Names and Dates. By and large, the names of countries, states, provinces, cities, counties, months, and days are not abbreviated in prose:

> United States   Nova Scotia   New York
> Great Britain   South Carolina   Antwerp, Belgium
> Switzerland   Los Angeles   Eugene, Oregon
>   Friday, May 13   Sunday, December 24
>   Christmas
>   New Year's Day

There are a *few* place names that, because of their length when written in full, are abbreviated. Principal among these are

> USSR (Union of Soviet Socialist Republics)

and

> Washington, D. C. (District of Columbia).

Numerals and Units of Measurement. The treatment of numerals varies from one style sheet to another. The easiest system is that used by *The New York Times* and many other newspapers: Numbers from one through ten are spelled out, numbers greater than ten are written as numerals. Thus:

> Diane is three years old but Clare is 13.
> There are 5,280 feet in a mile.

Note that in this last sentence we have used *feet,* not *ft.* In formal writing, most expressions of time, weight, size, and velocity are customarily written out. Only when giving directions, recipes, references, and so on, may units be abbreviated—and even then, only when they are used in conjunction with numerals.

> When born, Diane weighed eight pounds 13 ounces.

but

> 4 oz. butter [in a recipe]

> It takes only an hour to fly from New York to Chicago.

but

> Let cook for 3 hrs.

Here you must note just how continuous writing differs from technical or instructional writing (directions, recipes, and so on).

Scientific Terms, Technical Terms, Trade Names. Items that are familiar and that might be of excessive length when written out may be abbreviated:

> DDT   TNT
> Rh factor   TWA
> LEM   IBM
> AM (radio)

If you are going to refer to something frequently in your writing, you may abbreviate it, after explaining the abbreviation to the reader:

> *The Oxford English Dictionary* (hereafter, OED) consists of 13 massive volumes.

Finally, abbreviations may be used for technical terms used together with numerals:

> The SST flew at 720 mph.
> Although we own some old records, our new turntable only operates at 45 and 33 1/3 rpm (revolutions per minute).
> After thorough testing and 20,000 miles of driving, the Volkswagen still averaged 28 mpg (miles per gallon).

Latin Expressions. There are several Latin expressions, and their abbreviations, that are common in scholarly and technical writing. The most important of these are

cf.	*confer* (compare)
e.g.	*exempli gratia* (for example)
etc.	*et cetera* (and so forth)
ibid.	*ibidem* (in the same place)
i.e.	*id est* (that is)
loc. cit.	*loco citato* (in the place or passage cited)
op. cit.	*opere citato* (in the work cited)

Note that while the Latin words and phrases are italicized (because they are foreign words), the abbreviations are not.

Finally, let us remark that the ampersand (&) should never be used in continuous prose unless it appears in the material that is being copied:

> *U. S. News & World Report*

EXERCISES

1. Punctuate the following sentences:

    THAT THAT IS IS THAT THAT IS NOT IS NOT
    IS THAT NOT TRUE
    MS JONES FED HER DOG BISCUITS

2. Why is it best to teach grammar within the writing curriculum?
3. Devise a lesson plan for teaching prose organization skills to children.

To read is to translate, for no two persons' experiences are the same. A bad reader is like a bad translator: he interprets literally when he ought to paraphrase and paraphrases when he ought to interpret literally. In learning to read well, scholarship, valuable as it is, is less important than instinct; some great scholars have been poor translators.

—W. H. Auden

10 THE PROCESS OF READING

This chapter includes an overview of the reading process and a historical account of the approaches that have been used to teach reading in the United States. Methods of teaching decoding and comprehension are also included along with lesson plans and activities. The chapter also contains a section on evaluation, including a discussion of diagnosis, readability, and assessment.

WHAT IS READING?

What is reading? Most broadly, reading is the acquisition of information from printed materials. If information is not processed, if comprehension has not taken place, then reading has not occurred. Reading *is* comprehension.

Menyuk and Flood (1981) have pointed out that there are many viewpoints regarding the exact nature of the reading process. One group of theorists hold to a "bottom-up" view of reading; they claim that reading takes place in two stages: (1) decoding of words; and (2) reading for meaning. This viewpoint implies that reading takes place in the following way: through letter identification, letter-sound correspondence, the putting together of sounds, the lexical search for word meaning. The meaning of each word in a group is used to comprehend the meaning of the group.

The opposite point of view, held by a second group of theorists, is a "top-down" view of reading. These theorists hold that higher-order cognitive structures are used to comprehend lower-order morphemic (word) and phonological (sound) information.

A third viewpoint, held by yet another group of theorists (Menyuk, 1977; Rumelhart, 1981), postulates a parallel processing, or interactive, process. These theorists claim that letter-sound correspondences, letter-sequence correspondences, and syntactic structures are used in parallel fashion to arrive at the meaning of a string of words. This view is based on the premise that readers must be aware of what they are doing; that is, readers must bring their knowledge of language to conscious awareness in order to be able to derive meaning from texts.

When children become experienced competent readers, and when they are reading material that is lexically and structurally familiar to them, then the process of reading will become automatic. (*Photo by Linda Lungren*)

When children become experienced, competent readers, and when they are reading material that is lexically and structurally familiar to them, then the process of reading will become automatic. However, when reading material is lexically or structurally unfamiliar, readers have to bring their knowledge of language to a conscious level of awareness in order to be able to comprehend it.

It is important to note that reading requires many processes in addition to the recognition of grapheme-phoneme correspondences in a word (decoding abilities). Even in the beginning stage of reading acquisition, all levels of language knowledge are required in reading and comprehending sentences.

Menyuk (1981) further noted that different levels of language are required for different reading tasks. She illustrated these levels of language in the following diagram:

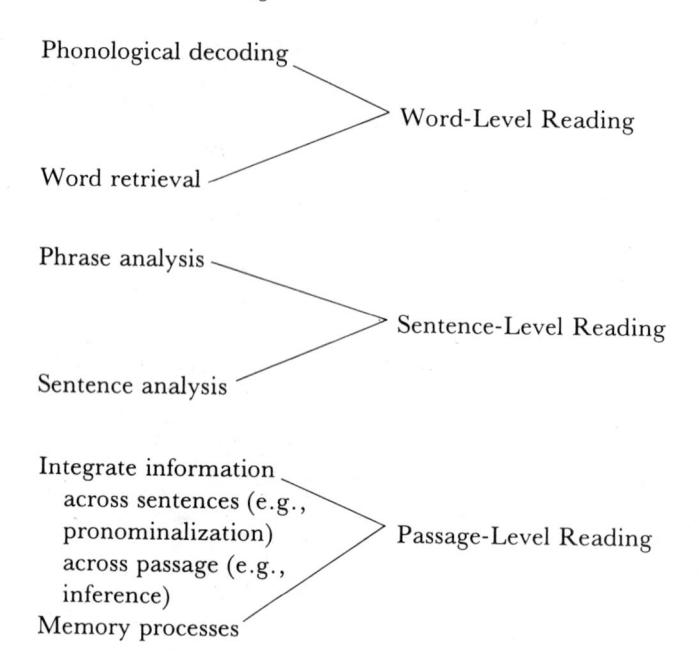

Phonological decoding ⟶ Word-Level Reading
Word retrieval ⟶

Phrase analysis ⟶ Sentence-Level Reading
Sentence analysis ⟶

Integrate information
  across sentences (e.g., pronominalization) ⟶ Passage-Level Reading
  across passage (e.g., inference)
Memory processes

INSTRUCTION IN READING

Reading instruction in the United States has changed radically over the three centuries of America's existence. The recorded history of reading instruction dates from the late 1700s, in the Colonial Period, when reading instruction relied on an alphabet-based spelling system. This oral process was based on single, then combined, letter-sound correspondences; then on letter recognition; next, on recognition of parts of words; and finally, on recognition of whole words. Mastery of pitch, stress, and enunciation was a priority in this type of instruction.

The alphabet approach was followed by the introduction of the whole-word method of reading. Developed by Horace Mann in the early 1800's, this method required that children memorize entire words before beginning their analysis of word parts. This development took place at the same time as the McGuffey Eclectic Reader, which emphasized controlled repetition of words, was introduced. These texts were an improvement over previous texts because they controlled sentence length and vocabulary complexity in an effort to match students' developmental levels with reading materials. Reprints from the McGuffey readers are included on the next page.

The Process of Reading 223

```
     McGUFFEY'S PRIMER.

        LESSON VII.

  sēe      sēeș      frŏḡ
```

[illustration: boy fishing on a fence with dog]

```
  ŏn                    lŏḡ
          ē
  a log              the frog

  See the frog on a log.
  Rab sees the frog.
  Can the frog see Rab?
  The frog can see the dog.
  Rab ran at the frog.
```

```
     ECLECTIC SERIES.

        LESSON VIII.
```

[illustration: boy and girl with kittens by a lamp]

```
  ĭt        stănd      Ann'ș
  iș        lămp       măt
                ĭ
  a mat           the stand

  See the lamp! It is on a mat.
  The mat is on the stand.
  The lamp is Nat's, and the mat
  is Ann's.
```

FIGURES 10-1 and 10-2.
From: McGuffey's Eclectic Primer, New York: American Book Co., 1909, pp. 13-14.

In the latter half of the nineteenth century, the phonetics method was introduced. Its strong emphasis on word analysis was not received well because teachers felt that it gave too little attention to comprehension. As a result, around 1910 the phonetics method was replaced by the "look and say" method. However, this too was abandoned since it proved tedious for a child to learn every word as a sight word.

In about 1920, schools adopted the silent reading method, which urged total abandonment of all oral instruction and testing. This was followed by a decade of widespread reading research (notably by Gray [1925]), which gave rise to the basal reading method in the early 1930s. Basals relied on the presentation of controlled levels of vocabulary and syntactic complexity that paralleled a child's development. This method was dominant until dissatisfaction with it in the 1950s and 1960s resulted in a return to phonics as a supplement to basals.

In the 1960s, a linguistic point of view was developed in which patterned word units were used as the focus of the basal reader, for example:

> Nat sat on the hat.
> A cat jumped out of the hat.
> Nat put the hat on the mat.
> The cat jumped up and sat in the hat.

Today, most reading educators agree that personalized reading programs offer the most effective method of reading instruction. However, time constraints often render this difficult if not impossible to carry out. Currently, attempts are being made to assist teachers in developing such individualized programs by the creation of management methods and techniques.

Two philosophies of reading instruction have always coexisted. One is the sequential reading approach, which encourages the use of materials designed to meet a child's current reading needs. The second is the spontaneous reading approach, based on the premise that materials should be designed to meet the interests of the child.

As a teacher of reading, you will want to develop a philosophy of reading, to establish objectives for your own program, and to select the methods and materials that you feel will best achieve your objectives. This historical review of reading instruction has been presented in an attempt to increase your awareness of past and current methods and trends in order to help you plan your reading program.

READINESS FOR READING

Now that we have explored some of the primary methods used to teach reading in the United States, it is necessary to determine the optimal time to begin reading instruction. You must determine when a child is ready to read. To assist in your determination of the onset of "reading readiness," it will be important for you to explore past and current practices, philosophies, and research in this area.

Beginning formal education and hence formal reading instruction at the age of six years was an accepted practice until 1931. Before 1931, only a few educators (specifically, Huey [1908], a psychologist) spoke against this practice, arguing that children should begin reading when they show an interest in it. Gesell, a medical doctor who was interested in the phenomena of biologically determined developmental stages, argued that reading ability must occur at a precise stage. He argued that reading instruction should be postponed until it could be demonstrated that a child had developed to that stage.

Based on the research of Morphett and Washburne (1931), it was found that the "perfect" moment for beginning formal reading instruction was a mental age of 6.5 years. Objections to the 6.5-year rule were raised in the later 1930s, when researchers began to acknowledge that the age that

You must determine when a child is ready to read. Matching colors and letters from a book to an electronic musical instrument reinforces letter and color recognition. (*Photo by Linda Lungren*)

was optimal for one child in one school using one method might not be optimal for another child using other methods in other schools. In short, it was determined that programs that did not make provisions for individual differences would not be effective programs.

As a result, researchers felt the necessity to develop indicators of readiness. These indicators became formal tests in the 1930s, 1940s, and 1950s. However, these proved inadequate, often testing factors that were only slightly related; for example, complex visual discriminating tasks were not necessarily related to reading potential. Other alternatives to formal testing were suggested. They included letter recognition, word knowledge, vocabulary knowledge, and visual discrimination.

Today, it is generally agreed that prereading programs should be developed to meet the needs of all children. Most contemporary programs should include the following objectives and strategies:

General Objectives and Strategies for a Prereading Program

Objectives	Strategies
1. Improvement of general language ability: phonology, morphology, syntax, semantics, and pragmatics. For bilingual children and non-English speaking children, support language development in the child's native language and provide opportunities for the acquisition of English as a second language where appropriate.	Language-experience approaches. Children who show interest in beginning reading instruction will be afforded the opportunity to begin a personalized language-experience reading program. These children can make word cards and will be taught to "read" single words.

General Objectives and Strategies for a Prereading Program (cont.)

Objectives	Strategies
2. Enjoyment of books and an understanding that they are resources. Books represent a wide variety of cultural and linguistic backgrounds. Children whose first language is not English should have the opportunity to hear stories in their own languages.	Reading to children individually and in small groups, in other languages (where appropriate) and in English. Asking questions relating to the story and encouraging children to retell it in their own words. Picture books readily available to children in a reading corner. Films of familiar stories. Trips to libraries and museums and other neighborhood places of interest.
3. Comprehension of material related orally such as understanding simple directions or a story that has been read.	Listening experiences via records and tapes of stories, songs, and nursery rhymes. Listening experiences that result in following simple directions. Musical listening, singing, and movement experiences.
4. Appreciation of the relationship between oral and written language.	Language-experience approaches. Children who show interest in beginning reading instruction will be afforded the opportunity to begin a personalized language-experience reading program. These children can make word cards and can be taught to "read" single words.
5. Confidence in their ability to create written materials—for example, stories dictated to a teacher.	Taking down children's dictated stories and helping children make their own books. Opportunities for dramatic play.
6. Recognition of the alphabet.	Games and other manipulative materials (felt letters and felt board; magnetic letters and magnetic board; alphabet bingo) that develop alphabet recognition and letter-sound associations.
7. Sight vocabulary that is familiar and important to the child, such as the child's name and the names of frequently used classroom materials (for example, door and window).	Use of labels in the classroom to indicate names of things and places for their storage. Use of children's names on lockers or tote boxes and on art work.

General Objectives and Strategies for a Prereading Program (cont.)

Objectives	Strategies

It is helpful to provide games and other manipulative materials that develop alphabet recognition and letter-sound associations. (*Photo by Linda Lungren*)

8. Letter-sound associations, particularly initial phonemes and consonants and recognition of familiar sounds.	Phonics training for those children who show interest and who will apparently profit from such a program.
9. Recognition of rhyming words.	Phonics training for those children who show interest and who will apparently profit from such a program.
10. Introduction to and/or development of effective viewing of educational television.	Use of educational television in selected classrooms.
11. Ability to communicate about concrete objects.	Use of referential communication games.
12. Recognition of sequence.	Use of recipe charts for cooking activities. Use of sequencing materials—for example, puzzles, stories (some without endings), and picture cards.
13. Simple categorization.	Work with children on visual discrimination skills (for example, matching letters, shapes, and designs).
14. Acquisition of directionality.	Exercises and games on directionality.

DECODING

It is generally accepted by researchers that children have acquired a sophisticated understanding of language structures by the time they reach four years of age. By the time formal instruction in reading begins, children can discriminate between most of the sounds in their language. As a reading teacher, your task is to help students decode graphic symbols into the language they already know. At first glance, this may seem to be a simple task, but when you actually consider the complexities of the task, you will realize that the job of teaching decoding skills is extremely difficult. The following is a brief description of the process involved in decoding.

Children can usually visually discriminate fine details by the age of four. However, differentiation among letter forms, while simple for competent readers, may easily confuse a child. For example, the graphemes *mn, EF,* and *db* are quickly discriminated by adults because competent adults use the following four distinctive features to discriminate graphemes: straight line segments found in *E, F,* and *H;* curved segments found in *o, c,* and *e;* symmetries found in *X* and *M;* and discontinuities found in *K, B,* and *G.* While competent readers are proficient at discriminating

Once children have acquired letter discrimination you may want to proceed to letter name knowledge. (*Photo by Linda Lungren*)

among these features, children may not have yet acquired the appropriate ability. A child may perceive only a part of a letter, or only one of its distinctive features, and thus label it incorrectly; for example, a child may attend only to the upper features of *J* and call it *T*.

Once children have acquired letter discrimination, you may want to proceed to letter names. It has been argued by a number of researchers (Durkin, 1972; Murphy and Durrell, 1972) that such a step is a necessary phase in initial reading instruction. While researchers have found that it does not necessarily affect later success in reading, it is generally agreed that knowledge of letter names is a useful skill in beginning reading. After your children have learned letter names, you may want to begin teaching the concept of letter-sound associations.

The following list may be useful as you begin teaching letter-sound correspondences:

Consonant Correspondence in Various Positions

Letter-Sound (Grapheme-Phoneme) Relationships

Phoneme	Grapheme	Phoneme in Initial Position	Phoneme in Medial Position	Phoneme in Final Position
/b/	b	bake baby	cabin	tub
/k/	c k ck x ch	cat kite charisma	become making tracking complexion anchor echo	tick work back monarch
	qu cc	queen	raquet account	bisque
/s/	s ss	suit	insert massive possessive	porous miss possess
	c	cite	pencil glacier	face
	st		gristle listen fasten	
	ps sc	pseudonym scissors	Pisces visceral	

Consonant Correspondence in Various Positions (cont.)

	Letter-Sound (Grapheme-Phoneme) Relationships			
Phoneme	Grapheme	Phoneme in Initial Position	Phoneme in Medial Position	Phoneme in Final Position
/č/	ch	cherry	lecher	such
	t		picture	
			nature	
			virtue	
/d/	d	dish	body	hard
	dd		middle	odd
/f/	f	fish	safer	knife
	ff		raffle	muff
	ph	phonograph	telephone	graph
		phrase	cephalic	
	gh			tough
/g/	g	good	rigor	bag
	gh	ghetto		ugh
		ghost		
	gg		trigger	egg
	gu	guest	beguile	rogue
			unguent	
/ǰ/	j	jug	prejudice	
	dg		dredger	hedge
			badger	
/h/	h	horse	behead	
	wh	who		
/l/	l	long	bailer	stale
	ll	llama	falling	doll
/m/	m	moon	hamper	game
	mb		tombstone	dumb
	mm		drummer	
/n/	n	nest	diner	pin
	nn		thinner	
	gn	gnat		
	kn	knight		
/ŋ/	ng		stinger	song
			think	
/p/	p	point	viper	hip
	pp		hopping	
/r/	r	rat	boring	tear
	rr		merry	
	wr	write		
	rh	rhyme	hemorrhage	

Consonant Correspondence in Various Positions (cont.)

Letter-Sound (Grapheme-Phoneme) Relationships

Phoneme	Grapheme	Phoneme in Initial Position	Phoneme in Medial Position	Phoneme in Final Position
/š/	sh	shadow	crashing	dish
	s	sure		
	ci		precious	
	ce		ocean	
	ss		obsession	
			assure	
	ch	chic	machine	
		chevron		
	ti		motion	
/t/	t	test	water	cat
	tt		letter	putt
	pt			receipt
	bt		debtor	debt
/θ/	th	thin	ether	wreath
			lethal	
/ð/	th	then	ether	bathe
/v/	v	violet	hover	dove
/w/	w	will	throwing	how
	ui		sanguine	
/ks/	x		toxic	box
	cc		accent	
/y/	y	yarn	lawyer	day
/z/	z	zipper	razor	blaze
	s		visit	logs
			amuser	
	zz		drizzle	fizz
			nozzle	
	x	Xanthippe		
		xylophone		
/ž/	z		azure	
	su		treasure	
	si		allusion	
	ss		fissure	
	g	genre		decoupage
/gz/	x		exhibit	
			exert	
			exact	
	gs			digs

The following list of vowel correspondences may also be helpful:

Vowel Correspondences

Sound Label	Vowel	Letter Label	Example
Glided or long	/ey/	a.e	pane, bake
		ai	rain
		ea	steak
		ei	feign
		ay	tray
		ey	obey
Unglided or short	/e/	e	pen
		ea	lead
		eo	jeopardy
		ei	heifer
		ai	stair
		ie	friendly
Glided or long	/iy/	e.e	mete
		e	he
		ea	heat
		ee	tree
		ei	conceive
		ie	believe
Unglided or short	/i/	i	hit
		ui	guild
Glided or long	/ay/	i.e.	write
		uy	buyers
		ie	tries
		ai	aisle
		ia	trial
		y	spy
		i	find
		ei	sleigh
		igh	night
Unglided or short	/a/	oo	not, fought, thought
Glided or long	/ow/	o.e	shone
		oa	goat
		ow	snow
		o	no
		ew	sewing
		ough	dough, through
		oo	floor
		eau	beau, bureau
		oe	hoe, doe
		jo, yo	fjord

Vowel Correspondences (cont.)

Sound Label	Vowel	Letter Label	Example
Unglided or short	/a/	u	nut
		oo	flood
		ou	enough, curious, pretentious
		ough	rough
		o	hover, cover, come
Glided or long	/yuw/	u.e	yule
		eau	beauty
		ew	dew
		ieu	lieu, lieutenant
Unglided or short	/u/	oo	good
		u	putt
		ew	grew
		ui	fruit
Unglided or short	/o/	a	walk
		au	maul
		o	frog
		aw	saw
Unglided or dipthong	/aw/	ow	down
		ou	cloud
Glided or dipthong	/oy/	oy	boy
		oi	loin
		ai	stair
Note: An unglided or short vowel followed by *r* is sometimes referred to as an *r*-controlled vowel	/ar/, /er/ /ir/, /or/ /ur/, /yur/ /ar/	ar, ea ea, oa oo, u.e e i	art, pear tear, boar poor, cure her sir

TEACHING WORD ATTACK SKILLS

Once a child is able to recognize letter-sound correspondences and apply rules of analysis to determine letter correspondences within words, the next step is to learn discrimination between whole words. There are several strategies for teaching this: phonics strategies, sight-word analysis, structural analysis, and contextual analysis.

Phonics Strategies

Phonics is a system of word analysis based on the sound system analysis called phonetics. Phonics instruction was introduced in the 1890s;

it replaced a method of reading instruction that had emphasized drills in the alphabet and letter naming. However, nineteenth-century phonics instruction often included using phonics only to sound out nonsense combinations of letters.

In recent years, Gibson and Levin (1975) found that presentation of the larger letter units, as in syllables, facilitates recognition and pronunciation in the decoding process. Further, it was found that knowledge of stress rules greatly facilitates decoding of unknown words.

In Chapter 1 we discussed the linguistic notion of phonology, and in Chapter 8 we discussed some spelling-sound correspondences. You can use this material in teaching reading.

To help you select the phonics rules that apply to language most frequently, we have included a list showing the frequency with which common phonics rules apply in English.

Forty-Five Phonics Generalizations

	Percentage of Utility		
	Clymer Grades 1–3	*Bailey* Grades 1–6	*Emans* Grades 4–
1. When there are two vowels side by side, the long sound of the first vowel is heard and the second vowel is usually silent. (leader)	45	34	18
2. When a vowel is in the middle of a one-syllable word, the vowel is short. (bed)	62	71	73
3. If the only vowel letter is at the end of a word, the letter usually stands for a long sound. (go)	74	76	33
4. When there are two vowels, one of which is final *e,* the first vowel is long and the *e* is silent. (cradle)	63	57	63
5. The *r* gives the preceding vowel a sound that is neither long nor short. (part)	78	86	82

Forty-Five Phonics Generalizations (cont.)

	Percentage of Utility		
	Clymer Grades 1–3	*Bailey* Grades 1–6	*Emans* Grades 4–
6. The first vowel is usually long and the second silent in the digraphs *ai, ea, oa,* and *ui.* (claim, beau, roam, suit)	66	60	58
ai		71	
ea		56	
oa		95	
ee		87	
ui		10	
7. In the phonogram *ie,* the *i* is silent and the *e* is long. (grieve)	17	31	23
8. Words having double *e* usually have the long *e* sound. (mere)	98	87	100
9. When words end with silent *e,* the preceding *a* or *i* is long. (amaze)	60	50	48
10. In *ay,* the *y* is silent and gives *a* its long sound. (spray)	78	88	100
11. When the letter *i* is followed by the letters *gh,* the *i* usually stands for its long sound and the *gh* is silent. (light)	71	71	100
12. When *a* follows *w* in a word, it usually has the sound *a* as in *was.* (wand)	32	22	28
13. When *e* is followed by *w,* the vowel sound is the same as that represented by *oo.* (shrewd)	35	40	14
14. The two letters *ow* make the long *o* sound. (tow)	59	55	50
15. *W* is sometimes a vowel and follows the vowel digraph rule. (arrow)	40	33	31

Forty-Five Phonics Generalizations (cont.)

		Percentage of Utility		
		Clymer Grades 1–3	*Bailey* Grades 1–6	*Emans* Grades 4–
16.	When *y* is the final letter in a word, it usually has a vowel sound. (lady)	84	89	98
17.	When *y* is used as a vowel in words, it sometimes has the sound of long *i*. (ally)	15	11	4
18.	The letter *a* has the same sound *(o)* when followed by *i, w,* and *u*. (raw)	48	34	24
19.	When *a* is followed by *r* and final *e,* we expect to hear the sound. (stare)	90	96	100
20.	When *c* and *h* are next to each other, they make only one sound. (charge)	100	100	100
21.	*Ch* is usually pronounced as it is in *kitchen, catch,* and *chair,* not like *sh.* (pitch)	95	87	67
22.	When *c* is followed by *e* or *i,* the sound of *s* is likely to be heard. (glance)	96	92	90
23.	When the letter *c* is followed by *o* or *a,* the sound of *k* is likely to be heard. (canal)	100	100	100
24.	The letter *g* is often sounded as the *j* in *jump* when it precedes the letters *i* or *e.* (gem)	64	78	80
25.	When *ght* is seen in a word, *gh* is silent. (tight)	100	100	100
26.	When a word begins *kn,* the *k* is silent. (knit)	100	100	100
27.	When a word begins with *wr,* the *w* is silent. (wrap)	100	100	100
28.	When two of the same consonants are side by side, only one is heard. (dollar)	100	100	100

Forty-Five Phonics Generalizations (cont.)

		Percentage of Utility		
		Clymer Grades 1–3	*Bailey* Grades 1–6	*Emans* Grades 4–
29.	When a word ends in *ck*, it has the same last sound as in *lock*. (neck)	100	100	100
30.	In most two-syllable words, the first syllable is accented. (bottom)	85	81	75
31.	If *a, in, re, ex, de,* or *be* is the first syllable in a word, it is usually unaccented. (reply)	87	84	83
32.	In most two-syllable words that end in a consonant followed by *y*, the first syllable is accented and the last is unaccented. (scary, dreary)	96	97	100
33.	One vowel letter in an accented syllable has its short sound. (banish)	61	65	64
34.	When *y* or *ey* is seen in the last syllable that is not accented, the long sound of *e* is heard. (monopoly)	0	0	1
35.	When *ture* is the final syllable in a word, it is unaccented. (future)	100	100	100
36.	When *tion* is the final syllable in a word, it is unaccented. (notion)	100	100	100
37.	In many two- and three-syllable words, the final *e* lengthens the vowel in the last syllable. (costume)	46	46	42
38.	If the first vowel sound in a word is followed by two consonants, the first syllable usually ends with the first of the two consonants. (dinner)	72	78	80

Forty-Five Phonics Generalizations (cont.)

		Percentage of Utility		
		Clymer Grades 1-3	*Bailey* Grades 1-6	*Emans* Grades 4-
39.	If the first vowel sound in a word is followed by a single consonant, that consonant usually begins the second syllable. (china)	44	50	47
40.	If the last syllable of a word ends in *le*, the consonant preceding the *le* usually begins the last syllable. (gable)	97	93	78
41.	When the first vowel element in a word is followed by *th, ch,* or *sh,* these symbols are not broken when the word is divided into syllables and may go with either the first or second syllable. (fashion)	100	100	100
42.	In a word of more than one syllable, the letter *v* usually goes with the preceding vowel to form a syllable. (ever)	73	65	40
43.	When a word has only one vowel letter, the vowel sound is likely to be short. (crib)	57	69	70
44.	When there is one *e* in a word that ends in a consonant, the *e* usually has a short sound. (held)	76	92	83
45.	When the last syllable is the sound *r,* it is unaccented. (ever)	95	79	96

A phonics program must be sequentially ordered. The following Scope and Sequence Chart from Prentice-Hall's *Phonics Plus* may serve as an ordered way in which to present phonics rules. Because many textbooks

The Process of Reading 239

on reading methods include rules and exercises for teaching phonics (for example, Lapp and Flood's *Teaching Reading to Every Child,* 2nd ed. New York: Macmillan, 1983), we will present only one sample lesson plan for implementing phonics strategies.

FIGURE 10-3.

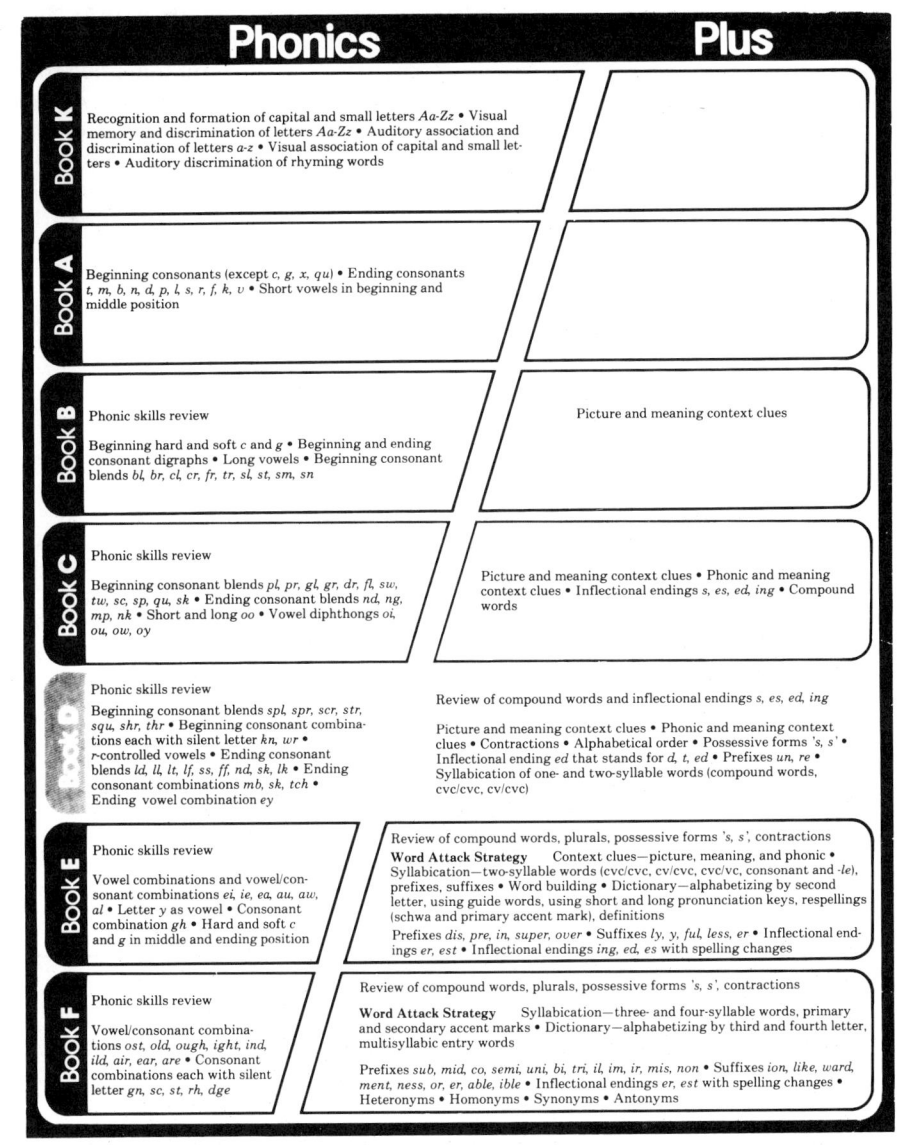

Phonics Plus

Book K
Recognition and formation of capital and small letters *Aa-Zz* • Visual memory and discrimination of letters *Aa-Zz* • Auditory association and discrimination of letters *a-z* • Visual association of capital and small letters • Auditory discrimination of rhyming words

Book A
Beginning consonants (except *c, g, x, qu*) • Ending consonants *t, m, b, n, d, p, l, s, r, f, k, v* • Short vowels in beginning and middle position

Book B
Phonic skills review

Beginning hard and soft *c* and *g* • Beginning and ending consonant digraphs • Long vowels • Beginning consonant blends *bl, br, cl, cr, fr, tr, sl, st, sm, sn*

Picture and meaning context clues

Book C
Phonic skills review

Beginning consonant blends *pl, pr, gl, gr, dr, fl, sw, tw, sc, sp, qu, sk* • Ending consonant blends *nd, ng, mp, nk* • Short and long *oo* • Vowel diphthongs *oi, ou, ow, oy*

Picture and meaning context clues • Phonic and meaning context clues • Inflectional endings *s, es, ed, ing* • Compound words

Book D
Phonic skills review

Beginning consonant blends *spl, spr, scr, str, squ, shr, thr* • Beginning consonant combinations each with silent letter *kn, wr* • *r*-controlled vowels • Ending consonant blends *ld, ll, lt, lf, ss, ff, nd, sk, lk* • Ending consonant combinations *mb, sk, tch* • Ending vowel combination *ey*

Review of compound words and inflectional endings *s, es, ed, ing*

Picture and meaning context clues • Phonic and meaning context clues • Contractions • Alphabetical order • Possessive forms *'s, s'* • Inflectional ending *ed* that stands for *d, t, ed* • Prefixes *un, re* • Syllabication of one- and two-syllable words (compound words, cvc/cvc, cv/cvc)

Book E
Phonic skills review

Vowel combinations and vowel/consonant combinations *ei, ie, ea, au, aw, al* • Letter *y* as vowel • Consonant combination *gh* • Hard and soft *c* and *g* in middle and ending position

Review of compound words, plurals, possessive forms *'s, s'*, contractions

Word Attack Strategy Context clues—picture, meaning, and phonic • Syllabication—two-syllable words (cvc/cvc, cv/cvc, cvc/vc, consonant and -*le*), prefixes, suffixes • Word building • Dictionary—alphabetizing by second letter, using guide words, using short and long pronunciation keys, respellings (schwa and primary accent mark), definitions

Prefixes *dis, pre, in, super, over* • Suffixes *ly, y, ful, less, er* • Inflectional endings *er, est* • Inflectional endings *ing, ed, es* with spelling changes

Book F
Phonic skills review

Vowel/consonant combinations *ost, old, ough, ight, ind, ild, air, ear, are* • Consonant combinations each with silent letter *gn, sc, st, rh, dge*

Review of compound words, plurals, possessive forms *'s, s'*, contractions

Word Attack Strategy Syllabication—three- and four-syllable words, primary and secondary accent marks • Dictionary—alphabetizing by third and fourth letter, multisyllabic entry words

Prefixes *sub, mid, co, semi, uni, bi, tri, il, im, ir, mis, non* • Suffixes *ion, like, ward, ment, ness, or, er, able, ible* • Inflectional endings *er, est* with spelling changes • Heteronyms • Homonyms • Synonyms • Antonyms

C. Mangrum & P. Messmore, *Phonics Plus* (Englewood Cliffs, N.J.: Prentice-Hall, Inc. 1981).

LESSON PLAN

GOAL: To introduce the grapheme *b* and its corresponding phoneme /b/

GRADE/GRADE LEVEL: Primary

CONSTRUCTION
AND UTILIZATION:
1. Write *b* on the board. Ask children if they can name words that begin with /b/.
2. Assess the degree to which children need this exercise. If some children have difficulty naming words, continue using this lesson. The children who have already mastered this information or who are not yet ready to pursue this lesson should be provided with activities to meet their needs.

PROCEDURE:
1. List on the board the words that children have named:
*b*irthday
*B*obby
*b*umblebee
*B*onny
*b*uddy
*b*unny
2. To reinforce this skill, divide an oak-tag board into four sections. In section one, draw a picture of a ball; in section two, a boy; in section three, a bat; and in section four, a boat. Ask children to name each picture, and then write the words *ball, boy, bat,* and *boat* under the appropriate pictures. Have the children copy the same pictures and words onto their own papers. When the children seem to have grasped the idea, have them present their pictures and help them write their own words under each picture.

EVALUATION: Put another *b* on the board and ask children to draw pictures and write words under each one.

Sight-Word Analysis

It must be emphasized that phonics is only one means of decoding—it is not the only strategy you can use to teach your children to decode. You should not hesitate to incorporate or supplement phonics instruction with other methods of instruction.

Sight-word strategies might also be used to teach decoding. Basal programs using this method stress the importance of teaching high-frequency sight words so that children can immediately take part in the reading process. After a core of sight words has been acquired, new sight words are presented in the basals. The new words are usually compared or contrasted with those already known (for example, known: cat—new words: pat, fat, bat). As in the case of phonics instruction, however, words should not be presented in a haphazard fashion. Lists of high-frequency functional words, such as the Dolch list of 220 words, will be helpful to you as you begin sight-word instruction.

Another alternative is to first present words that have a very high frequency and generally do not follow phonics generalizations.

The Dolch Basic Sight Vocabulary of 220 Words

a	call	from	jump	on	sing	under
about	came	full	just	once	sit	up
after	can	funny	keep	one	six	upon
again	carry	gave	kind	only	sleep	us
all	clean	give	know	open	small	use
always	cold	go	laugh	or	so	very
am	come	goes	let	our	some	walk
an	could	going	like	out	soon	want
any	cut	good	little	over	start	want
are	did	got	live	own	stop	warm
around	do	green	long	pick	take	was
as	does	grow	look	play	tell	wash
ask	done	had	made	please	ten	we
at	don't	has	make	pretty	thank	well
ate	down	have	many	put	that	went
away	draw	he	may	ran	the	were
be	drink	help	me	read	their	what
because	eat	her	much	red	them	when
been	eight	here	must	ride	then	where
before	every	him	my	right	there	which
best	fall	his	myself	round	these	white
better	far	hold	never	run	they	who
big	fast	hot	new	may	this	why
black	find	how	no	saw	those	will
blue	first	hurt	not	say	three	wish
both	five	I	now	see	to	with
bring	fly	if	of	seven	today	work
brown	for	in	off	shall	together	would
but	found	into	old	she	too	write
by	for	is		show	try	yes
		it			two	you
		its				your

Such instruction might then be followed by more complex word forms such as contractions and foreign language borrowings. The general rule to keep in mind when you are teaching sight words is to start with high-frequency, easy-level words, and then to move on to less frequently used, more complex words and word forms.

After you select which words to teach, you must think about your method of presentation. Since you are attempting to establish recognition by sight, your instruction should be highly visual. That is, words should be written in sentences and highlighted in italics or in bright colors. The following lesson plan illustrates the way in which sight words can be taught:

LESSON PLAN

GOAL: To introduce the word "live"

GRADE/GRADE LEVEL: Second grade

CONSTRUCTION: On a large piece of oak tag, paste a series of pictures of different dwellings common in your area: an apartment building in an urban setting, a small suburban house, a farmhouse, and so on. Above the pictures, write the question "Where do you live?"

PROCEDURE:
1. Ask the children to look at the pictures. Discuss with them what sort of structure each picture represents and where one would be likely to find these structures. Stress that these are all pictures of places where people live.
2. Explain to the children that the word *live* appears on the poster. Ask, "Who can read the question above the pictures?" Point to the words in the sentence as the children read. After the children have read the sentence, point to the word *live*. Discuss its meaning again in terms of the pictures and then have the children reread the sentence.
3. Ask the children, "Where do *you* live?" Repeat their answers and point to the appropriate picture. "Joey said, 'I live in a house.' Joey lives in a house."
To reinforce the word *live,* ask the children the same questions about pictures of places where animals might live. Discuss with them what kinds of animals live on a farm, in the jungle, or in the desert.
Have the children write a story describing where they live. You may want to provide them with the sentence starter, "I live in _____."

Structural Analysis

It is also necessary to help children develop skills in structural analysis. In order to do this, you will need a thorough knowledge of morphology as explained in the early chapters of this text.

Structural analysis usually includes instruction in root words and their affixes and suffixes as well as instruction in tense markers, inflectional endings, compounds, and contractions.

Prefixes. The following list contains some of the most frequently recurring prefixes in English and their meanings:

in (not)	de (from)
mis (wrong)	inter (between)
anti (against)	ex (out, from)
non (not)	en (in)
com (with)	op, ob (against)
con (with)	pro (in front of)
super (over)	im (not, in)
tri (three)	un (not, opposite of)

Suffixes. When the meaning of a word is modified by the addition of a new ending, a suffix has been added to the root word. Thorndike's text *The Teaching of English Suffixes* (1932) allows us some insight into the frequency with which some suffixes appear. For example, the five most common suffixes in English are

ion	tradition
er	brighter
ness	awareness
ity	levity
y	windy

The following lesson plan will help reinforce structural analysis strategies:

LESSON PLAN

GOAL: To teach the meaning and use of the prefix *re*

GRADE/GRADE LEVEL: Intermediate

CONSTRUCTION: Write on the chalkboard sentences using words that have the prefix *re*. Underline the *re* words. For example:

I'm going to *rearrange* the furniture.
Do you want to *reelect* me as your Class President?
Be sure to *recheck* your homework.
If you are late for lunch, we'll just *reheat* your soup for you.

PROCEDURE:
1. Have the children read each sentence. Then, erase the chalkboard, except for the underlined words.
2. Ask your students to pick out the similarities among the words. Once they have identified *re* as the common factor, put a slash mark between *re* and the base word, for example, *re/heat*.
3. Ask the children if they can use both the base word and its derivative in sentences. Finally, explain to the children that *re* is a prefix that can be added to some words to indicate an action that is repeated; *re* means "to do again."
4. Give your students additional examples and see if they can come up with some of their own.

Contextual Analysis

A final strategy that may be of great help to your children in word recognition is the use of contextual analysis. Rather than relying solely on letter-sound recognition as in phonics, it involves the analysis of a word within a given context. This strategy may be taught in a number of ways: The simplest way is to introduce new vocabulary words and define them within a context. You might also include synonyms, antonyms, similes, and examples within a single sentence. The following sample lesson plan may be helpful:

LESSON PLAN

GOAL: To teach the usefulness of relational clues in determining word meanings

GRADE/GRADE LEVEL: Intermediate

CONSTRUCTION: Prepare a series of cloze exercises in which a word known to your students has been omitted from a sentence; however, other words in the sentence should give the children enough clues to enable them to figure out what the omitted word might be. This should be a group activity. For example:

1. The bright, yellow _____ chirped with enthusiasm when I began to feed her.
2. The girl in the green bathing suit dove into the _____ with her arms stretched above her head.
3. The little white _____ meowed her thanks for the milk I gave her.
4. She had to _____ her car to get here.

PROCEDURE:
1. Explain to the children that sentences and paragraphs often contain clues to the meaning of individual words appearing in them. Reading each sentence in turn, ask the children to try to figure out the missing words by using clues provided by other words in the sentences.
2. Once the children have successfully completed the cloze exercises by providing the missing words, discuss with them in detail the strategies they used.
3. Working together with the children, make a list of questions that children might ask themselves when analyzing a sentence or paragraph to determine a word meaning.
4. You may wish to give your students additional practice by asking them to figure out new word meanings by utilizing the strategies they have identified. For example:

a. The small, striped *feline* meowed loudly at its owner.
b. The *obese* man was so fat he could barely squeeze into the bus seat.
c. *Poisonous* mushrooms will kill you if you eat them.

It must be remembered that these methods of decoding are meant to be modified, combined, and supplemented to meet the individual needs of each child. No one method is clearly "best," nor the sole means of teaching decoding skills.

In order to extract meaning from a text, readers must become active participants, applying their previous knowledge to the texts they are reading. (*Photo by Linda Lungren*)

COMPREHENSION OF TEXTS

If you were to define reading, somewhere in your definition you probably would include the word *understanding* or the phrase *get the meaning from*. In fact, reading without comprehension is a meaningless exercise. In order to extract meaning from a text, readers must become active participants, applying their previous knowledge to the texts they are reading. However, the exact nature of such processing is not totally known.

Rumelhart (1980) views reading comprehension as an information processing activity. Specifically, he believes that a reader processes printed information by relying on input at the graphic, orthographic, lexical, semantic, and syntactic level, bypassing any stage that is not needed. Further processing may proceed from either a top-down mode (the mind of the reader) or a bottom-up mode (the text). This means that it is not necessary to process features and then move "up" to meaning. Rather, it is possible that a reader may assume features and proceed to meaning first; then the reader will move "down" to verification of word patterns and features.

Rumelhart has generated a representation of reading based on a set of interactive stages:

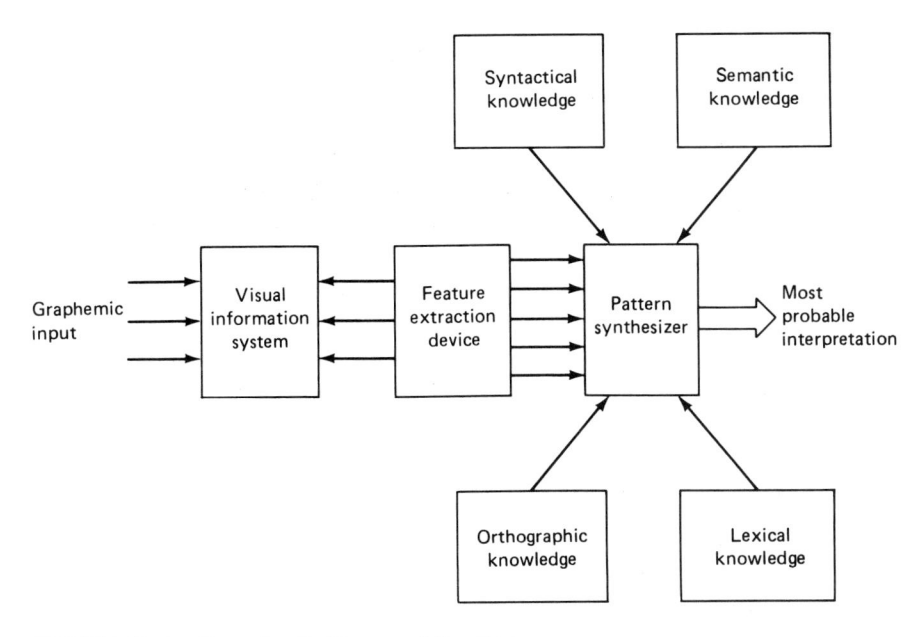

FIGURE 10-4. Rumelhart's Theory of Reading.

Bloom theorized that learning was a developmental process in which mastery of one level of cognitive functioning was necessary for mastery of the next.

FIGURE 10-5. Bloom's Taxonomy of Educational Objectives.

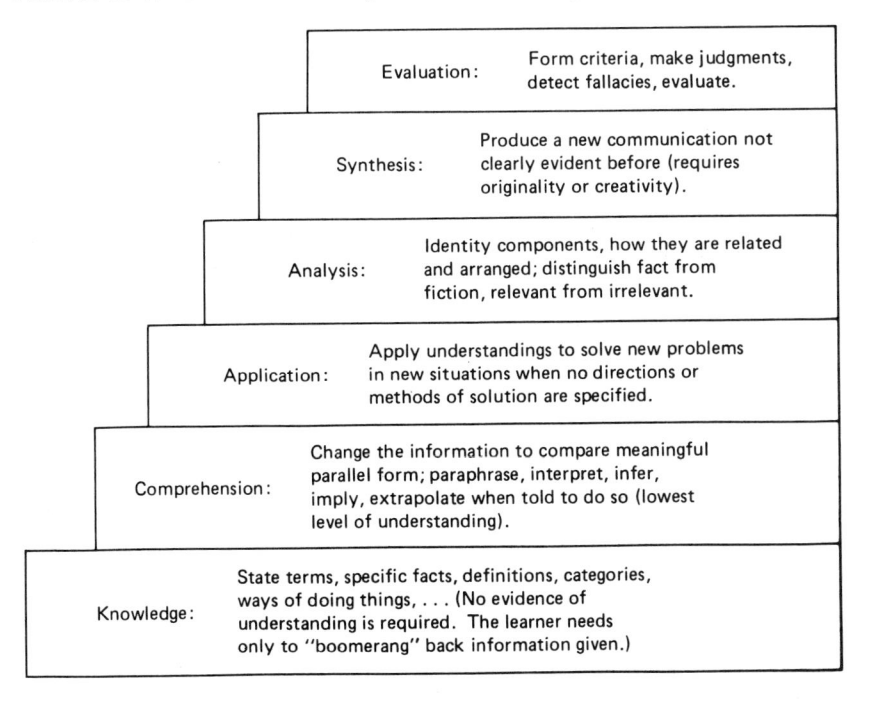

Level	Description
Evaluation:	Form criteria, make judgments, detect fallacies, evaluate.
Synthesis:	Produce a new communication not clearly evident before (requires originality or creativity).
Analysis:	Identity components, how they are related and arranged; distinguish fact from fiction, relevant from irrelevant.
Application:	Apply understandings to solve new problems in new situations when no directions or methods of solution are specified.
Comprehension:	Change the information to compare meaningful parallel form; paraphrase, interpret, infer, imply, extrapolate when told to do so (lowest level of understanding).
Knowledge:	State terms, specific facts, definitions, categories, ways of doing things, ... (No evidence of understanding is required. The learner needs only to "boomerang" back information given.)

Some reading educators have suggested that Bloom's taxonomy of educational objectives is closely related to the hierarchy of learning that encompasses reading comprehension processes. Several researchers in reading have thus based reading taxonomies on Bloom's model. These views are represented in the following ways:

Taxonomy of Reading

Levels of Cognitive Development	Reading Comprehension
	Text Emplicit Information (literal comprehension)

Knowledge (recall)	Identification of
	  sounds
	  letters
	  phrases
	  sentences
	  paragraphs
	Recognition and recall of
	  details
	  main ideas
	  sequence
	  comparison
	  cause-and-effect relationships
	  character traits
	  patterns

Comprehension (understanding)	Translation of ideas or information explicity stated:
	  classifying
	  generalizing
	  outlining
	  summarizing
	  synthesizing

Application	Text Implicit Information (inferential comprehension)

(abstracting)	Realization of one's experiences and textual exposures
	Inferring:
	  details
	  main ideas
	  sequence
	  comparisons
	  cause-and-effect relationships
	  character traits

Analysis (analyzing)	Predicting outcomes

Synthesis (production)	Interpreting figurative language, imagery, character, motives, and responses
	Synthesizing:
	  convergently
	  divergently

Evaluation	World Knowledge Information (critical comprehension)
(judging)	Making evaluative judgments of reality or fantasy fact or opinion adequacy and validity appropriateness worth, desirability, and acceptability Valuing

	Propaganda detection:
	  euphemism
	  fallacy of reasoning
	  statistical fallacy (maps, charts)
	  stereotyping
	  oversimplification
	
	Appreciation

	Emotional response to content Identification with characters or incidents Reactions to the author's use of language Reactions to the author's word pictures

CAUTIONS ABOUT USING THE "LITERAL, INFERENTIAL, CRITICAL" READING TRICHOTOMY

In many reading texts, reading comprehension is divided into literal, inferential, and critical components. However, certain objections have been raised regarding the validity of this three-level classification. These categories are too clear cut: they do not allow for overlap which exists in practice. Further, such a view does not account for operations of the reader during the reading process. It is through an understanding of the processes, as outlined in the theories of reading that we presented, that a more in-depth understanding of reading can occur.

A precise scope-and-sequence chart of comprehension skills is not available because most comprehension skills need to be retaught in progressively more difficult contexts. Unlike phonics skills, which are learned once and mastered for all contexts, comprehension skills need to be activated in many different reading situations. Prentice-Hall's *Comprehension Plus* program attempts to do this by repeating comprehension skills in several grades:

FIGURE 10-6. Scope and Sequence Chart of Reading Comprehension Skills.

The following scope and sequence charts list the Focus Skills throughout Books A-F of *Comprehension Plus*. A Focus Skill, shown with a ● symbol, has one or more complete lessons in a given book. Each Focus Skill is maintained within a book and in subsequent book(s). A Maintenance Skill, shown with a ○ symbol, appears as an activity within a lesson. This activity may appear in either the pupil's or the teacher's edition. A more detailed Skills Index is provided in the Annotated Teacher's Edition for each book.

COMPRESSION — A B C D E F

Skill		Skill	
Abbreviations and acronyms		Imagery	
Ambiguity		Making inferences	
Analogies		Main idea	
Antecedents		Mood	
Antonyms		Onomatopoeia	
Attribution		Paraphrasing	
Borrowed words and expressions		Picture clues	
Cause/effect relationships		Plot	
Characterization		Point of view	
Classifying		Predicting outcomes	
Comparisons		Propaganda devices	
Compound words		Questioning	
Conflict and resolution		Sequence of events	
Conjunction *and*		Setting	
Context		Shades of meaning	
Details		Simile	
Drawing conclusions		Supporting ideas	
Dramatizing		Symbolism	
Evaluating advertisements		Synonyms	
Fact/fiction		Theme (moral)	
Fact/opinion		Topic sentence	
Fantasy/reality		Word derivations	
Five W's		Word parts	
Flashback		Words from technology	

PLUS — A B C D E F

Skill		Skill	
Alphabetizing		Graphs	
Card catalog		Index	
Classified ads		Maps	
Comparing information sources		Metric conversion table	
Contents page		Note taking	
Diagrams		Outlining	
Direction words		Reference materials	
Encyclopedia articles		Schedules	
Following directions		Summarizing	
Glossary/Dictionary		Telephone directory	

J. Flood & D. Lapp, *Comprehension Plus*. (Englewood Cliffs, N.J.: Prentice-Hall, Inc. 1983).

LESSONS

When you are preparing lessons on the development of comprehension skills, it is important to consider reading as an interactive process so that you will select appropriate texts, create efficient questioning strategies, and develop effective instructional programs.

A sample lesson plan from *Comprehension Plus* has been included as an illustrative example on one comprehension skill:

FIGURE 10-7.

LESSON 7

What is the **main idea**? That is a good question to ask when you read a paragraph. A paragraph is a group of sentences that tell about a main idea. The main idea of a paragraph is the most important idea. Often the main idea is told in the first or the last sentence in a paragraph.

Read the following paragraph and look for the main idea.

When bubble gum was first made about eighty years ago, it was too sticky. The bubbles it made broke easily. People who chewed it ended up with a mess on their faces! The first bubble gum was not nearly as good as bubble gum is today.

Which sentence in this paragraph tells the main idea? If you think it is the last sentence, you are right. All the other sentences tell more about why the first bubble gum was not as good as bubble gum is today.

Read this paragraph and look for the main idea.

Major John Wesley Powell was the first person known to travel all the way through the Grand Canyon. He did it more than one hundred years ago. Major Powell went because he wanted to make a map of the canyon. The trip was a very dangerous one. Everyone was surprised when Major Powell made it through the canyon safely.

Which sentence in the paragraph tells the most important idea or the main idea? Look at the first sentence. It tells the main idea. All the other sentences tell more about Major Powell.

J. Flood & D. Lapp, *Comprehension Plus.* (Englewood Cliffs, N.J.: Prentice-Hall, Inc. 1983).

Read the story below and answer the questions that follow. Look for the main idea of each paragraph as you read.

Pilgrim Sailing Ships

The Pilgrims who first came to America had no gas or oil. They had no boats with engines. They had no steamboats, either. The Pilgrims had to go up and down rivers in sailing ships.

When there was no wind to push a ship upstream, the sailors would "walk the boat." They put the anchor of the ship in a rowboat and rowed as far ahead as the anchor rope reached. They dropped the anchor into the water and rowed back to the sailing ship. Then all of the sailors took hold of the rope and pulled as hard as they could. Slowly they pulled the ship forward. When they arrived at the anchor, they pulled it up, put it in the rowboat, and started all over again. It took a whole day to go only a few miles this way!

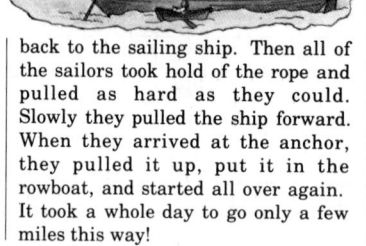

1. Underline the sentence that tells the main idea of the first paragraph.
    a. <u>The Pilgrims had to go up and down rivers in sailing ships.</u>
    b. They had no boats with engines.
    c. They had no steamboats, either.

2. Underline the sentence that tells the main idea of the second paragraph.
    a. Slowly they pulled the ship forward.
    b. It took a whole day to go only a few miles this way!
    c. <u>When there was no wind to push a ship upstream, the sailors would "walk the boat."</u>

3. The title of a story often tells the main idea of the whole story. Choose the title below that tells the main idea of the story you just read.
    Write the title you chose on the line above the story.
        a. Pilgrim Sailing Ships   b. Walking the Boat   c. Steamships

Here is a *tip*. Sometimes the main idea of a paragraph is in the first sentence. Sometimes it is in the last sentence.

FIGURE 10–8.
J. Flood & D. Lapp, *Comprehension Plus*. (Englewood Cliffs, N.J.: Prentice-Hall, Inc. 1983).

Read the following story about Doc Kimball and his horse.

Jenny

Doc Kimball was a country doctor who had a horse named Jenny. She carried him to visit sick people. Even if the roads were wet or snowy, Jenny took Doc wherever he wanted to go.

People who spent time on horseback learned to sleep while they rode. <u>Cavalry</u> men knew how to take short naps while riding. Country doctors knew how to do the same thing.

Doc knew that Jenny was <u>faithful</u>. She was always ready when Doc needed her. She always knew what to do. Jenny was a good horse.

One night, during the year of the big floods, Doc found out just how good a horse Jenny really was. That year it rained and rained. Many bridges were washed out. In some places the ground was so wet it couldn't hold trees with weak roots.

One of those trees fell on Jim McKay. When Doc found out, he saddled Jenny and rode to the McKay place. He set Jim's broken legs. It was dark when Doc was ready to set out for home.

"You can't go out in this storm," said Mrs. McKay. "Stay with us."

Doc wouldn't hear of it. The rain had nearly stopped and he knew he could count on Jenny to get him home. After the first mile he pulled up his collar and went to sleep.

Suddenly, Jenny stopped and Doc woke up. He didn't know how long he had slept, but he was sitting on Jenny's back outside his own home. His stable boy, Billy, was looking up at him. Billy looked worried.

"Are you all right, Doc?" Billy's voice shook.

"Yes, I'm all right. Why shouldn't I be?" Doc answered.

"Which way did you come home?" Billy asked.

Doc was <u>puzzled</u>. "Why do you ask? You know there is only one way home — across Brownsville Bridge."

"But that can't be true, Billy said. "That bridge was washed out hours ago. It's not standing anymore."

The next morning Doc and Billy went to look at the bridge. Sure enough, the bridge was gone. Only one narrow <u>beam</u> was left crossing the water. The beam was only a few inches wide. But there in the mud on the bank of the river they could see the <u>hoofprints</u> of old Jenny.

In the stormy darkness, old Jenny had crossed that narrow beam with Doc asleep on her back. Jenny had brought him home safely. *Sam Savitt*

FIGURE 10-9.
J. Flood & D. Lapp, *Comprehension Plus.* (Englewood Cliffs, N.J.: Prentice-Hall, Inc. 1983).

Word Hunt

Write the underlined word from the story that finishes each sentence.

[1. A _faithful_ friend is always honest and loyal.
2. The marks that a horse's feet make are called _hoofprints_
3. Soldiers on horseback belonged to the _cavalry_
4. You are _puzzled_ when you can't understand something.
5. A _beam_ is a long, thick piece of wood.]

Something to Think About

1. Underline the sentence that tells the main idea of the first paragraph.
   a. Even if the roads were wet or snowy, Jenny took Doc wherever he wanted to go.
   b. She carried him to visit sick people.
   c. Doc Kimball was a country doctor who had a horse named Jenny.
2. Underline the sentence that tells the main idea of the second paragraph.
   a. Cavalry men knew how to take short naps while riding.
   b. Country doctors knew how to do the same thing.
   c. People who spent time on horseback learned to sleep while they rode.
3. Underline the sentence that tells the main idea of the third paragraph.
   a. Doc knew that Jenny was faithful.
   b. Jenny was a good horse.
   c. She always knew what to do.
4. Underline the title below that would be another title for "Jenny."
   a. A Good Horse   b. Asleep at the Wheel   c. Country Doctors
[5. Underline the sentence that tells how Doc knew that Jenny had crossed the water on a narrow beam.
   a. He saw Jenny's muddy hoofprints on the beam.
   b. He woke up when Jenny was crossing the water.
   c. He heard about it from his stable boy, Billy.]

Something More

On another piece of paper, finish the paragraph that is started below. Add other ideas that tell more about your best friend.
I have a best friend.

FIGURE 10-10.
Flood J., & Lapp, D. *Book D Comprehension Plus*, Lesson 7, pp. 25-28.

QUESTIONING STRATEGIES

Once an appropriate selection has been made, it is necessary to develop meaningful and effective questioning strategies; questions have the ability to direct and focus a student's reading comprehension and serve as a source of ideas. Therefore, in order to tap a variety of mental operations, many different levels and types of questions should be developed. An array of question types may include:

Recognition or recall of facts, concepts, information	Convergence of concepts	Divergence from concepts	Evaluation of facts, information, concepts, situation

●————●————————●————————●————————●————→

narrowest questions   broadest questions

While questioning stimulates and directs thinking, it is also necessary to supplement your instruction with work in conception formation or schema development. This means developing students' knowledge, background, and experience so that they will have a large pool of knowledge from which to draw when they are reading. Through instruction in concept formation or schema development, you may positively affect a child's comprehension. Taba (1967) makes the following suggestions:

1. Ask students, "What did you see? hear? notice?" While students are enumerating items, they are also engaged in differentiating items.
2. After lists have been made, ask students, "Which items go together?" As they begin grouping, they are engaged in identifying common properties and abstraction processing.
3. Finally, ask students, "What label would you give each group?" In this labeling process, they are engaged in hierarchical grouping of subordinates and superordinates. The acquisition of each of these processing skills will contribute to the development of reading comprehension skills.

When you plan lessons to develop comprehension, remember the following points:

1. Establish a purpose for reading. Plan lessons that are related to the child's life. Questions should be appropriate to the type or types of comprehension you are teaching.
2. Choose materials that will further the purposes of the lesson. Sources from which you may choose include games, kits, and high-interest–low-vocabulary books.
3. Plan experiences that provide students with opportunities to develop the skills they will need to comprehend the book they are reading.

As you begin the task of developing your children's comprehension skills, it is vital that you be aware of the multitude of skills involved in the process of reading. These skills are not clear and concise, to be taught and learned once; rather, the process of comprehension development requires constant reinforcement. As a classroom language arts teacher, it is necessary for you to allow comprehension development the time and attention it demands.

ASSESSMENT OF READING

Every student is an individual, separate and unique. Just as instruction attempts to meet students' needs, assessment too must be tailored to each student.

The first stage in the assessment process is diagnosis. Before an instructional program can be developed, it is vital to assess each student's strengths and needs. This assessment may be formal, like intelligence testing, or informal. In either case, such information will facilitate your lesson planning, grouping, and instructional designs.

Formal Assessment

Two types of formal testing that may be used at this stage are criterion-referenced testing and norm-referenced testing. Criterion tests assess a student's performance in relation to a given or stated criterion, while norm-reference tests assess a child's performance in relation to other children's performance on the same measure. Many norm-reference tests are available from publishing companies.

Informal Assessment

In place of formal tests, informal teacher inventories can be used. The informal reading inventory (IRI) is used to determine a student's independent reading level, instructional reading level, or frustration reading level. The independent level is the level at which a student can read successfully without aid; the instructional reading level is the level at which a teacher's aid is required, and the frustration level indicates materials that are too difficult for the student to understand even with assistance. For further reading of IRI's, you may consult one of the following:

JOHNSON, MARJORIE S., and KRESS, RAY A. *Informal Reading Inventories.* Newark, Del.: International Reading Association, 1965.
POTTER, THOMAS C., and RAE, KENNETH. *Informal Reading Diagnosis.* Englewood Cliffs, N.J.: Prentice-Hall, 1973.

SILVAROLI, NICHOLAS J. *Classroom Reading Inventory.* Dubuque, Iowa: William C. Brown Company Publishers, 1973.

Another informal measurement technique is the cloze technique. To use the cloze, you must select a passage of 250 words. Delete every fifth word and substitute a horizontal line in its place. Ask students to replace the missing words. Each correct response receives two points. There are no time limits and misspellings do not count as incorrect responses. Score as follows:

> 58–100 points - material is at independent level
> 44–57 points - material is at instructional level
> Below 43 points - material is at frustrational level

The results of such a technique will indicate to you the possible uses for the text from which the passage was extracted; that is, if the text is at the instructional level of most students, you may use it during lessons. If the majority of students score at the independent level on a particular text passage, perhaps that text should be reserved for unassisted free reading in class or at home.

Formal and informal testing techniques can be valuable tools as you plan your curriculum.

EXERCISES

1. Describe and illustrate your theory of the process of reading as a language art.
2. Describe the relationships between your reading program and the rest of your language arts program.
3. Explain how reading instruction in the content areas is related to the goals of an effective language arts program.
4. Defend the following statement: "Reading problems often reflect oral language processing difficulties."
5. List the factors that affect reading performance. Make three lists to include the following:

Text Factors   Reader Factors   Interactive Factors
                 (Student)

REFERENCES

Dale, E., and Chall, J.   "A Formula for Predicting Readability." *Educational Research Bulletin* 27 (1948): 11-20.

Durkin, D.   *Children Who Read Early: Two Longitudinal Studies.* New York: Teachers College Press, 1966.

Durkin, D.   "A Language Arts Program for Pre-First Grade Children: Two Year Achievement Report." *Reading Research Quarterly* 5 (Summer 1970): 534-565.

Durkin, D.   *Teaching Them to Read.* Boston: Allyn & Bacon, 1974.

Durkin, D.   *Teaching Young Children To Read.* Boston: Allyn & Bacon, 1972.

Fairbanks, G.   *Experimental Phonetics: Selected Articles.* Urbana, Ill.: University of Illinois Press, 1966.

Gibson, E., and Levin, H.   *The Psychology of Reading.* Cambridge, Mass.: The MIT Press, 1975.

Gray, W. S., and Leary, B. E.   *What Makes a Book Readable?* Chicago: University of Chicago Press, 1935.

Huey, E. B.   *The Psychology and Pedagogy of Reading.* New York: Macmillan Publishing Co., 1908.

LaBerge, D., and Samuels, S. J.   "Toward a Theory of Automatic Information Processing in Reading." *Cognitive Psychology* 6 (1974): 293-323.

Lapp, D., and Flood, J.   *Teaching Reading to Every Child,* 2nd ed. New York: Macmillan Co., 1983.

Lapp, D., Lahnston, A., and Rezba, R.   "Is It Possible to Teach Reading Through the Content Areas?" Paper presented at Annual International Reading Convention, Anaheim, Calif., 1976.

Lorge, I.   "Predicting Readability." *Teachers College Record* 45 (March 1944): 404-419.

Menyuk, P.   "Language Development and Reading." In J. Flood, ed. *Understanding Reading Comprehension: Cognition, Language and the Structure of Prose.* Newark, Del.: International Reading Association. In press.

Menyuk, P., and Flood, J.   "Linguistic Competence, Reading, Writing Problems and Remediation." *Orton Society Bulletin.* 31(1981): 13-28.

Morphett, M., and Washburn, C.   "When Should Children Begin to Read?" *Elementary School Journal* 31 (March 1931): 496-503.

Murphy, H., and Durrell, D.   *Speech to Print Phonics.* New York: Harcourt Brace Jovanovich, 1972.

Rumelhart, David E.   "Toward an Interactive Model of Reading." Technical Report No. 56, *Center for Human Information Processing.* University of California at San Diego, 1976.

Rumelhart, D.   "Understanding Understanding." In J. Flood, ed. *Understanding Reading Comprehension: Cognition, Language and the Structure of Prose.* Newark, Del.: International Reading Association. In press.

Russell, D.   *Manual for Teaching the Reading Readiness Program.* Lexington, Mass.: Ginn and Company, 1967.

SMITH, F., *Understanding Reading.* New York: Holt, Rinehart and Winston, 1971.
SPACHE, G. "A New Readability Formula for Primary-Grade Reading Materials." *Elementary School Journal* 53 (March 1953): 410–413.
TABA, H. *Teacher's Handbook for Elementary Social Studies.* Palo Alto, Calif.: Addison-Wesley Publishing Co., 1967, pp. 91–117.

FURTHER READINGS

ANDERSON, R. C., SPIRO, R. J., and MONTAGUE, W. E., eds. *Schooling and the Acquisition of Knowledge.* New York: Lawrence E. Erlbaum, 1977. This book is a collection of articles written by experts in the field of reading research. Each author attempts to describe the relevance of current studies to classroom instruction. Authors include Rumelhart and Ortony, Meyer, Gagne, and Anderson.

FISHER, D. F., and PETERS, C. W., eds. *Comprehension and the Competent Reader.* New York: Praeger, 1981. Half of the chapters in this book review the research in various areas and the other half apply research to classroom practice. The book deals primarily with research into reading behaviors. Authors include Meyer, Marshall, and Flood.

FLOOD, J., and LAPP, D. *Language/Reading Instruction for the Young Child.* New York: Macmillan Co., 1981. A comprehensive methods text for teaching language and reading to young children from birth to eight years of age.

LAPP, D., and FLOOD, J. *Teaching Reading to Every Child,* 2nd ed. New York: Macmillan Co., 1983. A comprehensive reading methods text for teachers of school-aged children, kindergarten through high school.

SMITH, F. *Understanding Reading,* 2nd ed. New York: Holt, Rinehart and Winston, 1978. Presents an integrated and readable introduction to the theoretical framework upon which current research is based. It does not directly discuss instruction.

A child's reading is guided by pleasure, but his pleasure is undifferentiated; he cannot distinguish, for example, between aesthetic pleasure and the pleasures of learning or daydreaming. In adolescence we realize that there are different kinds of pleasure, some of which cannot be enjoyed simultaneously, but we need help from others in defining them. Whether it be a matter of taste in food or taste in literature, the adolescent looks for a mentor in whose authority he can believe. He eats or reads what his mentor recommends and, inevitably, there are occasions when he has to deceive himself a little; he has to pretend that he enjoys olives or War and Peace *a little more than he does.*

—*W. H. Auden*

11 LITERATURE FOR CHILDREN AND ADOLESCENTS

This chapter includes a discussion of the role of literature in your students' lives and a discussion of contemporary issues in children's literature. Instructional recommendations for teaching poetry, short stories, and journalistic writing have been included as well as instructional plans and techniques for teaching all forms of children's literature. The final section of the chapter includes titles of award-winning books that may be included as part of your literature program.

IMPORTANCE OF FAMILIARIZING CHILDREN WITH LITERATURE

By reading books, children learn to appreciate and cope with life. Books can make children see that other people have emotions similar to their own and, in turn, they can learn to deal with their emotions by seeing ways in which other people deal with similar emotions. Unless children become familiar with literature at an early age, their horizons will be limited. Through literature, children can be transported to unknown places, times, and cultures.

When choosing books for children, you should always keep in mind their needs, desires, and interests, so that they can discover books as sources of information and entertainment. Before selecting books, you may want to consider children's development of language and personality.

LANGUAGE DEVELOPMENT

As we discussed in detail in Chapter 2, children's language grows extremely quickly. It can be developed further by establishing a rich language environment in the classroom. Books can help increase children's language development. For example, in a study by Cazden (1976), it was pointed out that children's skills were positively affected by exposure to stories, poems, magazines, and novels.

By reading books children learn to appreciate and cope with life. Through literature, they can be transported to unknown places, times, and cultures. (*Photo by Linda Lungren*)

PERSONALITY DEVELOPMENT

Books play an important role in the personality development of children, helping both to instruct children in various subjects and to point out the essential values in a particular culture. Exposure to various forms of literature can help children form opinions, draw conclusions, and evaluate data. It is important to expose children to many forms of literature by many different writers from many different cultures. Although this may seem like an overwhelming task, it is critical that children experience their own world and the world around them through books.

CONTEMPORARY ISSUES IN CHILDREN'S LITERATURE

In recent years, several topics have become important and controversial issues in children's literature. Two of these topics, sex stereotyping and racial/cultural stereotypes will be discussed here.

Sex Stereotyping

Sex stereotyping has become an important issue in today's society. Formerly, it was considered taboo for a story to be written about a female in a male role or a male in a female role. This has changed only slightly according to Jennings (1975), who pointed out that it is now easier for preschool girls to accept females in traditional male roles in stories than for boys to accept males in traditional female roles in stories.

The teacher should select literature for young children that contains some or all of the following elements:

1. Males in many different roles
2. Females in many different roles
3. Females and males in compassionate and empathetic situations

Racial and Cultural Stereotypes

When selecting books, you should try to include some books that depict all races in all situations working and playing together. It is very important to establish racial equality in the minds of children at a young age.

TEACHING CHILDREN ABOUT GENRES IN LITERATURE

In the next few pages, we will discuss three genres in the field of literature: poetry, short stories, and journalistic writing. Although this is not a typical breakdown of the genres within a literature program, the authors believe that such information might serve as models for you in planning each part of your literature program.

Teaching Poetry

"poetry must say something significant about a reality common to us all, but perceived from a unique perspective."

W. H. Auden

Why Teach Poetry? Poetry is a natural beginning for language study since it is richer linguistically than any other genre and is unique in its use of language. It is a most economical entree to the reading of literature because it forces students to be sensitive to different levels of language and can heighten their responses to the language of drama, fiction, and nonfiction.

Through the ages, poetry has been enjoyed by many people—kings and queens, farmers and merchants, the old and the young. As a literary form, it has endured the test of time. In contrast to the way in which essays and articles convey information, poems combine, blend, and shape information in such a manner that they create new experiences for the reader.

In poems, sentences are put together and words are used in a way that is often quite different from the way language is used in other kinds of writing. The order of words in sentences may be shifted around, and words may be used in combinations that are startling. Some words may even be archaic or old-fashioned.

Dylan Thomas, for example, wrote, "The force that through the green fuse drives the flower, drives my green age" meaning that "nature" or "life" causes the flowers to grow up through the grass. We do not usually think of the growing flower as being driven (like a nail, rather than like a car) through a green glassy surface ("fuse"). However, by making us look at the level of green grass as a solid surface, by making us think of the flower as being hammered, or driven, up through it from below, Thomas has forced us to think of "nature" (or "life") in a forceful, rather than a passive, way. He has done this by using words in an unusual way and by putting them in an unfamiliar order. None of us, for example, would use the same order to describe an event such as the following:

> The force that through the grinder pushes the meat,
> also shapes it into hamburgers.

An example using a whole poem will help to illustrate the differences between poetry and other types of writing. Let us suppose that you had an interest in daffodils. If you wanted factual information about daffodils, you could turn to the encyclopedia, where you would find information about the family to which daffodils belong, the distinguishing characteristics of daffodils, and the geographical location and growth patterns of all daffodils. However, unless you are researching for facts, this account of daffodils may leave you cold, without the sense of the beauty of a daffodil. An encyclopedia can make a daffodil appear to be an inanimate object. However, if you want a description that imparts the real beauty of a daffodil, you may want to read Wordsworth's poem "Daffodils."

Daffodils

I wandered lonely as a cloud
    That floats on high o'er vales and hills,
When all at once I saw a crowd,
    A host, of golden daffodils;
Beside the lake, beneath the trees,
Fluttering and dancing in the breeze.
Continuous as the stars that shine
    And twinkle on the Milky Way,
They stretched in never-ending line
    Along the margin of a bay:
Ten thousand saw I at a glance,
Tossing their heads in sprightly dance.
The waves beside them danced; but they
    Outdid the sparkling waves in glee:
A poet could not but be gay,
    In such a jocund company:
I gazed-and gazed-but little thought
What wealth the show to me had brought:
For oft, when on my couch I lie
    In vacant or in pensive mood,
They flash upon that inward eye
    Which is the bliss of solitude;
And then my heart with pleasure fills,
And dances with the daffodils.

William Wordsworth

Unlike the factual description of daffodils found in the encyclopedia, the poet creates an image, or picture, of daffodils. The poet here allows the reader to share in his experience of daffodils, whereas an encyclopedia writer simply describes the qualities of the flower. In order to better understand how Wordsworth achieves his goal of communicating experiences and emotions, it is important to examine the language of the poem.

Let us look at some of the things that Wordsworth says and does in this poem. Do you think that inanimate objects can feel loneliness? Each of us has seen a clear blue sky with only one small cloud floating in this sea of blue. "Lonely" here means "solitary." In the very next line, Wordsworth uses "o'er." He does this for metrical reasons—he is trying to achieve a certain rhythm. If he had used "over," the line would have had too many syllables; therefore, he has contracted the word to one syllable. In the next line, Wordsworth takes you from the generality of the first two lines to a specific situation. "A cloud," "vales," and "hills" are all indefinite; the "golden daffodils," "the lake," "the trees," and "the breeze" are all definite. It is as though Wordsworth had thought of *some* or *any* hills, but was imagining a *specific* lake, next to which some daffodils grow.

By closing in on a specific instance, the poet has made the image, or picture, sharper; he has focused the imagination of the reader. His effect would have been quite different if he had written: "One day, when I was out walking by myself, I came across a field of daffodils beside a lake." Yet that is all the information Wordsworth has conveyed; all the rest is merely for effect.

General Suggestions for Reading Poetry. In order to help develop your children's understanding and appreciation of poetry, you might share with them the following guidelines:

1. Read the poem aloud. This will help you hear the sounds of the words as well as the rhythm within the lines. Poetry is meant to be read aloud; read each poem as slowly as possible so that you may appreciate each image.
2. Read each poem several times. The first reading will help you with an overall understanding of its meaning. A second or third reading will help you understand several aspects of the language that the poet uses.
3. Pay attention to what the poem is saying. Do not become so caught up in the rhythm that the meaning of the poem becomes lost.
4. When you practice reading poetry aloud, follow these rules:
   a. Read naturally, avoiding monotones and excessive emotion.
   b. Read more slowly than your normal reading rate so that the poet's language is comprehensible.
   c. Observe punctuation rules as you would when reading prose (do not stop at the end of every line unless punctuation requires a pause).

Reading Figurative Language. In most types of poems, poets use language devices to convey their emotions, experiences, and thoughts. Just as an artist creates with paints, so does a poet use figurative language.

Poets are not the only people who use language figuratively. We all use figurative language in normal conversation. When we say that someone is running around "like a chicken with its head cut off," we do not really mean that the person is headless. We do not mean the comparison literally; we mean it figuratively. By using this figure of speech to describe a person who is frantically busy, we are able to create a vivid effect or impression.

A poet usually uses figurative language for the same reason we do when we talk. By using figurative language, the poet can communicate vividly, powerfully, in the poems he or she writes.

The most common types of figurative language include imagery, metaphor, simile, and symbol. The poet is able to convey meaning in a minimum of words when using these literary devices. Several such devices are defined as follows:

Imagery:	The representation of an experience, an object, or an idea through descriptive language.
	Example: Romance can be represented by the glow of a full moon over a shimmering sea.
Simile:	Comparison of two objects using the words *like* or *as*.
	Examples: as cold *as* ice; run *like* the wind
Metaphor:	A comparison of two objects without using the words *like* or *as*.
	Example: All the world is a stage.
Symbol:	Something (such as a familiar object or person) used to stand for something else.
	Example: In "Ode on a Grecian Urn" by John Keats, pp. 268f., the urn may be interpreted as a symbol of abstract beauty.

IMAGERY. Imagery has been defined as the representation of an experience, an object, .or an idea through descriptive language. Frequently, when a poet uses imagery, he or she creates visual pictures for the reader. But images may also be created to make you hear something, smell something, or feel the particular texture of an object. The following poem, "Ode on a Grecian Urn," uses imagery beautifully.

Ode on a Grecian Urn

Thou still unravished bride of quietness,
   Thou foster child of silence and slow time,
Sylvan historian,[1] who canst thus express
   A flowery tale more sweetly than our rhyme:
What leaf-fringed legend haunts about thy shape
   Of deities or mortals, or of both,
     In Tempe[2] or the dales of Arcady?[3]
What men or gods are these? What maidens loathe?
   What mad pursuit? What struggle to escape?
     What pipes and timbrels?[4] What wild ecstasy?

[1] Sylvan historian: The urn first presents a woodland (sylvan) scene.
[2] Tempe: (tĕm′ pē): a pleasant valley in Greece; in poetry a synonym for rural beauty.
[3] Arcady: (är′ kə dē): Arcadia, in ancient Greece; a carefree paradise.
[4] Timbrels: small hand drums.

Heard melodies are sweet, but those unheard
  Are sweeter; therefore, ye soft pipes, play on;
Not to the sensual ear, but, more endeared,
  Pipe to the spirit ditties of no tone:
Fair youth, beneath the trees, thou canst not leave
  Thy song nor ever can those trees be bare;
    Bold Lover, never, never canst thou kiss,
Though winning near the goal—yet, do not grieve;
  She cannot fade, though thou hast not thy bliss,
    Forever wilt thou love, and she be fair!

Ah, happy, happy boughs! that cannot shed
  Your leaves, nor ever bid the Spring adieu;
And, happy melodist, unwearièd,
  Forever piping songs forever new;
More happy love! more happy, happy love!
  Forever warm and still to be enjoyed,
    Forever panting, and forever young;
All breathing human passion far above,
  That leaves a heart high-sorrowful and cloyed,
    A burning forehead, and a parching tongue.

Who are these coming to the sacrifice?
  To what green altar, O mysterious priest,
Lead'st thou that heifer lowing at the skies,
  And all her silken flanks with garlands dressed?
What little town by river or sea shore,
  Or mountain-built with peaceful citadel,
    Is emptied of this folk, this pious morn?
And, little town, thy streets forevermore
  Will silent be; and not a soul to tell
    Why thou are desolate, can e'er return.

O Attic[5] shape! Fair attitude! with brede
  Of marble men and maidens overwrought,[6]
With forest branches and the trodden weed;
  Thou, silent form, dost tease us out of thought
As doth eternity: Cold Pastoral![7]
  When old age shall this generation waste,
    Thou shalt remain, in midst of other woe
Than ours, a friend to man, to whom thou say'st,
  "Beauty is truth, truth beauty"—that is all
    Ye know on earth, and all ye need to know.

John Keats

---

[5] Attic: Athenian; Greek.

[6] Brede . . . overwrought: ornamented with a connected pattern.

[7] Pastoral: a country scene, or poem.

SIMILE. A simile is a comparison of two objects using the words *like* or *as*. The following poem makes use of this form of figurative language.

The Eagle

He clasps the crag with crooked hands;
Close to the sun in lonely lands,
Ringed with the azure world, he stands.
The wrinkled sea beneath him crawls;
He watches from his mountain walls,
And *like* a thunderbolt he falls.

Alfred, Lord Tennyson

METAPHOR. Like a simile, a metaphor is a comparison of two objects. However, a metaphor does not require the use of the words *like* or *as*. The following poem contains an example of a metaphor. Try to find this metaphor by discovering what the "it" in this poem represents.

I Like to See It Lap the Miles

I like to see it lap the miles,
And lick the valleys up,
And stop to feed itself at tanks;
And then, prodigious, step
Around a pile of mountains,
And, supercilious, peer
In shanties by the sides of roads;
And then a quarry pare
To fit its sides, and crawl between,
Complaining all the while
In horrid, hooting stanza;
Then chase itself down hill
And neigh like Boanerges;
Then, punctual as a star,
Stop-docile and omnipotent
At its own stable door--

Emily Dickinson

SYMBOL. Often, a poet uses an object or person to represent something besides itself. The following poem relies heavily on this technique. This device is called symbolism.

The Tiger

Tiger! Tiger! burning bright
In the forests of the night,
What immortal hand or eye
Could frame thy fearful symmetry?

In what distant deeps or skies
Burnt the fire of thine eyes?
On what wings dare he aspire?
What the hand dare seize the fire?

And what shoulder, and what art,
Could twist the sinews of thy heart?
And when thy heart began to beat,
What dread hand? and what dread feet?

What the hammer? what the chain?
In what furnace was thy brain?
What the anvil? what dread grasp
Dare its deadly terrors clasp?

When the stars threw down their spears,
And water'd heaven with their tears,
Did he smile his work to see?
Did he who made the Lamb make thee?

Tiger! Tiger! burning bright
In the forests of the night
What immortal hand or eye,
Dare frame thy fearful symmetry?

William Blake

Rhyme. Young children like poetry for many reasons; one of the principal elements they enjoy is rhyme. Young children especially enjoy listening to and reciting nursery rhymes because they can feel the beat and hear the rhyme. The following nursery rhymes can be used to introduce children to the concept of rhyme.

Old Mother Hubbard

Old Mother Hubbard
Went to the cupboard,
To get her poor dog a bone;
But when she got there,
The cupboard was bare,
And so the poor dog had none.

Hickory Dickory Dock

Hickory, dickory, dock!
The mouse ran up the clock;
The clock struck one,
The mouse ran down,
Hickory, dickory, dock!

Little Jack Horner

Little Jack Horner sat in the corner,
 Eating a Christmas pie;
He put in his thumb, and he pulled out a plum,
 And said, "What a good boy am I!"

Little Bo Peep

Little Bo Peep has lost her sheep
 And can't tell where to find them;
Leave them alone, and they'll come home,
 Wagging their tails behind them.

Little Boy Blue

Little Boy Blue, come blow your horn;
The sheep's in the meadow, the cow's in the corn.
Where's the little boy that looks after the sheep?
He's under the haystack, fast asleep.

Resources for Teaching Poetry. The following sources will enable you to develop effective instruction in poetry for your children and to select poems that your children will enjoy:

A Beginning Book of Poems, selected by Marjorie Laurence. Reading, Mass: Addison Wesley Publishing Co., 1967.

Childcraft, Poems and Rhymes, Vol. I. Chicago, Ill.: Field Enterprises Educational Corporation, 1974.

Just My Size, compiled by Charlotte S. Huck, William A. Jenkins, and Wilma J. Pyle. Glenview, Ill.: Scott, Foresman and Co., 1971.

Poems Children Will Sit Still For, compiled by Beatrice Schenk de Regniers, Eva Moore, and Mary Michaels White. New York: Citation Press, 1969.

Poems for Weather Watching, compiled by Laurie Israel. New York: Holt, Rinehart and Winston, 1963.

Teaching Short Stories

In addition to exposing children to the traditional elements of story grammars as presented in Chapter 4, you must acquaint children with the elements of short stories. It is important to explain the origin of the short story in the history of humankind as well as to introduce children to the four important elements of the short story: plot, setting, characterization, and theme.

Although we do not know precisely when the first short story was recited, we can assume that it happened as soon as people could talk. The first recorded story dates back to at least 3000 B.C. One of the earliest stories, "The Shipwrecked Sailor," was told by the sons of Cheops, the Egyptian Pharaoh, to amuse their father. The oldest written collection of stories that we know about is the *Panchatantra*. It is a collection of stories written in India more than 2,000 years ago.

Another ancient collection of stories, *The Arabian Nights,* tells about King Shar, who had his wife killed for her infidelity. He began to take vengeance on all women by marrying and killing a new wife every day. One wife, Scheherazade, was able to stop his killings by telling him stories for a thousand and one nights. Each night, she left her suspenseful story unfinished so that he would have to let her live until the next night. One of the most famous stories in *The Arabian Nights* is "Aladdin and the Magic Lamp."

The short story has three primary attributes: (1) It is "created" by a storyteller. (2) Its purpose is to have an effect upon the reader. This planned effect varies from author to author, depending upon his or her theme, method of presentation, and the expected audience. (3) It has a story line, a plot.

Reading for Plot. Plot is the sequence of events in a story. It includes the words, thoughts, and actions of characters. It usually contains a conflict—a clash between characters' actions, ideas, desires, or wills. Three common conflicts in stories are man vs. man, man vs. nature, and man vs. himself. Usually, these conflicts are resolved to create the story's ending. In most "good" stories, plot is inseparable from setting, character, and theme. Even when a story consists of a limited series of related events, it is said to have a plot. A plot by itself is like a map—it tells the direction of a story, but it does not tell us about the quality of the journey.

Reading for Setting. A story usually takes place in space and time. Most stories have a locale; they occur in a specific geographical location. They usually occur at a specific time in history, for example: the eighteenth century; July 4, 1887; or Tuesday, May 13, 1997. Stories often use settings to help them convey meaning. They may use a night setting for a suspenseful, eerie story, or they may use a nineteenth-century European city as a setting to tell the story of a runaway princess. Short-story writers usually integrate a setting into their stories to help convey plot and enhance characterizations.

Reading for Characterization. There can be no movement of plot without characters. Reading for characters, however, is more difficult than reading for plot or reading for setting because characters are, by definition, more complex than plots or settings of stories. It is easy to recount what a character has done or the place where it was done, but it takes considerably more skill to explain the essence of a character. When you are reading for characterization, it is important to read without preconceived notions. For example, you should never expect the main character to be virtuous and good, because such expectations limit the story and may disappoint you.

Within the framework of many short stories, it is important not to expect the development of more than one or two characters. The length of a story automatically limits the number of characters that can be developed thoroughly. After you examine the plot, setting, and characters of a story, it is important to understand the main idea—the theme—of a short story.

Reading for Theme. The theme of a short story is its controlling idea. In order to determine the theme of a story, it is necessary to ask: "What is the central purpose of the story?" Not all stories have a theme. Some horror stories, for example, are simply intended to scare the reader, and some adventure stories have a single purpose: to provide entertainment for the reader. Theme exists only when an author is attempting to reveal some truth about life that is illustrated in the story. Theme, like plot, may be stated briefly. However, this statement must be a *central* thought explaining the greatest number of elements possible within the story. Explain to your students that when they are trying to locate the theme of a story, they should use the following guidelines:

1. Theme must be expressible as a statement. Motherhood is not a theme; it is a subject. However, when the idea of motherhood is expanded to "Motherhood is rewarding," a theme has been expressed.
2. The theme must be a generalization about life. "John is left homeless and must fend for himself" is not a theme, but "Man attempts to survive alone" is a theme.
3. Theme is a central and unifying concept. Therefore, it must account for all the major details of the story without contradictions.

Teaching Journalistic Writing

Children need to be taught how to read journalistic writing. In the following pages, we will discuss magazine writing.

Children's Magazines. Many magazines have been published for children. These magazines encompass a variety of topics, interests, and reading abilities. They can become an extremely important part of your reading curriculum.

Most children's magazines contain essays and feature articles about topics of general concern to your students. In addition, they contain excellent language arts activities, such as puzzles and anagrams, that will reinforce word recognition and vocabulary instruction. Before asking children to read the essays and feature articles contained in these magazines, it is important to point out that essays/feature articles are primarily concerned with informing, entertaining, and persuading readers. Such works are written in many presentation modes and are published in many different forms. They are often published in magazines, newspapers, periodicals, and journals.

You may want to point out to your students that writers of essays/feature articles give the commonplace, everyday activities of life a refreshing twist and a new perspective. They are frequently written to capture a reader's attention quickly and thoroughly. The author of an effective essay/feature article often follows a lead statement with the major elements of journalistic writing: the who, what, when, where, why, how, and "so what" of an event. The writing style of an essay/feature article is usually crisp, simple, and direct in the same way as journalistic writings.

Many essays/feature articles are written by journalists who write from the perspective of astute observers. They write about people's feelings and emotions, motivations, beliefs, and behaviors. Essays/feature articles rarely have a single stylistic pattern. Their primary purpose is to broaden the dimensions of facts by informing, entertaining, or persuading the reader to a particular point of view. As one reads an essay/feature article, it is important to determine the purpose of the article. Has it been written to provide information, to entertain, or to persuade? After making this decision, it is useful to try to discern the focus of the article and the biases of the author as regards the information that is presented in the article. Frequently, essay/feature article writers, due to personal beliefs, are unable to write about events or people from a totally objective viewpoint. As readers, it is your students' responsibility to determine whether objectivity or subjectivity exists and to read the article from that perspective.

When your students are reading essays/feature articles, they should beware of the slippery boundary between fact and opinion. For example, suppose someone says, "I have a wonderful car; it's the best car on the road." This would be the car owner's opinion. But, if someone says, "My car has gone 70,000 miles and has never needed any repairs," this would be a fact.

An important point to remember when your students are reading essays/feature articles is that pictures are a vital part of each article. Sometimes these articles are so short that a picture or illustration is used to supplement the amount of information that is presented in the article.

Pictures and illustrations have many purposes:

1. An author can portray a character for readers.
2. An author can portray the setting of the article; it may take place in an unfamiliar place and the author may feel that a picture will serve to clarify the setting.
3. An author may wish to illustrate a point.

Regardless of the exact intent of the picture or illustration, it provides readers with additional information about the article. You may want to suggest the following guidelines for your students to use when reading essays/feature articles:

1. As you read, try to answer the questions: who, what, where, when, why, and how. Answers to these questions are often found at the beginning of the article.
2. Try to determine the purpose of the article. Is the article informative, entertaining, or persuasive?
3. Try to determine whether the article is based on opinions or facts.
4. As you read, be careful to examine all the pictures that accompany the article.

Children's Magazine Resources. There are so many magazines available to children that it may be difficult for you to select appropriate periodicals. Three author/editors—Lavinia Dobler, Marian Scott, and Lois Winkel—have categorized some of the leading children's magazines by interest level, reading grade level, and children's age level.

DOBLER, LAVINIA, ed. *The Dobler World Directory of Youth Periodicals,* 3rd ed. New York: Citation Press, 1970.

SCOTT, MARIAN H., ed. *Periodicals for School Libraries: A Guide to Magazines, Newspapers and Periodical Indexes.* Chicago: American Library Association, 1973.

WINKEL, LOIS, ed. *The Elementary School Library Collection/A Guide to Books and Other Media,* 12th ed. Newark, N.J.: The Bro-Dart Foundation, 1979.

Name of Magazine and Category	Interest Level (Grade)	Grade Level	Age Level
	Winkel	Scott	Dobler
General Interest			
Children's Digest	4–6	K–6	7–12
Child Life	4–6	K–6	6–12
Children's Playmate	1–3	K–6	3–8
Children's World	4–6		
Highlights	1–6 +	K–6	3–12
Humpty Dumpty	K–2	K–6	3–8
Jack and Jill	2–4	K–6	4–10
Jabberwocky (Canadian)	K–2		
Time: The Weekly Newsmagazine	4–6		
Young World	6	K–9	

Name of Magazine and Category	Interest Level (Grade)	Grade Level	Age Level
	Winkel	Scott	Dobler

Natural Science

Animal Kingdom: N. Y. Zoological Society Magazine	1-6+	K-12	4-12
Audobon	6	K-12	5-12
Beaver (Canadian)	6+	K-12	K-12
Chickadee (Canadian)	K-3		
Current Science	6	K-9	
Kind (Kindness in Nature's Defense)	6+		
National Geographic	K-6+	K-12	
National Geographic World	4-6		
National Parks & Conservation (Canadian)	6	K-12	K-12
Owl (Canadian)	4-6		
Popular Science Monthly	6		
Ranger Rick	2-4	K-6	K-6
Science News	4-6	K-12	
Wildlife: The International Wildlife Magazine	4-6		
Zoonooz	4-6 (9th rdab.)	K-9	6-10

Literature

Cricket	4-6		
Kids	1-6	K-6	
Read	6+	K-9	
Stone Soup	6		

History and politics

American Heritage	6+	K-12	
Cobblestone	4-6		
Current Events			
Early American Life	6		
Natural History (title varies)	6	K-12	K-12

Sports

Baseball Digest		7-12	
Football Digest	6	7-12	
Sport	4-6+	K-12	
Young Athlete	4-6		

Name of Magazine and Category	Interest Level (Grade)	Grade Level	Age Level
	Winkel	Scott	Dobler
Arts and Crafts			
American Indian Art	6		
Creative Crafts	6	7-9	
Man & His Music	4-8	K-9	8-10
Pack-O-Fun	2-4		7-12
Plays: Drama Magazine for Young People	6	K-12	7-19
Smithsonian (Art, Science, History)	6+	K-12	
Geography			
Arizona Highways	1-6+	K-12	
Alaska: The Magazine of the Last Frontier	6+		
Illinois History			12-18
Maryland Magazine			
Nature Canada			
Nevada Magazine		K-12	
Pacific Northwest			
Texas Historian			
Wisconsin Trails		K-12	high sch.
Walkabout (Australian)			
World Traveler	4-6 (4th rdab.)	K-9	
Learning			
American Red Cross Youth News	2-4	K-6	6-12
American Red Cross Youth Journal			13-18
Scholastic News Pilot		1	
Scholastic News Ranger		2	
Scholastic News Trails		3	
Scholastic News Explorer		4	
Scholastic News Citizen		5	
Scholastic Newstime		6	
Junior Scholastic		6+	K-12
Scholastic Search, Scope, Voice (3 mag.)		7-9-12	
Senior Scholastic		7-12	
My Weekly Reader Surprise			K
My Weekly Reader Eye			1
My Weekly Reader News Reader			2

Name of Magazine and Category	Interest Level (Grade)	Grade Level	Age Level
	Winkel	Scott	Dobler
My Weekly Reader News Story			3
My Weekly Reader News Parade			4
My Weekly Reader News Report			5
Senior Weekly Reader			6
Know Your World Extra			11–15
You and Your World			
Specialty			
American Aircraft Modeler		K–12	
Animal Life	4–6		
Cat Fancy Magazine		K–12	
Coins	6	K–6	
Dogs		K–12	
Foxfire		7–12	
Horselover's National Mag.	6+	7–9	
MAD Magazine	4–6	7–9	high sch.
Magazine of Fantasy and Science Fiction	4–6+		
Modern Airplane News	4–6	K–12	12?
Modern Railroader	4–6	7–12	
Pet News	4–6		
Scott's Monthly Stamp Journal	4–6+	K–12	
Super-8 Filmmaker	4–6		
Bonjour	6	K–6	beginners in French

Before beginning to teach a children's literature program, you will want to assess your children's reading ability as explained in the preceding chapter. You will also want to gauge their attitudes toward reading and learn their reading interests so that you can help them select books that they will be able to read with enjoyment.

ATTITUDES TOWARD READING

As children begin to read, it is important to provide them with materials of interest. Students must be motivated by a desire to read, whether their reading is for leisure or information. You must establish a positive reading atmosphere in your classroom. You can do this in the following way:

As children begin to read, it is important to provide materials of interest to keep them reading. Students must be motivated by a *desire* to read whether their reading is for leisure or information. (*Photo by Linda Lungren*)

1. Establish a set time to read with your children each day.
2. Involve students in reading magazines and newspapers in addition to books.
3. Establish a pleasant reading corner as a "getaway" for leisure reading.
4. Read to students on a variety of topics to stimulate and broaden their interests.
5. Read from a variety of literary forms.
6. Make paperbacks available to students.
7. Encourage students to recommend books to you. By doing this, you will discover their major areas of interest.

You can also use parents to help you to promote a positive reading attitude in each child. This can be done in the following ways:

1. Encourage children to question parents about vocabulary words they do not know.
2. Parents can read humorous stories and poems aloud.
3. Parents can subscribe to a magazine of their child's choice.
4. Children and parents can read materials together.
5. Parents can encourage children to take frequent trips to the library.
6. Parents can give books to children as gifts.

The following instruments may prove helpful in assessing the attitudes of children:

Reading Interest/Attitude Scale

Right to Read Office, Washington, D.C. 1976

Date _____ Grade _____ Name _____

Directions: Read each item slowly twice to each child. Ask him/her to point to the face which shows how he/she feels about the statement. Circle the corresponding symbol. Read each item with the same inflection and intonation.

A	B	C
Strongly Agree	Undecided	Strongly Disagree
(Makes me feel good)	(OK or don't know)	(Makes me feel bad)

A	B	C	1.	When I go to the store I like to buy books.
A	B	C	2.	Reading is for learning but not for fun.
A	B	C	3.	Books are fun to me.
A	B	C	4.	I like to share books with friends.
A	B	C	5.	Reading makes me happy.
A	B	C	6.	I read some books more than once.
A	B	C	7.	Most books are too long.
A	B	C	8.	There are many books I hope to read.
A	B	C	9.	Books make good presents.
A	B	C	10.	I like to have books read to me.

The second instrument can be used with older students. You can read some of the following statements to students in order to assess their attitudes toward reading.

Reading Attitude Inventory

by Molly Ransbury, 1971

Yes   No

____   ____   1. I visit the library to find books I might enjoy reading.

____   ____   2. I would like to read a magazine in my free time.

Yes   No

___ ___ 3. I cannot pay attention to my reading when there is even a little noise or movement nearby.

___ ___ 4. I enjoy reading extra books about topics we study in school.

___ ___ 5. I would like to read newspaper articles about my favorite hobbies or interests.

___ ___ 6. I feel I know the characters in some of the comic books I read.

___ ___ 7. My best friend would tell you that I enjoy reading very much.

___ ___ 8. I would like to belong to a group that discusses many kinds of reading.

___ ___ 9. I would enjoy spending some time during my summer vacation reading to children in a summer library program.

___ ___ 10. My ideas are changed by the books I read.

___ ___ 11. Reading is an important part of my life. Every day I read many different types of materials.

___ ___ 12. I read magazines for many different reasons.

___ ___ 13. My friends would tell you that I'd much rather watch T.V. than read.

___ ___ 14. When I listen to someone read out loud, certain words or sentences might attract my attention.

___ ___ 15. I would only read a book if my teacher or my parents said I had to.

___ ___ 16. Magazines, comic books and newspapers do not interest me.

___ ___ 17. I do not enjoy reading in my free time.

___ ___ 18. I would enjoy talking with someone else about one of my favorite books.

___ ___ 19. I might go to the library several times to see if a special book had been returned.

___ ___ 20. I am too busy during vacations to plan a reading program for myself.

___ ___ 21. Sometimes the book that I'm reading will remind me of ideas from another book that I've read.

___ ___ 22. If my only reading was for school assignments, I would be very unhappy.

Yes   No

___ ___ 23. Reading is not a very good way for me to learn new things.
___ ___ 24. I think reading is boring.
___ ___ 25. If I see a comic book or magazine I would usually just look at the pictures.
___ ___ 26. I sometimes read extra books or articles about something that we have discussed in school.
___ ___ 27. I enjoy going to the library and choosing special books.
___ ___ 28. I do not read during any of my vacations from school.
___ ___ 29. I would not want to help set up a book exhibit.
___ ___ 30. It would be very, very nice for me to have my own library of books.
___ ___ 31. I don't try to read many different kinds of books.
___ ___ 32. If I do not read many things when I'm an adult, I will miss many important ideas about life.
___ ___ 33. I read because the teacher tells me to.
___ ___ 34. I read only because people force me to.
___ ___ 35. I must shut myself in a quiet room in order to read almost anything.
___ ___ 36. I never do extra reading outside of school work because reading is so dull.
___ ___ 37. I only read extra books if my parents say I have to.
___ ___ 38. Reading certain newspaper articles might make me happy, or sad, or even angry.
___ ___ 39. I should spend some of my time each day reading so that I can learn about the world.
___ ___ 40. Before I make up my mind about something, I try to read more than one writer's ideas.
___ ___ 41. When I read, I sometimes understand myself a little better.
___ ___ 42. Some characters I have read about help me to better understand people I know.
___ ___ 43. Reading is a very important part of my life. I read nearly every day in books or newspapers and I enjoy doing so.

Yes	No		
___	___	44.	I would like to read some of the novels my teacher reads to the class.
___	___	45.	I would like to read more books if I had the time.
___	___	46.	I might keep a list of the books that I wish to read during the next few months.
___	___	47.	My parents force me to read.
___	___	48.	If people didn't tell me that I had to read, I would probably never pick up a book.
___	___	49.	Sometimes I think ahead in my reading and imagine what the characters might do.
___	___	50.	I wish I could buy more books for myself.
___	___	51.	Sometimes I wish the author of the book had written the story a different way.
___	___	52.	Much of my free time is spent in reading, library browsing and discussing books.
___	___	53.	I read lots of different newspaper articles so that I can learn more about the world.
___	___	54.	Reading is as much a part of my life as eating, sleeping and playing.
___	___	55.	A story that I see on television might also be interesting to read in a book.
___	___	56.	Even a little reading makes me feel tired and restless.
___	___	57.	I try to read many different types of materials in my free time.
___	___	58.	I would always rather talk about things, than to read about them.
___	___	59.	I have never wanted to read a book twice.
___	___	60.	When I am an adult and work all day, I will not read.
___	___	61.	I would feel disappointed if I could not find a book that I was very interested in reading.
___	___	62.	I have sometimes told my friends about a really good book that they might like to read.
___	___	63.	I look for some main ideas that the writer presents when I read a magazine article.
___	___	64.	Reading is a very important part of my life when I am not in school.

READING INTERESTS

Witty (1963, p. 331) defined interest as:

> ... a disposition or tendency which impels an individual to seek out particular goals for persistent attention. The goals may be objects, skills, knowledges, and art activities of various kinds. The behavior patterns in seeking these goals may be regarded as particular interests such as collecting objects or viewing TV. They should be looked upon as acquired, although they are based upon such factors as the constitutional nature of the individual and his personality structure as affected by his unique experiences and his particular environment.

This quote suggests that the development of a student's positive interest in reading may depend upon the success with which you are able to know and understand the child's background and the experiences that have led the child to his or her present state. It also suggests that some understanding of individual personality is required.

In order to obtain information on children's reading interests, you may want to use the following interest inventory or one that is similar and appropriate for your students' age group. The information you collect from this inventory will help you in making suggestions as regards students' reading.

Interest Inventory

Name: _____

1. What do you like to do in your spare time?
2. How do you usually spend your summers?
3. How much reading do you do on your own?
4. How much television do you watch each day?
5. What are some of the programs you watch and enjoy?
6. What movies have you seen that you really liked?
7. Do you ever read a book after you have seen the television or movie version? Which ones have you read?
8. Have you ever been to any of the following places?

Art Museum	Circus	Theater
Any Museum	National Park	Library
Concert	Zoo	

9. What other countries have you visited or lived in?
10. What other cities or states have you visited or lived in?

Circle the school subjects you like, cross out the subjects you don't like:

Arithmetic	Science	Gym
Spelling	Social Studies	Health
Reading	Music	English
Art	Other Languages	

Circle the kinds of books and stories you like, cross out the books and stories you don't like:

Adventure	Mystery	Magazines
Animal stories	Motorcycles	Comic books
Hobby stores	Love and romance	Ghost stories
Biography	Science fiction	Family stories
Autobiography	Car magazines	Riddles and jokes
Science	Fables and myths	Horse stories
Western stories	Sports	Humor
Art and music	Religion	Fantasy
Fairy tales	People of other lands	History
Poetry	Newspapers	Geography

READING TO YOUNG CHILDREN

There are many educators who encourage you to read to young children in order to improve their language development, but few educators tell you *how* to read to young children. Sir Allan Bullock's report "A Language for Life" (1975) briefly discusses the *how to* of reading to young children: "The best way to prepare the young child for reading is to hold him on your lap and read aloud to him stories he likes—over and over again."

Flood (1977) found that the most effective way to read to young children was to follow these four steps during a reading episode:

1. Prepare children for the story by asking warm-up questions, for example, before reading *The Story of Ferdinand,* you may want to ask children some of the following questions:
    a. Have you ever seen a bull?
    b. What are bulls like?
    c. Are bulls scary?
    d. Do you like to smell beautiful flowers?
    e. Sometimes animals are tame and sometimes they are wild. How would you expect a bull to be?

   Then introduce the story, for example:
   "We are going to read a story about a tame bull who loves to smell flowers. His name is Ferdinand."

Sir Allan Bullock's report suggests that the best way to prepare the young child for reading is to hold the child on your lap and read aloud the stories he or she likes—over and over again. (*Photo by Linda Lungren*)

2. Verbally interact with the child during the reading. Ask and answer many different kinds of questions, for example:
   a. Why was Ferdinand's mother worried about him?
   b. Why did the men choose Ferdinand to go to the bull fight in Madrid?
3. Reinforce your student during the reading episode. For example, if one of your children says: "Ferdinand was a nice bull. He didn't want to be picked for the bull fight"; you might say: "That's right. You're paying very close attention to the story."
4. Finish the episode by asking children to evaluate the story. You may want to ask some of the following questions:
   a. Did you like the story?
   b. Do you think Ferdinand is happy now?
   c. Did you like Ferdinand?

SELECTING LITERATURE FOR BEGINNING READERS

When a child is just beginning to read, you should select stories that are short with large print, short sentences, appropriate vocabulary, and many pictures. A list of beginning books can be found in the back of the *Elementary School Library Collection* edited by Phillis Van Orden.

Educators have found that several topics appeal to young children, for example, stories about animals and stories containing humor. All the Dr. Seuss books contain humor that young children can understand and appreciate. Syd Hoff, an author-illustrator, includes humor in his books *Albert and the Albatross, The Horse in Harry's Room,* and *Danny and the Dinosaur.*

P. D. Eastman uses humor as his vehicle in *Go, Dog, Go* and *Sam and the Firefly*. Some other humorous beginner's books are *It's So Nice to Have a Wolf Around the House* by H. Allard, *Nothing Much Happened Today* by Christian, *Loosen Your Ears* by Farly, *McBroom Tells a Lie* by Fleischman, and *The Contests at Cowlick* by R. Kennedy.

Another popular type of book with young children is the mystery book. Such stories as *The Alligator Cure* by William Pene du Bois, *The Case of the Cat's Meow* by Crosby Bonsall, *Rooftop Mystery* by Joan M. Lexan, and *Big Max* by Kin Platt are popular mysteries that can entertain and intrigue children. Other mystery stories are *The Stolen Spoon Mystery* by I. Bowan, *Secret of the Crazy Quilt* by Hightower, and *The Chocolate Chip Mystery* by McInness.

Books that deal with new adventures for young children, such as the first day of school, are also interesting to the beginning reader. Some adventure stories on this subject are *New Teacher* and *Will I Have a Friend?* by Miriam Cohen, and the *Moose Goes to School* by B. Wiseman.

Books that contain content-area information are becoming very popular with young children. Some titles include *The Big Dipper; The Sun, Our Nearest Star;* and *Mickey's Magnet* by F. M. Branley, and *The Carrot Seed* by Ruth Krauss. In addition, several publishers have data-filled informational beginning reading books: *I Can Read Books* by Martha and Charles Snapp, the *Let's Read and Find Out* books by Thomas Y. Crowell, Publisher, and the *Beginner Books* series by Random House.

When children are beginning to read, you should read aloud to them. When you are reading to a class, try not to read to a group of more than five to seven students in order to ensure that everyone can hear and understand what is happening. Also, try to show the book to the children as you read so that they can get used to seeing print and pictures. This will help them enjoy the story more.

TEACHING EPISODES

When teaching reading to children, you should try to create exercises that make reading fun. These exercises should help introduce a story before it is read, occur during the reading of the story, and serve as a discussion or postreading of the story. The following are some prereading, actual reading, and postreading exercises.

Prereading Exercises

When you first present a book to be read, you should review difficult vocabulary with the children. You should also look over the pictures and talk about them.

To introduce the characters in a story, you might ask children to bring in pictures of various people and have the children select the ones that best depict the characters in the story. You should have ready a picture that you selected of the main character in case your students do not bring appropriate pictures. Another useful prereading activity is to tell your students the names of the characters in the books and ask them to guess what the characters will be like.

Pictures are also an excellent way to introduce the setting of a story. You can show your students several pictures and try to make them guess what might be happening in the story. As you begin reading the story, you might say, "Let's see who is right as we read the story."

The following activity may help you teach vocabulary before reading the story. Write on cards the difficult vocabulary words from the story. Divide the class into three or four small groups. Hold up the vocabulary cards in front of the groups and discuss each word's meaning. Give each group a pile of blank cards and have the groups write as many of the vocabulary words as they remember while they are reading the story. Give each group a space in the room where they can display their vocabulary words. The group that has the most correct meanings will be the vocabulary winners.

Reading Exercises

When you are actually reading the story, you should allow time for children to monitor their own comprehension. With very young children, you should stop frequently and show them the pictures and the printed text.

A useful reading exercise is to stop reading in the middle of a story and ask the children to guess the outcome. This helps children focus their attention and develops their interest; each child wants his or her ending to be the correct one.

Postreading Exercises

After you have read a story, you may want to conduct a discussion. One technique you can use to have children test their own comprehension is to ask them to write or tell a different way in which the story could have ended. A variation of this exercise is to ask your students to tell what the story might have been like if it had been told by another character in the story. This may encourage children to think about the storyteller's point of view.

You may want to ask young children to draw a picture of their favorite part of the story. After reading *Baby Sister for Frances* by R. & L. Hoban, two kindergarteners were asked to do this and drew the following pictures:

A Baby Sister For Frances

My favorite part of the story was when Frances ran away under the dining room table

By: Sarah
Age: 5½

A Baby Sister For Frances

My favorite part of "Frances" was when Frances came back again.

By: Anna
Age: 5

ORGANIZING YOUR CHILDEN'S INFORMATION SEARCHING

In addition to having children select their own books based on their interests, it is important to help children choose appropriate books when they are reading for information. The creation of a "web of possibilities" based on multiple sources is an effective vehicle for organizing study on a particular topic. Charlotte Huck popularized this British notion in American education. It provides children with an organizing scheme for collecting, analyzing, and evaluating information.

CREATING STIMULATING ENVIRONMENTS FOR READING

The reading environment for any new reader in a classroom should be appealing and reassuring. It should be a comfortable, cozy place, where the new reader can feel at ease. If the reading environment is comfortable, your students may develop a positive attitude toward reading.

In your classroom, it is a good idea to section off a quiet place for reading. If possible, you should cover it with carpeting or blankets. Pillows, chair cushions, inner tubes, or beach chairs can make the reading area very attractive. Children love reading lofts—you may want to try to build one in your classroom because it gives the student a sense of being apart from the rest of the class.

Another very comfortable reading area can be made from an old bathtub. If you are fortunate enough to acquire one, line it with a furry rug or blanket and your students will enjoy hours of pleasurable reading.

The reading environment in the home should be similar to that found in the classroom. Again, it should be highly conducive to pleasurable reading. It should be a spot where one child can feel comfortable, but it should be large enough so that the child can invite friends over for the purpose of reading together.

TREASURE CHEST OF AWARD-WINNING BOOKS

Beginning in 1938, the Caldecott medal has been awarded to the artist who best illustrated a children's book published in the United States during the preceding year.

CALDECOTT MEDAL BOOKS

Author	Award Winner	Title	Year	Grade
Lathrop	Lathrop	Animals of the Bible	1938	2-5
Handforth	Handforth	Mei Li	1939	K-2
Aulaire	Aulaire	Abraham Lincoln	1940	2-4
Lawson	Lawson	They Were Strong and Good	1941	3-6
McCloskey	McCloskey	Make Way for Ducklings	1942	K-2
Burton	Burton	The Little House	1943	K-2
Thurber	Slobodkin	Many Moons	1944	1-4
Field	Jones	Prayer for a Child	1945	K-3
Petersham	Petersham	The Rooster Crows	1946	K-2
Brown	Weisgard	The Little Island	1947	K-2
Tresselt	Duvoisin	White Snow, Bright Snow	1948	K-2
Hader	Hader	The Big Snow	1949	K-2
Politi	Politi	Song of the Swallows	1950	K-2
Milhous	Milhous	The Egg Tree	1951	K-3
Lipkind	Mordvinoff	Finders Keepers	1952	K-2
Ward	Ward	The Biggest Bear	1953	K-3
Bemelmans	Bemelmans	Madeline's Rescue	1954	K-2
Perrault	Brown	Cinderella	1955	2-4
Frog...	Rojankovsky	Frog Went a Courtin'	1956	K-3
Udry	Simont	A Tree Is Nice	1957	K-2
McCloskey	McCloskey	Time of Wonder	1958	2-5
Chaucer	Cooney	Chanticleer and the Fox	1959	K-3
Ets	Ets	Nine Days to Christmas	1960	K-3
Robbins	Sidjakov	Baboushka and the Three Kings	1961	1-4
Hitapadesa	Brown	Once a Mouse	1962	K-3
Keats	Keats	The Snowy Day	1963	K-2
Sendak	Sendak	Where the Wild Things Are	1964	K-2
De Regniers	De Regniers	May I Bring a Friend?	1965	K-2
Alger	Hogrogian	Always Room for One More	1966	K-3
Ness	Ness	Sam, Bangs, and Moonshine	1967	K-2
Emberley, B.	Emberley, Ed.	Drummer Hoff	1968	K-3

CALDECOTT MEDAL BOOKS (cont.)

Author	Award Winner	Title	Year	Grade
Ransome	Shulevitz	The Fool of the World and the Flying Ship	1969	2-4
Steig	Steig	Sylvester and the Magic Pebble	1970	K-2
Haley	Haley	A Story, a Story	1971	K-2
Hogrogian	Hogrogian	One Fine Day	1972	K-3
Mosel	Lent	Funny Little Women	1973	K-2
Zemach, H.	Zemach, M.	Duffy and the Devil	1974	K-3
McDermott, G.	McDermott, G.	Arrow to the Sun	1975	1-up
Aardema, V.	Dillon & Dillon	Why Mosquitoes Buzz in People's Ears	1976	K-3
Musgrove	Dillon & Dillon	Ashanti to Zulu	1977	3-6
Spier	Spier	Noah's Ark	1978	K-3
Globe		The Girl Who Loved Wild Horses	1979	1-3
Hall	Cooney	Ox-Cart Man	1980	1-3
Lobel		Fables	1981	K-3

The Newbery medal has been awarded annually since 1922 to the author of the most distinguished contribution to children's literature published in the United States during the preceding year.

NEWBERRY MEDAL BOOKS

Author	Title	Year	Grade
Van Loon	The Story of Mankind	1922	7-9
Lofting	The Voyages of Dr. Doolittle	1923	4-7
Hawes	The Dark Frigate	1924	7-9
Finger	Tales from Silver Lands	1925	5-7
Chrisman	Shen of the Sea	1926	5-8
James	Smoky, the Cowhorse	1927	6-9
Mukerji	Gay-Neck	1928	6-9
Kelly	The Trumpeter of Krakow	1929	7-9
Field	Hitty	1930	5-8
Coatsworth	The Cat Who Went to Heaven	1931	4-7
Armer	Waterless Mountain	1932	5-8
Lewis	Young Fu of the Upper Yangtze	1933	7-9
Meigs	Invincible Louisa	1934	7-9
Shannon	Dobry	1935	5-8

NEWBERRY MEDAL BOOKS (cont.)

Author	Title	Year	Grade
Brink	Caddie Woodlawn	1936	6-8
Sawyer	Roller Skates	1937	6-8
Seredy	The White Stag	1938	6-9
Enright	Thimble Summer	1939	5-7
Daughtery	Daniel Boone	1940	5-9
Sperry	Call it Courage	1941	5-8
Edmonds	The Matchlock Gun	1942	4-6
Vining	Adam of the Road	1943	6-9
Forbes	Johnny Tremain	1944	6-9
Lawson	Rabbit Hill	1945	3-6
Lenski	Strawberry Girl	1946	4-6
Bailey	Miss Hickory	1947	4-6
DuBois	The 21 Balloons	1948	6-9
Henry	King of the Wind	1949	5-8
DeAngeli	The Door in the Wall	1950	3-6
Yates	Amos Fortune, Free Man	1951	6-9
Estes	Ginger Pye	1952	4-7
Clark	Secret of the Andes	1953	4-7
Krumgold	... And Now Miguel	1954	5-9
DeJong	The Wheel on the School	1955	4-7
Latham	Carry on, Mr. Bowditch	1956	6-9
Sorensen	Miracles on Maple Hill	1957	5-7
Keith	Rifles for Waite	1958	6-9
Speare	Witch of Blackbird Pond	1959	6-9
Krumgold	Onion John	1960	6-9
O'Dell	Island of the Blue Dolphins	1961	5-8
Speare	The Bronze Bow	1962	6-8
L'Engle	A Wrinkle in Time	1963	6-8
Neville	It's Like This, Cat	1964	6-8
Rodman	Shadow of a Bull	1965	6-8
Trevino	I, Juan de Pareja	1966	6-8
Hunt	Up a Road Slowly	1967	6-9
Konigsburg	From the Mixed up Files of Mrs. Basil E. Frankweiler	1968	4-6
Alexander	The High King	1969	5-9
Armstrong	Sounder	1970	7-9
Byars	The Summer of the Swans	1971	5-6
O'Brien	Mrs. Frisby and the Rats of NIMH	1972	5-7
George	Julie of the Wolves	1973	4-6
Fox	Slave Dancer	1974	5-6
Hamilton	M. C. Higgins the Great	1975	5-6

NEWBERRY MEDAL BOOKS (cont.)

Author	Title	Year	Grade
Cooper	The Grey King	1976	5-7
Taylor	Roll of Thunder, Hear My Cry	1977	3-6
Paterson	Bridge to Terabithia	1978	3-5
Raskin	The Westing Game	1979	5-9
Blos	A Gathering of Days	1980	6-8
Paterson	Jacob Have I Loved	1981	6-8

RESOURCE BOOKS ON LITERATURE FOR CHILDREN

If you are having trouble finding specific books that deal with specific situations, you may want to consult one of the following resource books:

ADELL, JUDITY, and KLEIN, HILARY DOLE. *A Guide To Non-Sexist Children's Books.* Chicago: Academy Press Limited, 1976.

CARDOZO, PETER, and MENTEN, TED. *The Whole Kids Catalog.* New York: Bantam Books, 1975.

CHILDREN'S BOOK COUNCIL. *Children's Books: Awards and Prizes.* New York: The Children's Book Council, 1975.

EXERCISES

1. Design a language arts program with literature as its base.
2. Design a "web of possibilities" for a theme that will be interesting to your students. Select the theme based on your students' needs, interests, and abilities.
3. Create a lesson plan for teaching a poetry unit for your students. In your plan, list suggestions for using several types of media and make recommendations for integrating all the elements of poetry that you have studied in this chapter.
4. If you have students reading below grade level, select ten books that would be enjoyable and important for them to read. Specify the criteria you use in selecting these titles.
5. Select three stories that you may want to read with your students. Design lesson plans that will enable your students to integrate their knowledge of plot, setting, characterization, and theme.

REFERENCES

Bullock, A. "A Language for Life." Report of the Government of the United Kingdom, London, England, 1975.

Cazden, C. *Child Language and Education.* New York: Holt, Rinehart and Winston, 1976.

Cullinan, B. *Literature and the Child.* New York: Harcourt Brace Jovanovich, 1981.

Flood, J. "Parental Styles in Reading Episodes With Young Children." *The Reading Teacher* 30 (May 1977).

Jennings, S. "Effects of Sex Typing in Children's Stories on Preference and Recall." *Child Development* (March 1975): 220–223.

FURTHER READINGS

Cullinan, Bernice. *Literature and the Child.* New York: Harcourt Brace Jovanovich, 1981. A beautifully written, edited, and illustrated treasure on teaching children's literature.

Huck, Charlotte. *Children's Literature in the Elementary School,* 3rd ed. New York: Holt, Rinehart and Winston, 1976. A classic on teaching children's literature.

Smith, Dora. *Fifty Years of Children's Books.* Urbana, Ill.: NCTE, 1963. An excellent collection of book titles for children.

If we only used words as a communication code, then it seems probable that, as with animals, the human species would have only one language with, at most, dialect variations like the song of the chaffinch.

—*W. H. Auden*

12 LANGUAGE VARIATION

In this chapter, two topics are dealt with in some detail: nonstandard dialect, especially Black English, and English as a second language. To a certain extent, these are related topics, for the child from either a nonstandard dialect background or from a home where English is not primary (and may not be spoken at all) may come to school with apprehension about an "alien" environment.

DIALECTS

At the beginning of Chapter 2, we remarked that everyone talks. However, not every individual talks in the same way; nor does each of us speak in the same way all the time. Differences in speech (within the same language) that can be physically localized are referred to as geographical dialects. Thus, we can talk about Bostonian or Texan or Hoosier English. Even in specific locations, however, speakers in different socioeconomic strata express themselves differently. Furthermore, each of us speaks differently depending on the social context of the conversation. An individual's variations are customarily referred to as registers, or levels, of language (one of these is the baby talk register mentioned in Chapter 2).

Such diversity of speech apparently is found in every mature speaker of every language: He or she reflects geography, social class, and context in everything said. Thus, not only do the natives of Brooklyn, New York, speak differently from the natives of Tucson, Arizona (and have in some respects a different vocabulary), but the Brooklynite speaks differently when talking to his or her boss, mate, cronies at a bar, or dog. Further, Brooklynites of different socioeconomic status speak differently even when within the same social context (at the beach with their families, for example). The study of regional and social variation in language is called dialectology; the study of language in its social context generally is called sociolinguistics.

It is important that the teacher be aware of the social and regional variations within American English because one's students tend to come from a variety of geographical areas (Americans move around a good deal)

It must be obvious that not every individual talks in the same way; or that each of us speaks in the same way all the time. (*Photo by Linda Lungren*)

and from a variety of educational backgrounds and socioeconomic classes. It is also important to recognize that it is very difficult to brand one regional or social variant as better than another. The entire school of American descriptive linguistics, in fact, was dedicated to the inherent equality of all social and geographical dialects: Dialects were not better than one another, just different.

While a belief in the equality of dialects may be held by the linguist, it is not a commonly held belief within our society. At present, Southeastern American English has less prestige than New England or North Central English. It is only within recent years that radio and TV announcers were permitted to use anything but the dialect referred to as "Mid-Atlantic English" which was a hybrid of the speech of Ohio/Indiana and London, England. Furthermore, variants such as Appalachian or Black English are still looked down upon, although there is no objective reason for them to be seen as inferior.

In fact, many geographical terms used to refer to English dialects refer more to lower-class labels in terms of education, income, or ethnic origin than they do to geography: Both "Brooklynese" and "Cockney" are good examples of this phenomenon, since they can hardly be said to refer to the speakers of certain parts of New York or London, respectively. In fact, most speakers of "Brooklynese" switch freely between that dialect and regionally standard New York English, depending on their emotional state when they are speaking and on their audience.

Every speech community beyond a minimal size has a variety of dialects and language levels used within it, which are referred to as a verbal repertoire. There are special varieties within each repertoire (for example, "hippie" talk, mariner's talk, farm or ranch or microbiology talk) as well as social and regional varieties. In multilingual communities, where more than one language is spoken, all these varieties may exist within each of the languages used for intragroup communication: for example, Hebrew, English, and Yiddish among Jewish groups in New York; Hindi and English among upper-class speakers in India; and so on. We will return to the question of multilingual speakers later in this chapter.

LANGUAGE IN SOCIETY

While geographical varieties of a language (New York English, Parisian French, Peking Chinese, Viennese German, Cairene Arabic) are spatially determined, social dialects and individual language levels are governed by societal rules. We laugh at the verbal antics of parrots and macaws because these birds do not know societal rules and are thus delightfully indiscreet.

Varieties of language, then, are indicative of certain interests, backgrounds, and origins. They reveal the interests as well as the limitations of the speakers. The symbolic status of the variety comes to represent educational status or intimacy; racial or national status or ideology; employability or formality. We automatically mark speakers as being unintelligent or sexist or authoritarian, depending on their use of language. In this chapter, we will look at some varieties of English and their functions in the classroom. The later portion of this chapter will concern itself with speakers of languages other than English and how to cope with them in the classroom.

VARIETIES IN THE CLASSROOM

Well before the American Revolution, English travelers noted differences between the speech of white colonials and black colonials. Some of the earliest travelers saw Black English as a degenerate and debased form. One of the first preconceptions any teacher must get rid of is the notion that "different" means "inferior." It is important to realize that deviance in language variety is not intrinsically bad. While we attempt to instruct our students in "standard" American English, any of the regional dialects and Black English are acceptable communication vehicles.

While sociolinguists generally talk of seven different varieties of language, we are generally confronted by four in a teaching/learning environment: the standard language, usually the language of the literati, the government, and the schools; the vernacular, or general speech; the dialect; and the creole. The last is a language that has arisen from an earlier pidgin, which is a "contact" language, native to no one. It is a reduced form of two (or more) languages that are in contact, as in the Caribbean, the South Atlantic, and the South Pacific. In general, it is used in a simple range of situations and has a reduced structure. When children grow up basing their speech on such a pidgin, they enrich and expand it so that it can be used in all of life's many situations. Such an elaborated pidgin is a creole. A pidgin is the native language of no one; a creole has native speakers. Haiti possesses a creole variety of French, and several areas of the Caribbean have English creoles. Along the coast of South Carolina, Gullah, a true English creole, is still spoken.

By and large, we teach the standard language in the classroom, although we accept the vernacular in many situations. For the most part, we frown upon use of the dialect, and pidgins and creoles are definitely "out."

It is not important for the classroom teacher to attempt to do away with dialect differences, save in written expression. It *is* important for the classroom teacher to attempt to do away with the social stereotypes that traditionally have been associated with the speakers of some dialects.

SOME STEREOTYPES

One of the most common misconceptions about nonstandard dialects is that they are unsystematic, incomplete, or inferior versions of the standard language. Speakers of such dialects are frequently thought of as being less intelligent, of having cognitive handicaps, or of having slower language development. Basil Bernstein, for example, has associated what he terms "social deprivation" with cognitive deficits and lack of intellectual ability. It has been conclusively shown that Bernstein's claims (and those of other British and American sociologists and psychologists who have claimed to find racial components in higher mental functions) are false. It is important for us to try to deal with language attitudes because unfair evaluations may result: Teachers' attitudes influence their expectations, and teachers' expectations influence their students' achievement levels. The teacher's attitude towards the student's language thus influences the quality of the education the student receives.

In order to change language attitudes, we must develop a respect for linguistic diversity. Knowledge about specific dialects can reduce the misconceptions and the negative attitudes we have concerning them.

DIALECT DIFFERENCES

There are many ways in which dialects can differ from one another. They may have different phonologies, morphologies, syntaxes, and vocabularies. The phonological differences are the most obvious. We all note that the Bostonian

Pahks his cah in Hahvahd Yahd

dropping all the /r/ sounds. Or, we note the nasalization of many vowels in Brooklynese or the "drawl" of the South or of the Southwest.

Vocabulary differences are quite noticeable, too. In different parts of the United States, one can buy a "hero," or a "sub," or a "submarine," or a "grinder." With it one might get a "float," or a "soda," or a "phosphate," or a number of other things. In some parts of the country you can carry things in a "pail," in others the same object is a "bucket." And you can ask for the "check," the "bill," or the "ticket," depending on just where you are.

But it is the morphological and syntactic differences which cause the greatest classroom problems. In some varieties of American English, for example, the auxiliary verb *be* does not exist. We thus get forms like

He goin' home

and

Fred ridin' his bike now.

As further examples of differences in varieties of English, read the following samples of Black English:

1. A twelve year-old boy from Detroit.
Sometimes we think she's absolutely crazy. She come in the classroom she be nice and happy . . . the next minute she be hollering at us for no reason, she never have a smile, she'd be giving us a lecture on something that happened twenty years ago. (collected by Roger Shuy)

2. . . . all black poems ain't the same kind . . . certain poets hip you to something, pull the covers off or something or run it down to you, or ask you to just dig it—your coat is being pulled . . . every poet has written a bein poem. In fact, most poets start off writing them. Just writing about the way they be, they friends be, they lovers be, the world be ... We do not want subhumans defining what we be doing ... black poetry is becoming what it has always been but not quite beed.*

SOME ALTERNATIVES

Given that there are dialect differences, there appear to be three possible alternatives: (1) that we accommodate all dialects; (2) that we insist on standard American English at all levels of all schools; and (3) some intermediary position.

The first alternative would be founded in a general democratic belief that all dialects are equal and that no individual should be penalized because his or her dialect is held in lower esteem than that of someone else. This would entail our attempting to make use of each student's native form of English in the schools and setting up special programs to lessen interference between the native dialect and the acquisition of skills and information in the learning environment of the school. It would also require the full acceptance of dialectal variation within the industrial and business world, for otherwise the school-leaver would be unemployable, as so many nonstandard dialect speakers are.

The second position, requiring the use of standard English at every stage, is supported by the belief that possession of such a standard dialect is the prerequisite to future success. Following this notion would require that we set up special programs to instruct nonstandard dialect speakers in the standard dialect. We might set up special programs to teach standard English. The native dialect would be discouraged outside of school contexts, too. Slightly less extreme would be some acceptance of the native dialect, resulting in some form of "bidialectalism," much like the two-language situation known as bilingualism.

The third alternative falls between the two extremes and is the course usually followed. The native dialect is accepted for some uses while the standard dialect is required for others.

For example, in aiding the student in mastering certain skills in your school, you might develop a plan such as the following:

> In recognition of the fact that the vast majority of the written messages the student will encounter during his or her life will be in standard English, every student will be expected to develop the capability of reading and writing standard English. The students would not be required to eliminate their native dialect in their speaking, but their efforts would be directed

---

*Carolyn Rodgers, "Black Poetry—Where It's At." *Black World* (September 1969):7-16.

toward acquiring competence in dealing with the standard written forms of the language (the newspaper, letters applying for jobs, advertisements, instructions, etc.) both in reading and in writing. In this way, different dialects would be used by the student for different purposes.

In a classroom dedicated to instructing and raising the competency of students, such a middle road enables the teacher to teach the student to read and write the language he or she will encounter in the working world; at the same time, the student's confidence is maintained by not insisting on abandonment of the home dialect and by not making the nonstandard dialect speaker feel inferior. Over the years, the interactions have tended to change the dialect more and more. But the generally common southern background and the common reaction to ghetto life cannot explain completely the salient features of contemporary Black English. It appears that the unique character of Black English can only be understood in the context of a long separation from White English. Further, Black English still carries traces of its African ancestry.

While Americans in general appear to be quite tolerant of most regional variations, Black English has not been viewed as a social and cultural equivalent of standard geographical variants. This unquestionably reflects the longstanding inferior social position of the American black. Such attitudes are not merely common among whites. Blacks who have struggled for an education and have acquired the appropriate White English dialect have little patience with the language of the lower class.

It is the dismissal of his or her speech as inferior or incorrect that offers an insuperable problem to the black child in a primarily white school system. Communication with parents and with age peers on the street requires an entirely different language from the one required in school. The other side of the coin is that if the black child learns standard English in school, he or she cannot possibly use it at home or among cohorts. The language first acquired by the child is a rich and flexible medium and can be used expressively and effectively in most situations encountered in everyday life. It is for this reason that teachers have so little success in attempting to persuade black pupils to abandon their own language for a dialect that is quite unnatural—almost foreign. Thus, many students reject their education and all it stands for.

Years of classroom drills as well as exposure to radio, TV, and the movies have had a profound effect: Many blacks, even if they do not achieve the standard white dialect, go a good way toward it. They become excellent dialect switchers and control a middle-class dialect when talking to employers, and so on, but revert to their black dialect among family and friends. An interesting example of the rejection of dialect switching is:

> Robert Park was just another cat walkin' and workin' ... now this was a white dude trying to trick us into diggin' what some slave owners developed

about us (remember that they counted us as three-fifths of a man) . . . Park was the man most responsible in the social sciences for a liberal white game to run on Black people . . . in other words, we need to get this shit on, and for that we need a revolutionary script for the terrible black drama and cosmic forces we're about to rain down on these pitiful ofays.*

It is interesting that McWhorter, who holds a doctorate from the University of Chicago, has chosen to write in this style (which, incidentally, is neither Black English nor the standard dialect of American scholarly English).

A more genuine variety of Black English is found in this description of gangs in Los Angeles:

See, there's all kin'a li'l ol' groups on d'streets. Like you have you little clique—dey yo' tight partners—dey like d' set you get down with, get high, thump, you be together in d' neighborhood. Gots yo' so-called gangs—jus' make' em up. Like we call ourselves The Magnificent Seven! Seven people all we had. It was a gang to me. Like a hang-out at d' taco stand over near Broadway. Dat be our base. Like our territory around it, nobody mess wid us. They knew we had a hellified thang goin'! Den you got yo' righteous hope-to-die gangs—Parks, Outlaws, Businessmen, a few buildin' up now—Brim Boys. East side got Pueblos. Got they own little territory. You cross d'line, dey jam you! (T. J., in E. A. Folb, *runnin' down some lines*. Cambridge, Mass.: Harvard University Press, 1980, p. 77.)

Yet another register of Black English is the following, a part of the Gospel according to St. John (from *The Bible Translator* 2.2 [1969]: United Bible Societies):

John 3: 1–17: Black English Version
It was a man named Nicodemus. He was a leader of the Jews. This man, he come to Jesus in the night and say, "Rabbi, we know you a teacher that come from God, cause can't nobody do the things you be doing 'cept he got God with him."

Jesus, he tell him say, "This ain't no jive, if a man ain't born over again, ain't no way he gonna get to know God."

Then Nicodemus, he asks him, "How a man gonna be born when he already old? Can't nobody go back inside his mother and get born."

So Jesus tell him, say, "This ain't no jive, this the truth. The onliest way a man gonna get to know God, he got to get born regular and he got to get born from the Holy Spirit. They body can only make a body get born, but the Spirit, he make a man so he can know God. Don't be surprised just cause I tell you that you got to get born over again. The wind blow where it want to blow and you can't hardly tell where it's coming from and where it's

---

*Gerald McWhorter, "Ideology of a Black Social Science." *Black Scholar* (December 1969):28–35.

going to. That's how it go when somebody get born over again by the Spirit."

So Nicodemus say, "How you know that?"

Jesus say, "You call yourself a teacher that teach Israel and you don't know these kinds of things? I'm gonna tell you, we talking about something we know about cause we already seen it. We telling it like it is and you-all think we jiving. If I tell you about things you can see and you-all think we jiving and don't believe me, what's gonna happen when I tell about things you can't see? Ain't nobody gone up to Heaven 'cept Jesus, who come from Heaven. Just like Moses done hung up the snake in the wilderness, Jesus got to be hung up. So that the peoples that believe in him, he can give them real life that ain't never gonna end. God really did love everybody in the world. In fact, he loved the people so much that he done gave up the onliest Son he had. Any man that believe in him, he gonna have a life that ain't never gonna end. He ain't never gonna die. God, he didn't send his Son to the world to act like a judge, but he sent him to rescue the peoples of the world.

Some Characteristics of Black English

Linguistic differences can be phonological or morphosyntactic. We have selected a few characteristics in each category for mention in this section.

Phonological. In Black English, there is a tendency for the distinctions between /θ/ and /f/ and /ð/ and /v/ to disappear (be neutralized) in final position. This results in words such as *Ruth* and *death* being pronounced as homophones of *roof* and *deaf*.

/ay/ and /aw/ as in *find* and *found* lose their off-glides and merge with /a/, as in *fond*. Other vowels are neutralized before /l/ and /r/, so that *boil* and *ball*, *beer* and *bear*, and *poor* and *pour* become homonyms.

Postvocalic and preconsonantal *r* tends to be dropped, so that *guard* and *God*, *sore* and *saw*, and *fought* and *fort* become homophones.

Postvocalic *l* is dropped: *toll* and *toe*, *tool* and *too*, *help* and *hep*, *all* and *awe*, and *fault* and *fought* become homophones. (Note that this means that *fort*, *fault*, and *fought* are all pronounced in the same way.)

Final clusters tend to be simplified: *past* and *pass*; *men*, *meant*, and *mend*; *wind* and *wine*; and *hold* and *hole* become homophones.

Suffix loss. Contracted suffixes are generally dropped. Thus, *you're tired* become *you tired* and *he's tired* becomes *he tired*; *I'll go* becomes *I go*.

Tense changes. In several cases, Black English has a richer mode of expression than standard American English. A notable example of this is in forms such as *he busy* ("he is busy at the moment") as opposed to *he be* *busy* ("he is busy all the time" or "he is habitually busy"). Our standard dialect has no simple way of expressing this habitual form.

Plural markers. In working-class black communities, phrases such as *two card* or *all them book* are used. In Appalachian White English, the plural suffix *s* is similarly dropped in weights and measures: *six pound* and *fifteen mile* are heard, for example. A few black communities in the South normalize English in a different way: Instead of *two feet, two foots* is used, and in place of *some sheep, some sheeps*.

Other noun markers. The possessive, the comparative, and the superlative are also different in Black English. *My friend car* and *Henry seat taken* are examples of the way in which the possessive *'s* is omitted in black dialects.

As regards the comparative and the superlative, Black English has normalized the standard system. While standard English adds *er/est* for many words (*stronger, tallest*), for some two-syllable and for all longer words we use *more/most* (*more beautiful, most friendly, most sensational*). Black English uses the suffixes throughout: *beautifuler, awfulest*.

However, it must be repeated again: These are differences—they are not "reductions." Black English is as capable of expressing nuances and ideas as any other natural language. In some instances (as in the normalization of forms), it is carrying forward a normal historical process. In some cases (as with the habitual marker), it has "invented" a form that standard English does not possess. The obvious question then is, Why do we insist on our students learning standard English?

BLACK ENGLISH

Without wishing to get into either a detailed linguistic description or a history of Black English, let us make a few generalizations.

First, the language of most of the blacks in the United States shows many characteristics of Southern American English. Throughout the South, black speech has traditionally approximated white speech. In recent decades, the influx of southern blacks into northern cities, and their ghettoization, has given rise to a black speech that is different from that of the white speakers within the same metropolitan area. Thus, the general tendency to merge /i/ and /e/ before /n/ means that *pin* and *pen* are homophonous to most New York black speakers. This is not true of New Yorkers in general.

Furthermore, the northern black ghettos created their own social climate and gave rise to several changes in the southern speech style, so that there are generational differences between the native northern black and the more recent southern black immigrant to a northern city.

Black English and the Language Arts

Language is crucial at every stage of education. There is nothing we teach in the schools and in the universities that we do not teach by means of language. As a result, the language arts, and the teaching of them, are central within the educational system.

The answer to the question, "Should standard English be taught to all students?" is not a simple one. As we have said before, the middle-of-the-road position seems to be the best one: Yes, standard English should be taught to every child, because without the ability to read and understand, to speak and write in that standard dialect, we are cutting off a number of the routes the student may wish to follow in later life. By not teaching the student to communicate in the standard dialect, we may well be preventing him or her from entering the profession she or he is best suited for; from pursuing the educational choices offered; from achieving his or her potential in life. On the other hand, we must be careful not to destroy the student's social identity by scorning the nonstandard dialect, by making the student feel that the home dialect is an inferior or lower-class speech form.

But it is not easy to teach standard English quickly and easily to groups of students from diverse cultural backgrounds. What may be most important is not the insistence on the standard dialect, but the awareness of the classroom teacher and the school administration. Information about the language and culture situation and its consequences may be the most important tool in your teaching.

As has been said earlier, the two basic positions toward dialects may be labeled the difference and deficit points of view. It must be obvious that we feel most strongly about the difference viewpoint.

The fact that language differences do not reflect deficiencies is an important one, whether or not you decide to teach standard oral English in your classroom. The next most important fact is that you must set up a list of priorities. Sociolinguistic studies have shown that the use of nonstandard forms is viewed far more negatively than dialectal pronunciation. Thus, it may be of great importance for you and your school to make a conscious decision that grammatical usage rather than pronunciation should be the focus in the classroom. Alternatively, you might decide that capability in written communication is far more important than capability in oral communication. That the ability to read and write the standard dialect is more important than speaking it. Robbins Burling has identified the following as the priority list in terms of language skills in the classroom:

1. Ability to understand the spoken language of the teacher.
2. Ability to make oneself understood to the teacher.
3. Ability to read and understand conventional English.
4. Ability to speak with standard grammar.

5. Ability to write with conventions of standard written English.
6. Ability to speak with standard pronunciation.

The first two of Burling's points cannot be overemphasized. If the students cannot understand you and you cannot understand the students because of dialect differences, the educational battle has been lost from the outset. Making yourself knowledgeable where the dialect spoken by the children is concerned will enable you to plan your lessons and to be more effective in the classroom. Too often, misunderstanding of the dialect or total lack of comprehension either by student or by the teacher leads to the branding of the student as retarded or uneducable. This can be shown to stem quite frequently from the student's lack of comprehension of instructions or requests or from the teacher's lack of comprehension of the student's attitudes or responses.

Information about dialects and levels of language generally, and about the variety spoken by your students, is the most important factor in planning a well-organized, well-thought-out, effective program.

INTERACTIONS

Your students continue to exist outside your classroom. This means that you must pay attention to group reference factors as well as to individual ones. Before they enter your room and after they leave it, your students must communicate with each other, with their family and friends, and with the people in their neighborhood. To maintain these ties, they will have to maintain their dialect at the same time as they are acquiring aspects of the standard dialect in the classroom.

As mentioned earlier, this situation is known as bidialectalism. To a certain extent, each of us lives in a world of multiple dialectal continua. We speak differently among our friends outside the working place from the way we speak at school or in the university. However, for the most part, this difference is varietal; it is not as great as the difference between Black English and standard American English.

Bidialectalism has existed among blacks in the United States for a long time. Just before the turn of the century, the novelist and critic William Dean Howells termed Paul Laurence Dunbar "the first Negro voice of the freed slave population." Dunbar was born in Cleveland in 1872. Both of his parents had been slaves. He was valedictorian of his high-school class and found employment as an elevator boy. From 1893, when he was twenty one, to his death in 1906, at only thirty-four years of age, he wrote a large number of poems, plays, and novels. His poetry is in two voices: dialect and standard English. The following two poems illustrate his bidialectal ability.

The Poet And The Baby

How's a man to write a sonnet, can you tell,—
How's he going to weave the dim, poetic spell,—
   When a-toddling on the floor
   Is the muse he must adore,
And this muse he loves, not wisely, but too well?
Now, to write a sonnet, every one allows,
One must always be as quiet as a mouse;
   But to write one seems to me
   Quite superfluous to be,
When you've got a little sonnet in the house.
Just a dainty little poem, true and fine,
That is full of love and life in every line,
   Earnest, delicate, and sweet,
   Altogether so complete
That I wonder what's the use of writing mine.

Little Brown Baby

Little brown baby wif spa'klin' eyes,
   Come to yo' pappy an' set on his knee.
What you been doin', suh—makin' san' pies?
   Look at dat bib—you's ez du'ty ez me.
Look at dat mouf—dat's merlasses, I bet;
   Come hyeah, Maria, an' wipe off his han's.
Bees gwine to ketch you an' eat you up yit,
   Bein' so sticky an' sweet—goodness lan's!
Little brown baby wif spa'klin' eyes,
   Who's pappy's darlin' an' who's pappy's chile?
Who is it all de day nevah once tries
   Fuh to be cross, er once loses dat smile?
Whah did you git dem teef? My, you's a scamp!
   Whah did dat dimple come f'om in yo' chin?
Pappa do' know you—I b'lieves you's a tramp;
   Mammy, did hyeah's some ol' straggler got in!
Let's th'ow him outen de do' in de san',
   We do' want stragglers a-layin' 'roun' hyeah;
Let's gin him 'way to de big buggah-man;
   I know he's hidin' erroun' hyeah right neah.
Buggah-man, buggah-man, come in de do',
   Hyeah's a bad boy you kin have fu' to eat.
Mammy an' pappy do' want him no mo',
   Swaller him down f'om his haid to his feet!
Dah, now, I t'ought dat you'd hug me up close,
   Go back, ol' buggah, you sha'n't have dis boy.
He ain't no tramp, ner no straggler, of co'se;
   He's pappy's pa'dner an' playmate an' joy.
Come to yo' pallet now—go to yo' res';
   Wisht you could allus know ease an' cleah skies;
Wisht you could stay jes' a chile on my bres'—
   Little brown baby wif spa'klin' eyes!

We have presented these two poems here to show just how effectively the bidialectal voices can be manipulated by a good poet. In all likelihood, none of your students will be good poets; yet, they too can function well and eloquently. It is your job to ensure that they can do so effectively.

GENERAL GUIDELINES

1. The teaching of standard English must take into account the importance of the group reference factor. There must be some external motivation for the student to learn the standard dialect.
2. The teaching program must recognize clearly the goals for teaching standard spoken English. Here it is important for the situational nature of bidialectism to be emphasized. That is, the students must realize that they are not being forced to eradicate their dialect, but that there are situations in which the standard mode of expression is more important, and others in which the dialect is more important.
3. The teaching of standard English should be coupled to information concerning dialect diversity, so that the students will recognize the integrity of their own dialect within the larger language system.
4. The teaching of English should be based on the systematic differences between the dialect and the standard language. The dialect should not be treated as though it were a random assortment of words and forms, but recognized as a language system of its own, corresponding to the system of the standard dialect.
5. The standard dialect taught should be a real dialect, not some fictitious, textbook dialect. A formal variety of "stage English" is not appropriate to the classroom.
6. The teacher must realize that the student will be speaking his or her ordinary dialect outside the classroom. While this will not obliterate the teaching, it will certainly have some influence. It is to the teacher's advantage to emphasize the situational nature of using the nonstandard dialect among friends and family and the standard dialect in the classroom and, eventually, in the working world.

TEACHING THE STANDARD DIALECT

The "Ann Arbor Decision" of July 12, 1979, required the school board to (1) "help the teachers... identify the children speaking black English..." and (2) "use that knowledge in teaching such students how to read standard English." It has been our intention to provide you with enough information about dialects and Black English to enable you to come to grips with the problems and language capabilities of your students. With knowledge and good will, it should not be difficult for any school board to comply with the intent of Justice Joiner's decision.

BILINGUALISM

Many of the people living in North America speak one language at home and a different one at work or at school. Many, in fact, conduct their everyday lives in two, three, or four languages. Rather than differentiate between those who speak two languages and those who speak more than two, we will refer to the phenomenon of using more than one language as bilingualism, and to those using more than one language as bilinguals.

Because most of you will be teaching language arts in the classroom, in the pages that follow we will confine ourselves to questions that concern children.

NATIONAL LANGUAGE

In Switzerland, three languages are "official": French, German, and Italian. A fourth language (Romansh) spoken in the country, is tolerated, but is not an "official language." In Canada, French and English are both "official languages," but only on a federal level. On a more local level, each locale is either French or English.

The national language of the United States is English. For this reason, speakers of languages other than English must become bilingual if they wish to take advantage of what the country has to offer and to participate in the national life of the United States. Unlike many other countries, the United States does not encourage children born into English-speaking families to acquire some other language. Children from linguistic minorities are expected to become bilingual; children from the English-speaking majority are not.

Most of the children of the immigrants who came to this country before World War II wanted to assimilate to the dominant culture. Whether they were Czech, German, Greek, Irish, Italian, Russian, or Scandinavian, the immigrants wanted to move into the mainstream and to become successful economically and educationally. By the second generation of residence, they usually succeeded. (In many cases, there were children who subsequently could not communicate with their own grandparents.) Although the force was not as great, many of the nineteenth-century Asian immigrants also assimilated.

However, there were some groups who did not immigrate to the United States but had the United States imposed upon them: the Native American peoples; Spanish speakers in what had been the Mexican territory; the Acadian French who moved to Louisiana; and Puerto Ricans conquered by the United States. These groups have maintained linguistic and cultural identities for generations and have not become part of our great melting pot. It is unclear whether this is because these groups did not wish to assimilate, or because they have not been allowed to assimilate. The result is quite clear: a discouraging prognosis made up of poor housing, poor nutrition, poor education, poorly paying jobs, and resultant negative self-concepts.

INTERVENTION TECHNIQUES

Because English is our national language and because we recognize the price paid by the bilingual in terms of inadequate education (and all that goes with inadequate early schooling), a number of intervention techniques were established to aid these "disadvantaged" children.

Project Head Start was perhaps the most notable of these programs. It was intended to narrow the experiential gap between the "disadvantaged" child and the school's expectations.

The points that must be recognized by educational (and by minority) groups are as follows:

1. Teachers and children both come from backgrounds that have their own attitudes, expectations, and skills; these will rarely be identical.
2. Bilingual children come from environments and have experiences that are different from those expected or desired by the school.
3. Teachers' degrees and experiences are not clearly related to their students' needs.
4. It is social class membership that seems to determine teachers' attitudes and expectations.
5. Teachers' attitudes and expectations result in differential responses to linguistically and culturally different children.
6. As children tend to adopt the majority view of themselves as their own view, they tend to live up to the negative or positive expectations of teachers and other adults.

The most important time to begin working with the bilingual child appears to be in the preschool years, between the ages of three and five. But even later, in your classroom, it is the children's own experiences that must be built upon in forming the goals for your language arts program. These experiences are both linguistic and cultural and, as with the speaker of Black English, we cannot isolate the bilingual from his or her culture. It is of prime importance to recognize that we cannot enculturate a child into our dominant English society if we strip him or her of all respect or regard for the home society. We must appreciate and recognize the minority culture in bringing the child to appreciate the majority culture.

The most important time to start with the bilingual child appears to be in the preschool years, between three and five. (*Photo by Linda Lungren*)

LEARNING A SECOND LANGUAGE

For the child born into a bilingual environment, acquiring two languages appears to be no more difficult than acquiring one. While there have been several claims that being in a bilingual environment slows language development, there does not appear to be any conclusive evidence to support this. It is true that many bilingual children appear to acquire first words—in both languages—rapidly, then slow down in their development (perhaps they require a "sorting out" period). By puberty, they are either at "normal" level or, because of the enrichment of a second culture, above normal level.

Acquiring a first language (or languages) appears to be tied to the child's cognitive development. For this reason, a child acquiring a second language after acquiring a first is not in the same position as the child acquiring two languages simultaneously. In considering the child from a non-English cultural background entering first grade with little or no English, we must recognize that up to that time he or she has spent eight to twelve hours every day (for four or five years) in another language environment. The few hours spent in school for only five days a week are a mere fraction of the total immersion time dedicated to the home language. Yet, we attempt to bring children to levels of "equivalent" competence in this short space of time.

As we have said, first-language acquisition appears to have some relationship to cognitive development. But second-language acquisition is based on a first language. In the one case, the child must learn to express (new) meanings in terms of verbal expressions; in the other, the child must learn a new way to express concepts that are already there in another form. That is, if a Spanish-speaking child is acquiring English, there are few notions he or she must express in the "new" language that were not already there in the "older" language. For many people, learning words in a foreign tongue means relating sequences of sounds to English words, not relating those sequences of sounds to the things the English words represent. In other words, for many people the second language is always mediated through the first language.

It appears to be easier for children to make this transition than it is for teenagers and adults. Just why this is true is unclear, although it may be related to maturational events such as the onset of puberty. Younger children are also more likely to be affected by their age peers in the new linguistic environment of the school, to be more perceptive to nuances of sound differences, and to be more apt at relating speech to its context. The last, of course, is a direct function of the child's pragmatic attitude to language, which has been discussed in Chapter 2.

THE BILINGUAL CHILD IN THE CLASSROOM

Coming from a non-English cultural background, the bilingual child may well be bewildered by the Western classroom. Much of what is done there must appear to be strange, and the language used is not the one used at home or by the familiar authority figures of the home environment. This is even more true of children from Native American (Amerindian, Aleut, Eskimo) backgrounds than it is for children of Hispanic backgrounds. Fully 60 percent of the native population never reaches the eighth grade.

Here, as we have said before, you must try to understand just what the child's home culture and home community are like. The following will give you some idea of the problems encountered:

> His teacher is likely to be a Caucasian who knows little or nothing about his cultural background. He is taught to read the Dick and Jane series. Many things confuse him: Dick and Jane are two *gussuk* (Eskimo term for "white person," derived from the Russian Cossack) children who play together. Yet, he knows that boys and girls do not play together and do not share toys. They have a dog named Spot who comes indoors and does not work. They have a father who leaves for some mysterious place called "office" each day and never brings any food home with him. He drives a machine called an automobile on a hard-covered road called a street which has a policeman on each corner. These policemen always smile, wear funny clothing, and spend their time helping children to cross the street. Why do these children need this help? Dick and Jane's mother spends a lot of time in the kitchen cooking

a strange food called "cookies" on a stove which has no flame in it, but the most bewildering part is yet to come. One day they drive out to the country, which is a place where Dick and Jane's grandparents are kept. They do not live with the family and they are so glad to see Dick and Jane that one is certain that they have been ostracized from the rest of the family for some terrible reason. The old people live on something called a "farm," which is a place where many strange animals are kept: a peculiar beast called a "cow", some odd-looking birds called "chickens," and a "horse," which looks like a deformed moose.... (*Bilingual Schooling in the United States.* Washington, D.C.: Office of Education, 1972, p. 72.)

Keeping this in mind, is it at all strange that so many children from non-English backgrounds find our schools strange and repellent places? And as a result of feeling alienated by the materials, in an environment they do not comprehend, and confronted by a system which apparently considers the child's home culture as inferior, is it any wonder that so many bilingual and bidialectal speakers become discipline problems? Keep in mind that people identify with their language, and by maligning the non-English languages or nonstandard dialects, we are cutting down the child's self-image; effectively we are telling the child that he or she is not as good as other children from the dominant culture.

Knowledge and understanding are the keys to the language-learning environment.

Bilingual reading

It is over a decade since Paul A. Kolers of the University of Toronto demonstrated that fluent bilinguals read as well in one language as another and, in fact, read "mixed" passages without hesitation. That is, he presented readers with passages to be read aloud where some phrases were in French and others were in English. Obviously, for the adult bilingual, the two language systems are integrated to a very great extent.

But what of the child who speaks one language far better than the other, and who is just acquiring reading as a skill? For such a child, the chore is a more difficult one, but it is not insurmountable.

The most important factor is the conscious recognition that bilingual children are not disadvantaged. With proper teaching, sometimes in the native language, sometimes in English, the bilingual child will soon be able to communicate in two languages. Obviously, the capabilities of the teacher to handle more than one language will be of importance here, and will, of course, dictate the language to be used in reading instruction. But awareness of the constraints will enable even a monolingual teacher to achieve success.

The bilingual child's special needs are in three areas:

Self-Concept
Ethnic Heritage
Language.

We have already discussed the first two of these. Let us now turn to the third.

Language Needs of Bilingual and ESL Students

Bilingual children need to speak English before they learn to read English. This may seem like a silly thing to say, but adult learners, who already read their native language, frequently learn to read English before speaking it. But a child who does not read at all, apparently needs to learn to speak a language before learning to read in it.

With this understood, there are apparently four categories in which bilingual children may require instruction:

1. Experiential/informational/conceptual background. Children frequently find it difficult to read about things that are totally outside their experience. The Office of Education's report cited above has innumerable instances of such lack of background. The Eskimo anecdotes are good examples.

2. Auditory discrimination. Because the phonological structures of different languages are never identical, the child from a non-English background may have trouble learning which sounds are relevant in English and which are irrelevant. For example, the initial sounds of *key* and *cup* are "identical" in English, but significantly different in Arabic. Similarly, the "k" sounds of *key* and *ski* are identical in English, but different in Hindi.

3. Vocabulary. In dealing with Hispanic students, for instance, one must beware of "false cognates": words which look or sound similar, but have quite different meanings. For example,

libreria	bookstore, *not* library
chanza	joke, *not* chance

4. Syntax, especially word order. Many languages, such as French and Spanish, permit or prefer placement of adjectives after nouns.

La casa blanca	the white house
Les livres jaunes	the yellow books

Other languages, like Russian, do not use the copula verb in the present as English does. Speakers of other languages may be confused about the use of *to be* in English, resulting in forms like

> Lamp here
> Today he work in store
> Freddy in school

Plurals, comparatives, and possessives are other forms which tend to give language learners trouble:

> My tooths hurt
> This book is more heavy
> Is black the pen of Jim

EXERCISES

1. Survey members of your community, asking them to give their name for the following:

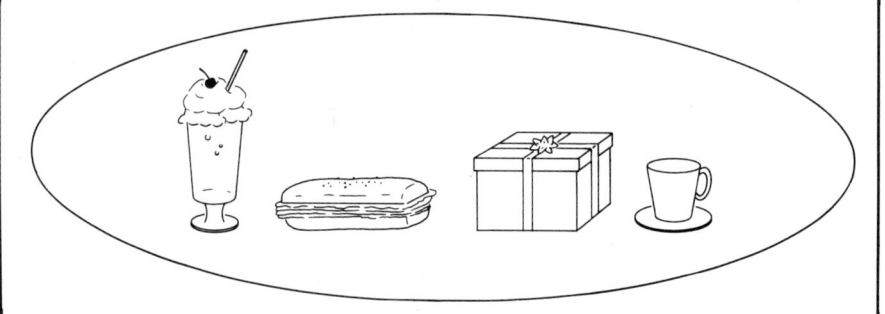

2. Begin to plan a language arts program for your bidialectal students by listing your criteria for correcting written and oral errors.
3. Design a beginning reading/writing program for a child from a bilingual back ground.

REFERENCES

Board of Education of the City of New York. *Nonstandard Dialect*. Urbana, Ill.: NCTE, 1968.
FISHMAN, J. A. *Sociolinguistics*. Rowley, Mass.: Newbury House, 1970.

KOCHMAN, T., ed. *Rappin' and Stylin' Out: Communication in Urban Black America.* Urbana, Ill.: University of Illinois Press, 1972.

LABOV, W. *Language of the Inner City: Studies in the Black English Vernacular.* Philadelphia: University of Pennsylvania Press, 1972.

REED, C. E. *Dialects of American English.* Amherst, Mass.: University of Massachusetts Press, 1967.

SHUY, R. W. *Discovering American Dialects.* Champaign, Ill.: NCTE, 1967.

SMITHERMAN, G. *Talkin' and Testifyin': The Language of Black America.* Boston: Houghton Mifflin, 1977.

TRUDGILL, P. *Sociolinguistics.* Harmondsworth, Middlesex: Penguin Books, 1974.

FURTHER READINGS

FISHMAN, J. A. *Sociolinguistics.* Rowley, Mass: Newbury House, 1970. Probably the best brief introduction to the sociology of language.

SMITHERMAN, G. *Talkin' and Testifyin': The Language of Black America.* Boston: Houghton Mifflin, 1977. An interesting discussion of the styles of Black English.

Most modern books on bringing up children warn parents against projecting their own ambitions onto their children and demanding of them a high standard of achievement. It seems to me that this warning is merited only in cases where there is no relation between the parents' ambition and the child's actual endowments.

—W. H. Auden

13 STUDENTS WITH SPECIAL NEEDS

After discussing "difference" and "disorder," this chapter concerns itself with the various types of disorders and disabilities you may encounter. Deafness and dyslexia are examined as well as speech and language disorders. The consequences of PL94-142 for your classroom are introduced. The last part of this chapter discusses other special children you may encounter: the gifted.

DIFFERENCES AND DISORDERS

Many school systems have screening procedures designed to aid in identifying children with oral language problems. Sometimes, it is left up to the individual classroom teacher to recommend specific children for speech therapy. It is important that you carefully distinguish between a dialect difference and a disorder.

The crucial consideration in determining what is a difference and what is a disorder is the standard of the student's home community: Even if the child does not appear to comprehend you or is not comprehensible to you, he or she has no disorder if family and playmates are comprehended and are spoken to. Only if the child has difficulty communicating with parents and peers should you consider referring him or her for therapy.

Thus, once again, the most important information you can have concerns the community dialect of the children in your classroom. Understanding normal language variation and possessing some knowledge of the local dialect will enable you to discriminate dialect difference from language disorder.

You may also need some information to react to the classifications made by others. For example, a black working-class child might use *f* in *birfday, toof,* or *baf* and thus be diagnosed as having a pronunciation disorder. But an alert teacher would note that the child uses *f* for *th* in the middles and ends of words, never initially (*thick* would be pronounced appropriately); and, furthermore, that other speakers in the child's community use such forms. You would thus be able to note that the child was using a regular rule of the speech community and would argue against the diagnosed need for therapy.

When you are in your classroom, it is important that you carefully weigh just what is a dialect difference, and what is a disorder. Our classrooms encompass a wide range of oral language abilities. (*Photo by Linda Lungren*)

SPEECH AND LANGUAGE DISORDERS

Language disorders are not the same as speech disorders. Of course, the first impression any child makes upon us is a visual one, but the next most important impression is the verbal one. If the child speaks with good articulation, even if she or he does not say much, we mark him or her as being "O.K." If the pronunciation is notably deviant, we immediately classify the child as slow, or behind grade or age level, or defective. It is only later that we may notice that the child speaks very little or only one or two words at a time or in only a few sentence types. In Chapter 2, we discussed language acquisition at length. You will recall that age is a very poor basis on which to predict linguistic development in children. Not only first words and first sentences, but every other milestone occurs at a wide range of onset times. Putting a child together with age peers does not guarantee that the language (or the dentition) of the children will "match."

When a speech pathologist speaks of language disorders, one or more of the following are most often meant:

1. Delay—a significant lag in expected linguistic development; the child's productive speech is that of a much younger child.

2. Childhood aphasia—severely delayed language development, frequently accompanied by a number of other problems including articulatory ones and neurological "soft" signs (those behaviors that are exhibited by children with demonstrable brain damage, when found in other children who do not have that damage).

3. Psychological problems—emotional disorders, psychoses, and so on. Some children, especially those from home environments dramatically different from that of the school (usually for cultural reasons), refuse to speak at all in school, although they indulge in oral expression with family and peers away from school. These children are referred to as electively mute, because they have "decided" not to participate. Because many electively mute children are from bilingual environments, this problem was discussed in Chapter 12.

4. Autism—this is sometimes termed childhood schizophrenia and involves strange habitual behaviors on the part of the child (rocking back and forth, running on tiptoe, and other more violent and self-destructive activities).

5. Learning disability—which many consider to be the result of subtle language problems.

6. Mental retardation—from whatever cause, mental retardation usually results in language "delay," together with general developmental slowness.

Speech disorders, in general, may be classed under the following categories:

1. Articulation—disturbances in speech-sound production. The majority of children in public-school speech correction are there because of "functional" pronunciation problems with no accompanying organic problem.

2. Voice—this refers to an excess or an insufficiency along three parameters: loudness, pitch, and vocal quality. These may be either or-

ganic or functional (see below) and are primarily the result of faulty respiration (breath control), phonation (control of the glottis and larynx), or resonance; this disorder may be linked to the neurological and endocrine systems (as in the voice control in pubescent boys).

3. Fluency—this generally refers to two phenomena: stuttering and cluttering. Stuttering is usually confined to sound and syllable repetitions that disrupt the flow of speech. Cluttering is the introduction of extraneous sounds into the flow of speech (*uh,* gasps, wheezes, and so on). Cluttering is frequently confused with stuttering and is sometimes considered to be a subclass of it.

In talking about voice, we referred to organic and functional disorders. Organic disorders are those that arise from observable physical and neurological defects: cleft palate, cerebral palsy, traumatic aphasia, dental problems, and so on. Functional disorders are those resulting from psychological problems, environmental influences, and bad habits. Within this framework, fluency problems are always functional, while articulation and voice problems may be either organic or functional. In our view, traumatic and childhood aphasia and mental retardation are always organic. There are debates within the field of speech pathology about this, but it is not necessary for us to go into the arguments here.

DEAFNESS

You cannot learn to talk adequately if you cannot hear. Your speech will be imperfect in quality if you cannot hear well. It is therefore of great importance to know whether every child in your class can hear adequately. If any child has a hearing impairment, it is necessary to have him or her tested by a competent audiologist and, if necessary, equipped with an aid or supplied with special instruction by teachers of the deaf. A child who cannot hear you, or cannot hear you well, will not profit from your teaching, no matter how good it is.

There are a variety of causes of deafness: genetic factors, disease (both on the part of the young child and on the part of the pregnant mother-to-be), trauma (blows to the head, objects in the ear), and so on. There are also varying degrees of severity of hearing loss.

By and large, most audiologists and teachers of the deaf recognize the following:

Mild hearing impairment
Moderate impairment
Severe impairment
Profound hearing loss

Whatever method of assessing or evaluating degrees of hearing loss your school district uses, it is vital to the deaf child's well-being that you and the other teachers understand his or her handicap.

The deaf are not retarded; they are not uneducable. These may be the most important things we can say about the subject. Far too many people, even teachers who ought to know better, act as though deafness was intimately associated with other cognitive or mental deficits. It is not. While we do not treat the blind—who suffer from a sensory loss—as though they were feebleminded, we tend to treat the deaf in that way.

Nevertheless, it is foolish to maintain that the deaf child is like any other child, save for an auditory deficit. Deafness, in whatever degree, necessarily brings a modification to the entire individual. Psychologically, there is a difference between the child with five senses and one with four.

The effects of deafness are the same, no matter what the cause. Obviously, the child who loses the ability to hear at age five, after he or she has acquired speech and language, will not be as handicapped as one born profoundly deaf. Still, deaf babies are no different from other babies during their first months. They babble and coo, much as other babies do. However, because the baby cannot hear its own or other voices, these babbling sounds never develop into articulate speech.

THE SPEECH OF THE DEAF

By and large, deaf people do not speak well. Their voices, when they speak, often do not sound "right." This is because the deaf person cannot hear himself or herself. There is no feedback from the speech mechanism as there is with most of us. When you say something, you hear yourself say it. You sometimes correct yourself if what you have heard yourself say does not sound right. This is impossible for the deaf. Because deaf students cannot hear you, nor themselves, they cannot monitor what they are saying.

Depending on how literate the deaf person is, and on whether he or she has been brought up using American Sign Language of the Deaf (ASL), finger spelling, or Exactly Signed English, his or her speech may be grammatically correct or it may lack certain markers. ASL, for example, has a different word order from English and has no definite article. Signed sentences are thus quite different from their spoken equivalents. The speech of a good signer may be quite poor. On the other hand, Exactly Signed English gestures all the grammatical markers of spoken English in the order of spoken English. While the pronunciation of such a signer may be no better than that of an ASL signer, the speech produced may be better grammatically.

It is important to note that in your classroom the deaf child may well be like a foreign child in the same room: The language he or she is required to read and write is different from that signed, in much the same way as the language of the classroom differs from that of the foreign child's home.

THE LANGUAGE OF THE CEREBRAL PALSIED

Cerebral Palsy is the result of damage to the motor portions of the nervous system. It may affect only a small part of the victim's body (one arm, for example) or it may be quite general. As with the deaf, there is no concomitant intellectual deficiency, although there may be some cognitive deficits. The main problem is one of motor control. Just as the palsied may have trouble walking or holding a pen, he or she may have severe problems coordinating the muscles involved in speech. In general, the speech of the palsied is slower in rate and more poorly articulated than that of normal children. Because there is usually no problem where the input channels are concerned, the speech of the palsied does not generally differ in terms of grammar or vocabulary from that of normal children, although there are tremendous articulation problems.

THE SPEECH OF THE RETARDED

The speech of the retarded individual is just that: retarded. Although the mentally retarded do learn to speak and to comprehend, their speech and comprehension are frequently like those of a much younger child. The rate of speech may be quite slow, and the syntax and variety of sentence types generally will be impoverished. One of the problems that occurs when working with the retarded child is assuming understanding where there is none. The retarded child is not likely to ask questions or to interrupt to have something explained. In many cases, the child will merely sit and let things go by. As the vast majority of mentally retarded people are mildly, not severely, retarded, it is important for you to attempt to bring them into your classroom, to make them active rather than docile.

SOME LAST WORDS

We have discussed all these issues because as a teacher of the language arts you must know something about the varieties of language you will encounter in the classroom. Such language variation encompasses not only the regional and social dialects of English we have discussed but also the defective forms of English caused by various speech and language disorders and by deafness. Within your school district, there are a variety of professionals who will know how to diagnose and prescribe for the deviant speaker (or nonspeaker) in your classroom. Do not hesitate to use this expertise. If you discover, for example, that Freddie does not turn around when a balloon is popped, have him sent for hearing testing. If Alice has not said a word in the first two weeks of school, she should be referred to a qualified psychologist. If she comes from a nonstandard language background or from a dramatically different culture, someone from her own background should try to extract some communicative behavior from her, if possible. It will prove invaluable in the long run to seek help for the child, and possibly professional intervention, as early in the child's school career as possible.

If our goal is to educate the child, then we must attempt to deal with every aspect of the child. We must try to understand dialects not our own so that we do not handicap children who speak those dialects in their quest for an education (and a better future as a result of that education). We must try to comprehend the problems of the physically handicapped so that these children too will receive the best education available. We must try to comprehend the limitations of the intellectually handicapped so that they will be educated to the extent that they are able. Finally, we must try to enable every child to reach whatever goals he or she can attain so that the children will become happy and productive members of our society.

PL94–142

PL94–142 requires that our schools integrate, as far as is possible, the handicapped and disadvantaged into our classrooms. This is a wise move as regards both "normal" children and the disabled, but it makes your job as a classroom teacher more difficult.

It is good for normal children because it makes them aware of the nature of specific handicaps; it is good for handicapped children in that they are not kept segregated and have greater contact with "reality" than they would if they spent all their time in special classes or special schools. The situation is difficult for you, the teacher, because it requires that you differentiate among your children in terms of workload and activity level to a greater extent than previously. It may mean that for many activities you will have to divide your class into different groups: sometimes by ability level, sometimes by activity level. It means that you must have a better understanding of both the abilities and special needs of your children. Assignments that are beyond the abilities of some of your children will not educate them, but will merely frustrate them. Just because a child is hard-of-hearing, partially sighted, or confined to a wheelchair does not mean that he or she cannot be educated or that she or he should be shunted away from the other, "normal" children.

The handicapped can and should be productive members of our society; integrating them into the mainstream classroom is a first step in this direction.

LANGUAGE ARTS AND THE EXCEPTIONAL CHILD

Generally, when educators talk of exceptional children, they are referring to the exceptions from the norm on only one end of the curve: children with language deficits or those from different home environments. While we acknowledge that this is the result of a longstanding belief that something must be done to help the development of the linguistically different learner, we wish to take issue with the other half of this proposition: that the gifted need no special attention. The usual attitude in our schools has been that gifted children can take care of themselves, that an additional book or two will keep them busy and quiet.

Unfortunately, this is not enough. The gifted need as much help as exceptional children at the other end of the scale. Merely adding work will not suffice; the gifted and talented child will see this as a time waster and may well become disruptive in innovative ways.

THE GIFTED CHILD

It may be worth making a few points about gifted children.

1. Gifted children are still children. They enjoy children's activities as much as their fellows. They need affection as much as any other child and, perhaps because they are different, they need reassurance, too.

2. Gifted children may be advanced in vocabulary, syntax, and reading ability, but they are still children of their own age. Just because a five-year-old is reading on the third-grade level does not mean that she or he will want to read *Charlotte's Web*. Most likely, the precocious reader will read the same books that his or her age peers enjoy having read to them.

3. There are degrees of creativity within the group we designate as gifted.

4. The gifted child tends to have broader interests than the normal child.

5. While some class leaders are among the gifted, many of these children, especially those who are creative in the arts or in conceptualization or imaginative play, may suffer socially because of their intellectual abilities. These children may need as much help in adjusting as do the handicapped exceptional students.

TEACHING THE GIFTED

The teacher of the gifted must possess several traits to face the challenge posed by the exceptionally able child. He or she must be sensitive to the classroom activities and must be able to react to the interests of the students with flexibility. The teacher must possess a great deal of resourcefulness, because the gifted child is apt to go off on tangents and a lesson in literature may well turn into an exercise in social studies or current events.

Nelson and Cleland (1967) studied gifted children and asked them about the characteristics of good teachers. The children said the important characteristics were a sense of humor, firmness and fairness, knowledge of the subject, an ability to encourage responsibility, understanding of children, enjoyment of teaching, and the ability to create a feeling of hope, not fear.

There are a variety of ways to teach the gifted student. Only two will be considered here: acceleration and ability grouping.

Acceleration

Acceleration is the method by which the gifted child is moved beyond his or her age peers in some way. "Skipping" grades, combining grades, and "covering" four years of material in three years are ways of accomplishing this. This experience may not be welcomed by the young gifted child. We know of the case of a girl who entered first grade with a tested reading level of 4-2. Her teacher arranged for her to do reading with a mixed 1-2 reading group, rather than with her regular K-1 group, into which she had been placed because she was the youngest first grader in the school. After a few weeks, the child complained to her parents, and after a month was placed back in her original class: She had felt ostracized, not elevated, by being sent to another class. Such feelings are not uncommon, and the teacher must always keep in mind that the gifted six-year-old is still a six-year-old.

Ability Grouping

Ability grouping mixes children according to their ability: Usually, this is judged by means of an IQ test. This procedure frequently results in whole classes with roughly similar abilities. The top and bottom groups of such students are thus in "special" classes; the middle groups in "regular" or "normal" classes. This appears to work quite well in the lower grades and in junior high school.

When dealing with a high IQ-ability group or an individual with a high IQ, one of the best things to do with the curriculum is to let the child's (or children's) varied interests determine the directions to be taken beyond the normal curriculum.

One of the units done in a sixth-grade class might be on ancient civilizations. Should students become interested in the pyramids or in the Roman ruins, one of the projects that might be suggested could deal with architecture: religious, domestic, and so on. We know about the pyramids and the Colosseum, but how did people live? What were Egyptian or Roman houses like? One child approached his teacher in sixth grade with an interesting question: If Marco Polo brought noodles to Italy from the East, and if rice was also a late import, and if potatoes came from the New World after the fifteenth century, what did Italians eat when they had no tomato sauce, no spaghetti, and so on? Questions about food and diet rarely come up in class, yet they make fascinating projects for gifted children.

It is because of instances such as these that the teacher of the gifted must be both flexible and resourceful: All the work, all the research these children do on their projects will be related to the language arts. They will have to read, digest, interpret, and write. Further, if you ask the child who has gone off on a tangent to explain to the class what he or she has learned, speaking will be involved, too.

Finally, if you have a gifted group or a gifted class, newspapers and magazines, dittoed or mimeographed, and written and laid out by the students themselves are of tremendous value. Everyone loves to see his or her name in print. Also, the rewards of having a story or poem, a memoir of a trip, or a factual report "published" to garner the praise of parents, grandparents, relatives, and friends cannot be underestimated.

EXERCISES

1. Walk around your school, college, or university. What sort of special access has been provided for the handicapped? What is missing? Are there places a person in a wheelchair might not be able to go?
2. Here is a list of special facilities available at one international airport:
    a. A TTY (telephone for the deaf)
    b. A "regular" pay telephone with amplification
    c. Two pay telephones at wheelchair height
    d. Special "stalls" in restrooms for wheelchair access
    e. Braille marking on signs
    f. Ramp access (no stairs)
    g. Water fountains at two heights

    How many of these are available at your facility? Can you think of other conveniences that might be made available?
3. You have been teaching a unit on Rome. A gifted child has asked about the way ordinary Romans lived. Set up a project involving everyday life in Rome, as well as life on a Roman farm, that would enable this child to satisfy his or her curiosity.

REFERENCE

Nelson, J. B., and Cleland, D. L. "The Roles of the Teacher of the Gifted." *Education* 88 (September 1967): 47–51.

FURTHER READINGS

Bery, M. F. *Language Disorders of Children.* New York: Appleton-Century-Crofts, 1969. An excellent survey of speech disorders.

Farnham-Diggory, S. *Learning Disabilities.* London: Open Books, 1978. The best recent summary of what we know about learning failure.

Knight, L. N. *Language Arts for the Exceptional: The Gifted and The Linguistically Different.* Itasca, Ill.: F. E. Peacock, 1974. A remarkable, succinct resource; one of the few books to talk about both the gifted and the "different."

Moores, D. F. *Educating the Deaf: Psychology, Principles and Practices.* Boston: Houghton-Mifflin, 1978. A good handbook on education for the deaf.

It is difficult, perhaps impossible, for us to form a complete picture of life because, for that, we have to reconcile and combine two completely different impressions—that of life as each of us experiences it in his own person, and that of life as we all observe it in others.

—*W. H. Auden*

14 ORGANIZING AND MANAGING YOUR PROGRAM

As you begin to organize your classroom for effective instruction, you will want to tailor your program to the needs of each of your students. The best way to do this is to individualize your instruction. However, before you plunge into this, it is important for you to consider several issues, which we will discuss throughout the chapter.

DEFINING INDIVIDUALIZATION

Simply stated, individualized instruction is instruction that meets the learning needs (built upon the learning strengths) of each child. You are individualizing by interest when you permit students to choose reading materials or to select topics for a writing assignment. However, there is

There is more to individualizing than permitting choices by interest. It also includes instruction based on children's abilities, skills, and knowledge. (*Photo by Linda Lungren*)

much more to individualizing than permitting choices by interest. You must also consider children's abilities, skills, and knowledge. Individualized instruction is not solely one-to-one instruction. It can encompass every possible teaching format as long as it meets students' needs. It uses whole-class presentations, small-group work, and individual work.

There are several ways that students can be grouped to accomplish the goals of individualization. They can be grouped on the basis of knowledge, interest, or skills. They can work on the same material (multiple copies) or they can work on individual tasks. The following is an illustration of the possible grouping formats:

Basis of Grouping	Types of Groups			Materials
	Small Groups	Whole Groups	One-to-One	
Knowledge Interest Skills	X	X	X	Same Materials
	X		X	Difficult Materials

DESIGNING AN EFFECTIVE PROGRAM

Now that you have a workable definition of individualized instruction, you can begin to establish your own program. The following seven steps will help you design an effective curriculum:

Step 1: Establish goals for your program.
Step 2: Assess students' abilities, needs, attitudes, and interests.
Step 3: Assess and select appropriate materials.
Step 4: Establish appropriate, flexible grouping patterns.
Step 5: Design your physical environment.
Step 6: Design appropriate instruction.
Step 7: Evaluate your program.

Step 1: Establish Goals for Your Program

It is important that you specify the goals of your program so that you can later evaluate whether you have met your goals. In addition to specific goals, most language arts teacher will want to have the following general goals:

Skills. To improve students' language skills in reading, writing, speaking, listening, and viewing.
Knowledge. To enable students to acquire basic information (knowledge) about forms of literature, film, and modes of writing.
Interest. To encourage students to broaden their interests in the communication processes.

As you consider these goals, you will realize that each is totally dependent upon the experience of the individual student. Improving one student's skills in reading will be quite different from improving another student's skills in reading. The second step in the process of establishing an individualized program, then, is to assess each student's needs, abilities, and interests in order to plan a personalized program.

Step 2: Assess Students' Abilities, Needs, Attitudes, and Interests

Assessment can be conducted in several ways—there is no single best method. Standardized paper-and-pencil tests are only one way to gather information when designing programs. In addition to norm-reference standardized tests, you can use diagnostic tests that include valuable information about the component skills of each of the general language arts. In a reading diagnostic test, you will be given information about each student's abilities in several of the skills and different aspects of comprehension. You can also gather valuable information from your own observations and informal teacher-made–criterion-referenced tests. When you construct your own test, you can design it for particular students or classes.

In addition to information about students' skills and knowledge, you should gather information about students' interests:

Interest Inventory

Name _____ Date _____

1. My favorite animal is _____ because _____.
2. My favorite color is _____.
3. The best book I ever read is _____.
4. My brothers and sisters _____.
5. My favorite sport is _____.
6. When I have free time, I _____.
7. My favorite television program is _____.
8. The movie I enjoyed most is _____.
9. The day of the week I like most is _____ because _____.
10. The person I admire most is _____ because _____ _____.
11. Reading is _____.

12. I like to read stories about _____.
13. The subject in school I like best is _____ because _____ _____.
14. The subject in school I don't like is _____ because _____ _____.
15. When it rains, I _____.
16. My hobbies are _____.
17. I am going to be a _____ when I grow up because _____.
18. Poetry makes me _____.
19. I wish my teacher would _____.
20. My parents _____.
21. Libraries are _____.
22. If I had three wishes, they would be
    1. _____.
    2. _____.
    3. _____.
23. My favorite food is _____.
24. I'd like to visit _____ because _____.
25. If I could be anywhere in the world right now I would be in _____ _____ because _____.
26. If I could do anything I wanted to do I would _____ _____.

To help you assess children's attitudes toward learning in language arts classrooms, you may want to ask them to complete Ransbury's Reading Attitude Inventory which was presented on page 281ff. As you begin to store this information, you will need a recordkeeping system to help you remember it. We will discuss this later in this chapter.

After you have compiled all this information, you can begin making text assignments. However, now you have a new problem. Which texts should you use?

Step 3: Select and Assess Appropriate Materials

As a first step in matching texts with students, you will want to determine the approximate readability levels of each of the texts you may use. In addition to using standardized readability formulas, you will also want to rely on your intuitive judgments about aspects of texts that are not assessed in the formulas: idiomatic language, concept complexity, syntactic complexity, and use of literary devices.

We have included one of the most popular readability formulas for you to use as a starting point in your assessment procedures.

Organizing and Managing Your Program

Graph for estimating readability
by Edward Fry, Rutgers University Reading Center, New Jersey

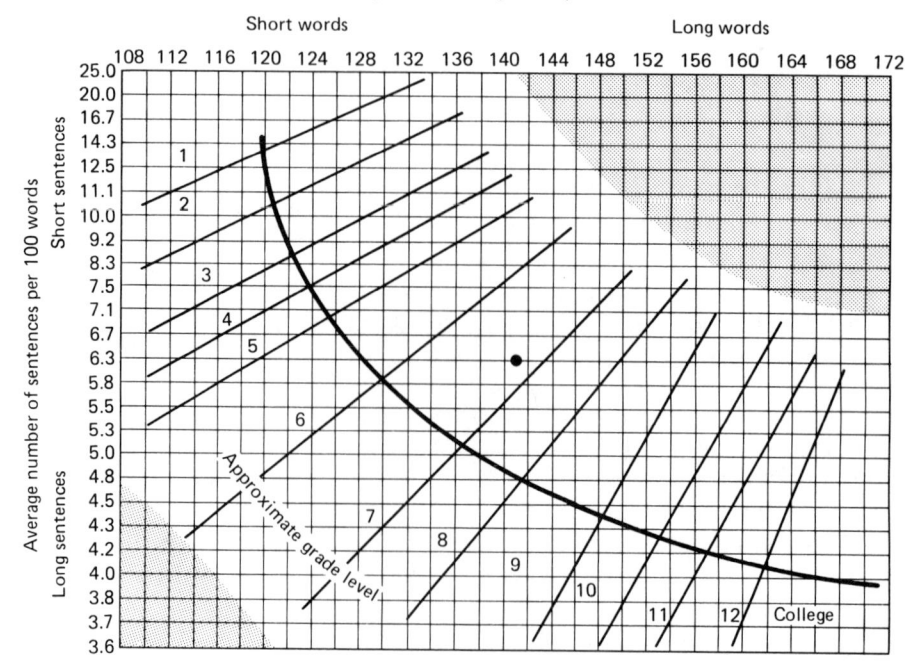

Directions: Randomly select 3 one hundred word passages from a book or an article. Plot average number of syllables and average number of sentences per 100 words words on graph to determine the grade level of the material. Choose more passages per book if great variability is observed and conclude that the book has uneven readability. Few books will fall in gray area but when they do grade level scores are invalid.

Example:

	Syllables	Sentences
1st hundred words	124	6.6
2nd hundred words	141	5.5
3rd hundred words	158	6.8
Average	141	6.3

Readability 7th grade (see dot plotted on graph)

How to Use the Fry Graph

1. Select three hundred-word passages from near the beginning, middle, and end of the book. Skip all proper nouns.

2. Count the total number of sentences in each hundred-word passage (estimating to the nearest tenth of a sentence). Average these three numbers (add together and divide by 3).

3. Count the total number of syllables in each hundred-word sample. There is a syllable for each vowel sound; for example: cat (1), blackbird (2), continental (4). Do not be fooled by word size; for example: ready (2), stopped (1), bottle (2).

4. Plot on the graph the average number of sentences per hundred words and the average number of syllables per hundred words. Most plot points fall near the heavy curved line. Perpendicular lines mark off approximate grade-level areas.

Cautions When Using Readability Formulas

When you are using a readability formula, you must be aware that it should be used *only* as an approximation of the difficulty of the material. In the following list, you will find the most frequent criticisms of readability formulas.

1. The resulting level is only an approximation of difficulty.
2. Varying degrees of reading difficulty may be found within one text.
3. The introductory chapters of a text are often the most difficult.
4. Content area materials often do not evidence a gradation of difficulty.
5. It is virtually impossible to hold constant all the factors that affect the difficulty level of reading materials; for example:

   Semantics
   Syntax
   Tone, mood, author's style
   context

Step 4: Establish Appropriate, Flexible Grouping Patterns

After gathering information on students' abilities and interests and on the difficulty level of texts, you will begin to wonder, "How do I teach all my students, who have such different needs and abilities?" You will want to begin by grouping students in ways that will help them begin at their own appropriate starting point and progress as rapidly and productively as possible. Writing single contracts for every one of your students for every day is not an efficient use of your time. Rather, you will want to use several different teaching formats: whole group, individual work, or small groups. You may want to use whole-group instruction when you are showing a movie or performing a play. You may want to use individual instruction when you are meeting to discuss a writing assignment.

If you are using small groups, you will want to construct your groups very carefully so that each child can learn as effectively as he or she is able.

340   Organizing and Managing Your Program

After gathering information on students' abilities and interests and on the difficulty level of texts, you will want to begin by grouping your students in ways that will help them begin at their own appropriate starting point and to progress as rapidly and productively as possible.   (*Photo by Linda Lungren*)

Group assignments should be based on three different criteria: skills, interests, and knowledge. Sometimes your students will be grouped by skills, sometimes by interests, and sometimes by knowledge. The following design illustrates these grouping patterns:

Grouping by Skills

Task: Learning capitalization rules	Task: Learning the use of the comma	Task: Learning the use of quotation marks
Sharon	Diane	Emily
Scott	Mary	Hanna
Anthony	Bart	Michael
Maggie	Robert	Frank
Linda	Karen	Lee
Keith	Lynne	Debbie
	Fran	

Grouping by Interests

Task: Library Research

Topic: Cookies	Topic: Sailing	Topic: Football	Topic: Beaches
Hanna	Lynne	Scott	Diane
Keith	Anthony	Sharon	Frank
Robert	Linda	Fran	Debbie
Lee	Bart	Michael	Maggie
Emily		Mary	
		Karen	

Grouping by Knowledge

Task: Learning the elements of plot in narratives	Task: Learning the authors of twentieth century America	Task: Learning the parts of the old Globe Theater
Sharon	Anthony	Linda
Diane	Lynne	Robert
Emily	Michael	Bart
Scott	Maggie	Lee
Mary	Karen	Keith
Hanna	Frank	Fran
		Debbie

It should also be pointed out that you can devise a system of group membership based on ability levels in whch each group performs the same task at different rates: for example, learning spelling words.

Step 5: Design Your Physical Environment

In order to establish a true language arts learning laboratory in which children have the opportunity to grow at their own pace, you will want to design a model classroom in which learning occurs quite naturally. Your room should include the following:

1. Learning centers
2. Work space
3. Quiet space
4. Library
5. Conference space

6. Access to materials
7. Adult space (for teachers, aides, volunteers)

You may design your room in the following way so that it includes access routes for all students to all parts of the classroom:

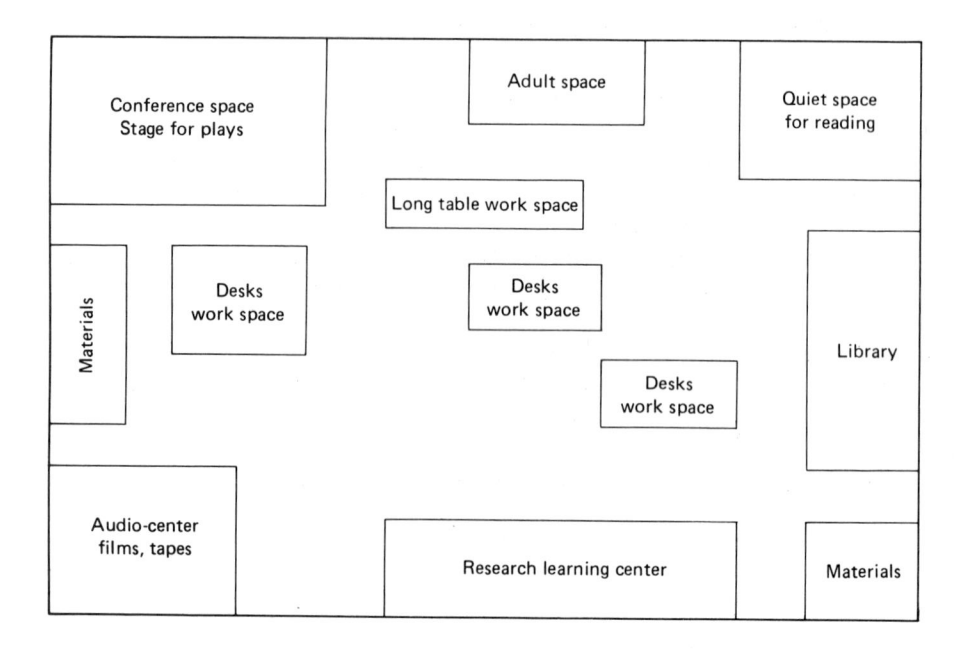

```
+------------------------------+------------------+------------------+
|                              |   Adult space    |                  |
|   Conference space           |                  |   Quiet space    |
|   Stage for plays            |                  |   for reading    |
|                              +------------------+                  |
+------------------+-----------+------------------+------------------+
|                  |           | Long table work space |             |
|                  |   Desks   |        Desks          |             |
|   M              |   work    |        work           |             |
|   a              |   space   |        space          |             |
|   t              |           |                       |   Library   |
|   e              +-----------+-----------+-----------+             |
|   r                                      |   Desks   |             |
|   i                                      |   work    |             |
|   a                                      |   space   |             |
|   l                                      |           |             |
|   s              +-----------+-----------+-----------+-------------+
|                  |           |                       |             |
|                  | Audio-center |                    |             |
|                  | films, tapes |  Research learning center  | Materials |
|                  |           |                       |             |
+------------------+-----------+-----------------------+-------------+
```

Step 6: Design Appropriate Instruction

Now that you have gathered information on each student's abilities, needs, and interests, as well as on textbooks, you have established a working physical arrangement for your classroom. You can design instruction that will meet these needs. The previous chapters of this book have provided you with ideas for structuring your lessons.

Step 7: Evaluate Your Program

It is important to evaluate your entire program, that is, your performance as a language arts teacher and the growth of each of your students in each of the language arts areas.

To help you evaluate your own performance, we have included a checklist of qualifications for language arts teachers, prepared by the National Council of Teachers of English. You should take time periodically to critically assess your own effectiveness.

Qualifications Needed by Language Arts Teachers

	Degree of development			
	Not developed			Highly developed
Qualification	1	2	3	4

KNOWLEDGE. Teachers of English need to know, and know how to draw on for their teaching, according to the needs and interests of their students:

1. processes by which children develop in their ability to acquire, understand, and use language, both oral and written, from early childhood onward;

2. the relations between students' learning of language and the social, cultural, and economic conditions within which they are reared;

3. the workings (phonological, grammatical, semantic) and uses of the language in general and of the English language in particular; and the processes of development and change in language;

4. linguistic, rhetorical, and stylistic concepts that furnish useful ways of understanding and talking about the substance, structure, development, and manner of expression in written and oral discourse;

5. the activities that make up the process of oral and written composing (these activities may differ among different students);

Qualifications Needed by Language Arts Teachers (cont.)

	Degree of development			
Qualification	Not developed 1	2	3	Highly developed 4

6. processes by which one learns to read, from initial exposure to language in early childhood, through the first stages of readiness-to-read, through more advanced stages by which the reader comes increasingly to understand and respond to details of meaning and nuances of expression;
7. an extensive body of literature in English (including literature for children and adolescents, popular literature, oral literature, nonwestern literature, and literature by women and minority groups);
8. varied ways of responding to, discussing, and understanding works of literature in all forms;
9. ways in which nonprint and nonverbal media differ from print and verbal media, and ways of discussing works in nonprint and nonverbal media;
10. ways in which nonprint and nonverbal media can supplement and extend the experiences of print and verbal media;
11. instructional resources (including educational technology) and varied sources of information (books, magazines, newspapers, tapes, recordings, films, pictures, and other nonprint and nonverbal

Qualifications Needed by Language Arts Teachers (cont.)

	Degree of development			
Qualification	Not developed 1	2	3	Highly developed 4

      materials) that will help students understand—through both intellect and imagination—the subjects and issues they are studying;

12. the uses and abuses of language in our society, particularly the ways in which language is manipulated by various interests for varied purposes;

13. problems faced and procedures used by teachers and educational leaders in designing curricula in English for students of different ages, abilities, and linguistic backgrounds;

14. the uses and abuses of testing procedures and other evaluative techniques for describing students' progress in the handling and understanding of language;

15. major research studies on acquisition and growth of language in children and adults, on reading, on response to literature, on the processes of composing, and on the building of curricula for different kinds of students in different settings.

ABILITIES: Teachers of English must be able:

16. to identify, assess, and interpret student progress in listening, reading, speaking, and writing;

Qualifications Needed by Language Arts Teachers (cont.)

Qualification	Degree of development
	Not developed 1 2 3 Highly developed 4

17. to take appropriate steps to help students improve their skill in responding to and using language;
18. to work effectively with students of different ethnic groups, including those who do not speak English as their native language;
19. to organize groups of learners for a variety of purposes appropriate to the English classroom, e.g., discussion, creative problem-solving, composing, and commenting on compositions;
20. to engage both the intellect and the imagination of students in their listening, reading, speaking, and writing;
21. to ask questions (at varying levels of abstraction) that elicit facts, opinions, and judgments that are appropriate to the subject and occasion;
22. to respond specifically and constructively to student discourse;
23. to communicate to students, parents, administrators, and officials the conclusions that can be legitimately inferred from results of tests purporting to measure progress in using and understanding language;
24. to set professional goals for themselves and evaluate their progress toward them;

Qualifications Needed by Language Arts Teachers (cont.)

		Degree of development			
	Qualification	Not developed 1	2	3	Highly developed 4
25.	to guide students in producing discourse that satisfies their own distinctive needs;				
26.	to help students distinguish between effective and ineffective discourse;				
27.	to help students experience the connection beween the experience of reading and the experience of writing;				
28.	to help students learn to observe and report accurately;				
29.	to help students distinguish among the language options (such as registers and levels of usage) open to them in various social and cultural settings;				
30.	to help students respond appropriately to the differing demands made on speech and writing by different contexts, audiences, and purposes;				
31.	to help both beginning and maturing readers apply varied techniques to improve reading comprehension;				
32.	to help students learn to listen effectively for information, for understanding and for pleasure;				
33.	to help students develop satisfying ways of responding to, and productive ways of talking about, works of literature;				
34.	to help students identify and weigh facts, implications, inferences, and judgments in both spoken and written discourse;				

Qualifications Needed by Language Arts Teachers (cont.)

	Degree of development			
Qualification	Not developed 1	2	3	Highly developed 4

35. to help students develop the ability to respond appropriately to and create nonprint and nonverbal forms of communication, including both symbolic forms and other visual and aural forms (including film, videotape, photography, dramatic performance, song, and other art forms).

ATTITUDES: Teachers of English at all levels need to reveal in their classes and in their work with individual students:

36. a conviction that by helping students increase their power to use and respond to language both creatively and responsibly they are helping those students to grow as human beings;
37. a respect for the individual language and dialect of each student;
38. a willingness to respond and help students respond to work in all the different media of communication;
39. a desire to help students become familiar with the diverse cultures and their art;
40. a recognition that, whatever their rate of growth and progress, all children are worthy of a teacher's sympathetic attention;

Qualifications Needed by Language Arts Teachers (cont.)

	Degree of development			
Qualification	Not developed 1	2	3	Highly developed 4
41. a sensitivity to the impact that events and developments in the world outside the school may have on themselves and their students;				
42. a flexibility in teaching strategies and a willingness to seek a match between students' needs and the teacher's objectives, methods, and materials;				
43. a commitment to continued professional growth.				

Source: From National Council of Teachers of English, *A Statement on the Preparation of Teachers of English and the Language Arts* (Urbana, Ill.: National Council of Teachers of English, 1976).

In order to assess your students' progress, you will want to examine standardized test results, observations, written reports, and the data from personal conferences with your children.

Recordkeeping

It will become critical for you to have a way to store all the information you are actively collecting from and about your students. The following checklists will help you keep all the information in one place.

Skills Checklist

	YES	NO	MOSTLY	COMMENTS
I. Reading/Thinking				
A. Structural Analysis				
tense markers				
morphemes				
affixes				
prefix				
suffix				
roots				
B. Vocabulary				

Skills Checklist (*cont.*)

	YES	NO	MOSTLY	COMMENTS
C. Comprehension				
Explicit Information				
details				
supporting evidence				
cause and effect				
main idea				
Implicit Relationships				
synthesis				
inference				
main idea				
transfer				
application				
judgment				
D. Study Skills				
Library				
reference books				
organization				
Dictionary				
II. Writing				
A. Structure				
Sentence structure				
Paragraphing				
Organization in passage				
Spelling				
Vocabulary				
B. Creative Expression				
C. Journalism				
Newspaper				
Magazine				
D. Language Usage				
Grammatical structures				
Mechanics				
agreement of verbs				
agreement of subject and verb				
consistency				
diction				
III. Listening				
A. Follow Directions				
B. Comprehension				
Details				
Evidence				
Cause and effect				
Main idea				

Skills Checklist *(cont.)*

	YES	NO	MOSTLY	COMMENTS
IV. Speaking				
A. Organization				
B. Expression				
C. Persuasion				
D. Creative Dramatics				
V. Viewing				
A. Comprehension				
Details				
Main idea				
Cause and effect				
Evidence				
B. Film Production				
Writing				
Filming				
Editing				

Knowledge Checklist

	Test 1	Test 2	Test 3	Test 4	Test 5	Test 6
I. Literature						
1 Short Story/Novel						
2 Poetry						
narrative						
ballad						
3 Drama						
comedy						
tragedy						
4 Nonfiction						
biography						
diary						
II. Film						
1 Short Selection						
2 Narrative						
3 Full length						
4 Documentary						
III. Written Composition						
1 Prose Writing						
narrative						
expository						
2 Expressive Writing						
poetry						
short story						
3 Journalism						
news						
editorial						

Knowledge Checklist (cont.)

		Test 1	Test 2	Test 3	Test 4	Test 5	Test 6
	4 Biography / diary / journal						
IV.	Oral Communication						
	1 Discussion						
	2 Folktales, Storytelling						
	3 Formal Presentations						
	4 Conversation						

This seven-step model detailed above will help you get started but it is only the beginning of a well-managed language arts program. You will have to assess your program constantly in order to be certain that it continues to meet the needs of each of your students.

EXERCISES

1. Design your model classroom, illustrating each section of the room.
2. Explain the procedures you would use in selecting appropriate learning materials for your students.
3. Prepare an evaluation design of your language arts program. Include in your design an assessment of each component of your program.

FURTHER READING

LAPP, D. *Making Reading Possible Through Effective Classroom Management.* Newark, Delaware: International Reading Association, 1980. An excellent overview of management-procedure issues and recommendations for implementation.

*Vacant the scholar's brain
Under his great hat.*

—*W. H. Auden*

Appendix WORD GAMES

This appendix consists of word games that will enable you to reinforce your children's language arts skills.

All children like to play games. Playing word games is a way for you to combine educational material and entertainment. Word games are a good way to make the children in your class more aware of the language they use. In this appendix, we will present a variety of word games at a variety of levels. A consideration of level is important because playing Boggle or Scrabble with a child under the age of eleven or twelve is pointless—it merely leads to frustration on the part of the child. You want to make the games in your class both relevant and enjoyable. You will have to be willing and able to vary the material you use depending on the level of ability of the children you are teaching.

Emily Salus and several of her friends have played these games with us and have suggested books to us. Without the aid of these children (in Toronto, Boston, Storrs, Connecticut, and Jacksonville), this chapter would be far poorer.

EASY GAMES

Perhaps the easiest game to play with children is one in which you ask them to rhyme words. This not only gives them a "feel" for the sounds of English, but it can be used to open the door to reading. Such families of words as

cat	hat	pat
fat	bat	rat
mat	sat	vat

are most useful, as are sets such as

> able   table   stable

and

> bang   rang   sang
> clang hang   gang
> fang   pang   tang

Another interesting activity is to involve the class with riddles. Solving the riddle usually means that the child has to think about the attributes of an object. Since children love to ask and be asked riddles, you can start the class off and then ask the children to supply more riddles. You might even pick one riddle a day and put it up on your bulletin board. Thus, each child gets a chance to read it and to try to solve it. You can have each child supply an answer at the end of the day (although usually children will all have the same answer).

Riddles such as

> Why do birds fly south in the winter?
>   (Because it's too far to walk.)
> What kind of cat eats lemons?
>   (A sourpuss.)
> Why is baseball like a cake?
>   (They both depend on the batter.)

both entertain children and make them aware of the language they are using. Even very simple jokes such as

> Why is a hill different from a pill?
>   (because a hill is hard to get up, but a
>   pill is hard to get down.)

and

> There are two things you can never eat for breakfast:
>   (Lunch and dinner.)

increase the child's consciousness of the possibilities of language: for example, that *batter* has several different meanings, that *puss* in *sourpuss* refers to face, not to cat.

Another interesting game to play is changing one word into another. For example:

Can you change a BALL into a GAME one letter at a time?

Word Games

```
B                                                               G
A                                                               A
L                                                               M
L                                                               E
Start
```

An animal with horns	A thing to ring	To say	Very big	A story	Not wild
B	B	T	T	T	T
U	E	E	A	A	A
L	L	L	L	L	M
L	L	L	L	E	E

A puzzle such as this both enables the child to achieve his or her goal and gives the class good practice in definitions and spelling. You might also have the children supply the clues, or you could leave the entire middle blank and see whether the class can make up the puzzle as a group.

Yet another good teaching device involves letter squares. For example, in

$$P\ I\ N$$
$$I\ C\ E$$
$$N\ E\ T$$

the same words appear across and top-to-bottom. Present your children with a scrambled square and let them straighten it out. For example:

$$N\ F\ U$$
$$U\ E\ S$$
$$E\ N\ W$$

They should be able to do this. A variant is to give them clues:

1. Games are _____.
2. Wasting time is no _____.
3. The opposite of old is _____.

MORE DIFFICULT GAMES

The word square is, of course, a form of crossword puzzle. It is a crossword puzzle in which all the items are, in some sense, "given." However, easy crossword puzzles are both educational and fun, although you must be careful not to present your class with too difficult a chore here. One way to avoid difficulty is to "violate" one or more of the rules of crossword puzzles. Perhaps the most important of these is the rule of symmetry: Adult crossword puzzles are symmetrical; they also interlock to a very high degree. Children will not be disturbed if the puzzles you use are neither symmetrical nor highly interlocking. The content of the puzzle itself is interesting to them; that interest can be heightened by making the topics in this form of word play interesting, too.

For example, you might make up clues to go with an array such as

```
                              S
          B A S E B A L L     F O O T B A L L
          O       V           C
    S     A       E           C
    K     T E N N I S    H    H O C K E Y
    A     I       T      W    R       R
    T     N       D I V I N G E       T
S K I I N G       M      D    S       R
    N             M      B A S K E T B A L L
    G O A L       I D E A     C
                  N      L    O
                  G I R L     R
                              E
```

Similar crosswords may be made up of animal names:

```
              H
              R O B I N
              R
        M O U S E           S
        O         E L E P H A N T        R
        N         K       I       A      C A T
        K                 G E C K O      T U R K E Y
  S H E E P                     E W E    T
        Y A K                   L A M B  L
        R   C                   G        E
        R O O S T E R           L O B S T E R
        O   W                   E
        T
```

or flowers:

```
            V
            I
         R  O  S  E
            L
            E        L
         T  U  L  I  P
      L              L
I R I S     P  A  N  S  Y
      L     E
   M  A  R  I  G  O  L  D
      C     N
            Y
```

or states:

```
         O  K  L  A  H  O  M  A
         E
         N        T
         T  E  N  N  E  S  S  E  E     U        V  I  R  G  I  N  I  A        G
      F  U        X                    T        E                 E           E
      L  C        A  L  A  B  A  M  A           R                 B           O
N E W Y O R K     S              R  H           M                 R           R
      R  Y                       I              O                 A           G
H A W A I I                      Z     I  L  L  I  N  O  I  S     S           I
      D                          O              T     O           K A N S A S
         A  L  A  S  K  A        N                    W                       A
                         C  A  L  I  F  O  R  N  I  A
```

The last scheme might be combined with learning (for example) the states and their capitals, the cities being given as the clues.

Finding hidden words is also a lot of fun for children. Confronted by a rectangle such as

```
C O M M E R C I A L
A P O G E E O S N O
R A V E N S L O T C
T V I D E O O R E A
O E E I W U R A N L
O A R A S N X Y N B
N L O L R D Q U A E
```

and asked to find COMMERCIAL, CARTOON, MOVIE, DIAL, SOUND, ANTENNA, VIDEO, RAY, SLOT, LOCAL, NEWS; or by a simple square such as

```
O B I G
V E R Y
E N O E
R E N T
```

and asked to find BIG, VERY, ONE, RENT, OVER, IRON, YET; most primary-school children do not find themselves out of their depth. By putting in an item such as ONE, which is backwards, you give the children the pleasure of achieving something they consider out of the ordinary.

ADVANCED GAMES

If your class is made up of older, or more able, students, you may wish to play more complicated games with them. Commercial games such as Scrabble and Boggle are excellent for children in or above the fifth or sixth grade. There are also several books of crosswords and of word squares that will tax, but not overtax, the abilities of your students. What you must always keep in mind, however, is that the games you play or that you have your children play with each other must be both entertaining and educational: If a game is either too easy or too difficult, it will not interest your students. Once you have lost their interest, the educational value of what you are doing will wane

SOME TYPES OF GAMES

Juggling letters is a game in which the players are given both a word and the definition of a different word. The new word can be found by rearranging the letters of the given word. Here are some examples of items you can use in playing the game:

Given	Definition	New Word
ate	something to drink	tea
add	father	dad
arm	a male sheep	ram
owe	sorrow	woe
pots	to halt	stop
pots	a stake of wood	post
pots	covers	tops
pots	chooses	opts
two	pull	tow
ink	relative	kin
ash	possesses	has

The given words and the new words are called anagrams. Other anagram word pairs are: *tone/note; tear/rate; abed/bead; meat/team; ripe/pier; felt/left; shore/horse; crate/trace; timer/merit; stone/tones; charm/march; lived/devil; livers/silver; drier/wetter; leader/dealer; live/evil; drawer/reward;* and *stage/gates.*

Palindromes might be considered the syntactic equivalent of anagrams. Palindromes are words or sentences that spell the same thing backwards and forwards. *Peep* and *deed* are examples of simple palindromes. The longest single-word palindromes in English are about seven letters long, but few of these words are likely to be known even to a high-school student: *deedeed, murdrum, sooloos,* and (better known) *repaper, reviver,* and *rotator.* There are only a few six-letter palindromes, and the only one likely to be known to students is *redder;* among five-letter palindromes are *civic, kayak, level, madam, radar, rotor,* and (less well-known) *minim* and *tenet.* However, English has a number of sentence palindromes, which ought to interest your classes. The most famous of these are probably *Madam, I'm Adam* and *Able was I ere I saw Elba,* presumably spoken in the Garden of Eden and by the former Emperor Napoleon. At one time, there was a shop in northern California called the *Yreka Bakery,* surely one of the few naturally occurring palindromes. The longest English palindrome we know is *Live dirt up a side-track carted is a putrid evil.*

Adding letters to words is a good way to develop word knowledge. This can be done in two ways. The simpler is merely to add a letter to the beginning or the end of the given item. For example:

Given:	r
a musical note	re
to be	are
to think about	care
to frighten	scare

A more complicated form is to combine this with letter juggling, as in:

Given:	g
to leave	go
one's self	ego
leaves	goes
a large bird	goose

or

Given:	i
not out	in
writing fluid	ink
stop floating	sink
a lizard	skink

or

Given:	o
either	or
mined metal	ore
ripped	tore
a place to shop	store
caretaker	storer
to fix up	restore

There are a great many words that can be built up in this way. Not wanting to waste too much time and space, we will merely list some progressions here. You can supply your own definitions.

a/an/van/vane/raven
b/be/bet/bite/tribe
c/co(mpany)/cop/cope/scope
d/do/dot/toad/today
e/me/met/meat/steam
f/if/fin/fine/knife
g/—above
h/he/her/here/cheer
i/see *f*
j/?
k/?
l/la/lap/pale/plate (or, petal)
m/—see *e*
n/no/not/note/stone
o/—see *n* and above
p/up/cup/puce
q/?
r/—see above
s/so/sop/soap or s/is/his/this/shirt
t/it/sit/this/hoist
u/us/sun/stun/turns or runts
v/—?
w/we/owe/wore/wrote
x/—?
y/by/bye/byre
z/—?

(Most of the question marks are there because there just aren't any two letter words with those letters. If you want to start your students out at a different level, or "skip" a step, then you can use things like x/ox/box . . . /boxes or z/ . . . /zoo/ooze/zoomer. But you mustn't feel constrained to have such a set for every letter of the alphabet, and it may be a wonderful discovery for your class that they can't play this game with some letters of the alphabet.)

Change-a-letter and *drop-a-letter* are other games you can play. Both of these involve word definitions, as well as spelling. In *change-a-letter*, you say "Change a letter in a word meaning ____ to get a word meaning ____" and the children have to fill in the two words. For example: "Change one letter in a word meaning low, wet clouds to get a word meaning enemy"—*fog* and *foe*. Or "Change a letter in a word meaning a fight to get a word meaning a glass container"—*battle* and *bottle*.

The alternative is to say "Drop a letter from a word meaning ____ to get a word meaning ____." For example, "Drop a letter from a word meaning departed to get a word meaning a single number"—*gone* and *one*; or "Drop a letter from a word meaning picture to get a word meaning a contest"— *image* and *game*.

You can make this more complicated by asking to drop two letters, as in

garden	drag
operate	opera
proof	for
protest	store
intrude	trend

The entire game can be made even harder by demanding responses in a specific category:
For example,

Trees

popular	poplar	-1
lame	elm	-1
sash	ash	-1
snipe	pine	-1
sample	maple	-1

or

sample	palm	-2
shall	ash	-2
flirt	fir	-2

Animals

bread	bear	-1
pact	cat	-1
stale	seal	-1
greets	egret	-1
crowd	crow	-1
crowd	cow	-2
scowl	owl	-2
shifty	fish	-2

Foods

pike	pie	-1
pearl	pear	-1
pearl	pea	-2
tamed	meat	-1
mistake	steak	-2
crony	corn	-1

and so on.

Sometimes, if you have introduced the notion of anagrams or of palindromes to your class, you can get them interested in looking at the words backwards. There are many words in English that are other words backwards and forwards. Here again you can give the two definitions: For example, "This word is a negative one way and two thousand pounds backwards" (not/ton). Some pairs of words like this are

on	no
am	ma
net	ten
bat	tab
but	tub
mat	tam (a hat)
tag	gat
raw	war
trap	part
trot	tort
emit	time
dual	laud
straw	warts
layer	relay
drawer	reward

There are literally hundreds of pairs of words like this. Your students will enjoy trying to think of new ones and will feel that they have achieved something when they come up with them.

Word Games

We have mentioned rhymes before, but we cannot overemphasize how rhyming will make the children in your class more conscious of the words they use. Rhymes will also aid them in both reading and spelling, for they will become more aware of the relationships between sounds and spellings.

The following is a good word game:

Something that rhymes with *hat*,
Is a household pet, the ____.   (cat)
Not at all like a *cake*,
Is a garden tool, the ____.   (rake)
A word that rhymes with *look*,
Is a new reading ____.   (book)
A word that rhymes with *freight*,
Is a wooden packing ____.   (crate)
Something that rhymes with *barge*,
Is a word for size that's ____.   (large)
When you put on something nice to *wear*,
Everyone knows that you ____.   (care)
A word that rhymes with *great*,
Means blackboard, it's a ____   (slate)

Another rhyming game is to put together what might be called a "crossword." On the chalkboard, draw a few sets of boxes—three by three, five by five—such as the following:

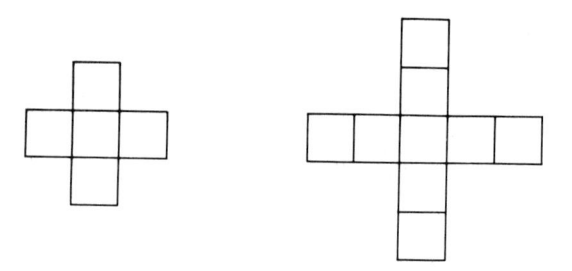

Then give a few definitions and see if the children can come up with the words to fill in the squares. For example, "An animal kept at home and a collection":

```
        P
      S E T
        T
```

or "A hamburger roll and a rifle":

```
        B
    G U N
        N
```

"Not at all and to cut off":

```
        N
        E
    S E V E R
        E
        R
```

or "Thick oil and to stop":

```
        G
        R
        E
    C E A S E
        S
        E
```

Note in this last example that we have used an asymmetrical model. As long as your drawn boxes match the letters of the words defined, you needn't worry about this.

There are a number of other word games you can play with great pedagogic effect. Sound-alikes (*to, too, two; sew, so, sow*) are very useful. Here, for example, you might ask your class for a word meaning "also"; then ask for a number that sounds like it. Or, you might ask for a word meaning "to fasten with thread," and then for "planting seeds." Other useful sound-alikes are *pale/pail, knight/night, knot/not, ate/eight, or/ore, through/threw, roll/role, knows/nose, pear/pair, hour/our, meat/meet,* and *fair/fare*.

With sound-alikes, we are dealing with two words that sound the same but are spelled differently. In English, there are also many words that are spelled the same but mean different things. Thus, *may* means "permitted" and *May* is the fifth month of the year. *Tap* is both "a faucet" and "to touch." You might ask your class to think of more than one meaning for a number of words. Some words with two meanings are *can, ape, rub, seal, foot, deed, honey, crank, might, cable, spring, hammer, tongue, tender,* and *change*.

A final pair of word games involves synonyms and antonyms. Asking your class for "another word for" or "the opposite of" provides them with an interesting task.

Games are fun; they can also teach. Playing word games, doing crossword puzzles, and working with rhyming words are ways both to teach and to keep your class involved in what is going on.

EXERCISES

1. Teach Pig Latin (or some other "secret language") to your class. Does using such an invented language make them more aware of their own English?
2. The Walbiri of Australia have an initiation rite that involves "upside-down" talk. See if your class can talk "upside down." This means that "She is going" means "He is coming." "We won't work with him" means "I will play with her." Ask the class what they consider to be opposites. Are *I* and *we* opposites like *up* and *down* or *work* and *play*?
3. Try to make up a crossword puzzle in class. Is it easy or hard to do?

FURTHER READINGS

ANDREW, JEAN, ed. *Hidden Words* #14. New York: Ace Books, 1974.

DOHERTY, LINDA. *Junior Scrambled Word Find Anthology 2.* New York: Grosset & Dunlop, 1975.

EPSTEIN, SAM and BERYL. *What's Behind the Word?* New York: Scholastic Book Services, 1964.

FELLOWS, LEN. *Puzzle Blast.* New York: Scholastic Book Services, 1977.

KLEIN, LEONORE. *Arrow Book of Tricks and Projects.* New York: Scholastic Book Services, 1960.

PETER, JONATHAN. *More Jokes and Riddles.* New York: Wonder Books, 1963.

PETERSON, JOHN. *How to Write Codes and Send Secret Messages.* New York: Scholastic Book Services, 1966.

WYLER, ROSE. *Real Science Riddles.* New York: Scholastic Book Services, 1971.

INDEX

A

Abbreviations, 214-217
Ability Grouping, 330-331
Acceleration, 330
Active, 16
Activities, Listening, 94-98
Adjectives, 15
Affixes, 13
Agreement, 202-203
Allomorphs, 12
Allophones, 12
Alphabet, 114-117
Alphabet Approach to Reading, 222
American Sign Language, 48, 326
Anatomy, 4
Animal Communication, 2, 3
Ape Language Experiments, 48
Apostrophe, 210
Approaches to Writing, 125-128
Articulation, 9
Articulation Disorders, 324
Aspiration, 7
Assessing Spelling, 182-184
Assessment of Reading, 256-257
Assimilation, 46
Autism, 324
Aztec Writing, 111, 112 (ill.)

B

Babbling, 26
Baby Talk, 26
Bantu, 53
Basal Reading, 223
Basic Sight Vocabulary, 241
Bidialectalism, 303; 309-311
Bilingualism, 312-318
Bilingual Reading, 316-317
Black English, 302, 304-309
Black English and the Language Arts, 308-309
Blake, W., 271
Bloom's Taxonomy of Objectives, 247
Brackets, 209-210

C

Caldecott Medalists (list), 291-293
Caxton, W., 57
Cerebral Palsy, 327
Chaucer, G., 52
Childhood Aphasia, 324
Childhood Schizophrenia, 324

Children's Magazines (list), 276-279
Chinese Writing, 110, 111
Choral Speaking, 93-94
Classroom Environment, 134-135, 291
Cluster Simplification, 46
Cluttering, 325
Coinages, 60
Colon, 209
Comma, 208-209, 211-213
Common Spelling Errors, 193-196
Communication Competence, 72-75
Communicative Acts, 26
Composition, Organization of, 205-206
Comprehension, 40-42
Comprehension and Performance, 38-39
Comprehension of Texts, 246-249
Comprehension Skills (Lessons), 251-254
Conjugation, 13
Consonants (of English), 8, 9
Contextual Analysis, 244-245
Controlled Levels of Vocabulary, 223
Controlling Function, 72, 73
Corrective Procedures in Spelling, 193-196
"Correct" Pronunciation, 45
Creative Dramatics, 93
Creoles, 301
Cultural Stereotyping, 264
Cuneiform, 105, 117 (ill.)
Cursive Writing, 160-162

D

Dash, 209
Deafness, 325-327
Declension, 13
Decoding, 220
Decoding in Reading, 228-229
Delay, 324
Demonstrative, 15
Descartes, R., 23

Designing a Writing Program, 133-139
Dialect(s) 298-300
Dialect Differences, 302-303
Dickinson, E., 270
Dictation, 80-81
Disorders, 322-328
Dolch List, 241
Dunbar, P. L., 309-311

E

Early Modern English, 58
Egyptian Writing, 108-110
Ellipsis, 211
English Spelling, 177
Environmental Design, 341-342
Errors, Spelling, 193-196
ESL, see *Bilingualism, Bilingual Reading*
Evaluating Handwriting, 164
Evaluation of Writing, 149-150
Exactly Signed English, 326
Exceptional Children, 322-331
Exclamation Point, 207-208
Explosive, 4

F

Families of Words, 62-64
Feeling Function, 73-74
Figurative Language, 267-271
First Words, 27
Fluency Disorder, 325
Following Directions, 81-83
Formal Grammar, 203-204
Forms, 149
Fricative(s), 5
Fry Graph, 338-339

G

Games, 354-366
Genetic Epistemology, 23

Index

Genres in Literature, 264-274
Germanic Languages, 55-58
Gifted Children, 329-331
Glides, 10
Goals, 335-336
Grimm, J., 56
Grouping (Examples), 340-341

H

Handwriting Assessment, 167
Handwriting, Evaluation of, 164
Handwriting, Improving Performance of, 170-171
Handwriting Program Objectives, 156-157
Handwriting Readiness, 158
Handwriting Samples, 164-167
Handwriting, Self-Analysis, 168-169
Handwriting Skills, 157-158
Hieroglyphics, 105, 108-109 (ill.)
Hyphen, 211

I

Iconography, 104-105
Ideographic Writing, 105
Imagery, 268-269
Imagining Function, 74-75
Implosive, 5
Improving Handwriting, 170-171
Improvisation, 93
Individual Differences, 322
Individualized Instruction, 334-335
Indo-European, 53-55, 62-64
Infant Perception, 24
Infix, 13
Information Questions, 35
Informing Function, 74
Instructional Grouping for Spelling, 192
Interactive Reading, 220
Interviewing, 84-85
Intonation, 11, 35-36

J

Journalistic Writing, 274-276
Juncture, 11

K

Keats, J., 268-269

L

Language Acquisition, 23
Language Attitudes, 301-302
Language Change, 42-43
Language Development, 23
Language Development and Reading, 262
Language Disorders, 323-325
Language Intervention, 313
Languages and Language Families, 53-55
Language Stereotypes, 301-302
Larynx, 4-6
Learning Disability, 324
Left-Handed Writing, 162-163
Lesson Plan (Contextual Analysis) 244-245
Lesson Plan (Prefixes), 243-244
Lesson Plan (Sight Word), 242
Lessons (Comprehension Skills), 251-254
Letter-Sound Correspondences (Table), 229-233
Letter Writing, 144
Levels of Competence, 75-77
Linguistic Method (Reading), 223-224
Linguistics, 4
Listening, 69-70
Listening Activities, 94-98
Listening Skills, 70-71
Listening/Speaking Program, 79-98
Literature for Beginning Readers, 287-288
Loanwords, 58-60

M

Making Books, 142-143
Manuscript Writing, 158-159
Maturational Processes, 24
Mayan Writing, 111, 112 (ill.)
Meaning, 17, 19
Mean Length of Utterance, 30
Mechanics of Composition, 205-206
Mental Retardation, 324, 327
Metaphor, 270
Middle English, 42, 57
Minimal Pair, 7
Minoan Writing, 110, 111
MLU, 30
Models of Writing, 123-124
Mongolian Writing, 106 (ill.)
Morphology, 12, 23
Morphology, Acquisition of, 33
Mother-Child Interactions, 26
Motivation (Reading), 279-280
Motivation (Writing), 128-131
Murray's Recommendations, 124

N

National Languages, 312-313
Negation, 33
Negatives, 34-35
Newberry Medalists (list), 293-295
Noun Phrase, 14

O

Objectives of a Prereading Program, 225-227
Old English, 52, 56
Oral Communication Programs, 67-68
Organization in Composition, 205-206
Overgeneralization, 39

P

Parallel Processing, 220
Parentheses, 209
Passive, 16, 42
Penmanship, see *Handwriting, Writing*
Period, 206-207
Personality Development and Reading, 263
Personalized Reading Program, 224
Phaistos Disc, 110-111 (ills.)
Pharynx, 4, 6
Philology, 4
Phoneme, 7
Phonetics, 4
Phonetics Method (Reading), 223
Phonetic Spelling, 176 (ill.)
Phonetic Writing, 113-117
Phonics Generalizations (list), 234-238
Phonics Lesson Plan, 240
Phonics Strategies, 233-240
Phonology, 4, 23, 44-45
Pictographic Writing, 113
Pictorial Signs, 105 (ill.)
Picture Writing, 103 (ill.)
Pidgins, 301
Pitch, 11
Pivot Grammar, 28-29
Plosives, 6
Plurals, 12-13, 32
PL 94-142, 328-329
Poetry, 264-272
Poetry Writing, 145-147
Postreading Exercises, 289-290
Pragmatics, 42-44
Prefixes, 13, 243
Prehistoric Drawings, 104 (ill.)
Prepositional Phrases, 15
Prereading Exercises, 288-289
Prereading Objectives, 225-227
Prestige Dialects, 300
Printing, 57
Program Design, 335-349
Program Goals, 335-336
Program Management, 334-352

Program Organization, 334-352
Pronouns, 32
Proofreading, 138-139
Psycholinguistics, 23
Psychological Problems, 324
Punctuation, 206-214
Puppetry, 91-93

Q

Questioning Strategies, 254-256
Question Mark, 207
Questions, 33, 35-37
Question Types, 255
Quotation Marks, 210

R

Racial Stereotyping, 264
Ransbury's Reading Attitude Inventory 281-284
Rask, R. K., 56
Reader's Theater, 86-88
Reading, 220-222
Reading Assessment, 256-257
Reading Attitude Inventory, 281-284
Reading Decoding, 228-229
Reading Exercises, 289
Reading for Characterization, 273-274
Reading for Plot, 273
Reading for Setting, 273
Reading for Theme, 274
Reading Instruction, 222-224
Reading Interest/Attitude Scale, 281
Reading Interest Inventory, 285-286
Reading, Personalized Program, 224
Reading Readiness, 224-225
Reading to Young Children, 286-287

Record-Keeping, 349-352
Reference, 202-203
Registers, 26
Relationships among Language Arts, 78-79
Relative Clauses, 33, 37-38
Replacive, 13
Report Writing, 147-149
Research Reports, 147-149
Revising, 138-139
Rhyme, 271-272
Ritualizing Function, 74
Role-Playing, 89-90
Rumelhart's Theory of Reading, 247
Runes, 55, 56 (ill.), 115 (ill.)

S

Sandburg, C., 93
Sanskrit Script, 106 (ill.)
Scribbles, 154-156
Segmental Phonemes, 11
Semantic Change, 60-62
Semantics, 17, 23, 46-48
Semicolon, 208, 211-213
Sentence, 14
Sex Stereotyping, 264
Short Stories, 272-274
Sight-Word Analysis, 240-241
Sight-Word Lesson Plan, 242
Silent Reading, 223
Simile, 270
Single Letter Spelling, 176 (ill.)
Speaking, 72-77
Speaking Skills, 77-78
Speech Disorders, 323-325
Speeches, 85-86
Spelling, Acquisition of, 174-176
Spelling Activities, 196-197
Spelling, Assessment of, 182-184
Spelling Curriculum, 184-185
Spelling Demons (list), 190-192
Spelling, English System of, 177
Spelling Games, 197-199

Spelling Instruction, 181–182, 192
Spelling Program Objectives, 182
Spelling Rules, 177–179
Spelling-Sound Relationships (table) 179–181
Stages (I-V), 30–33
St. Augustine, 23
Stereotypes in Language, 301–302
Stereotypes in Literature, 263–264
Stops, 6
Story-Telling, 90–91
Story Writing, 143–144
Stress, 11
Structural Analysis, 243–244
Stuttering, 325
Suffixes, 13, 243
Suppletive, 14
Suprasegmentals, 11
Symbol, 270–271
Syntactic Development, 30
Syntax, 14, 23, 39
Syntax (Acquisition), 33

T

Tacitus, 55
Tapes, 79–80
Taxonomy of Reading, 248–249
Teacher Evaluation, 342–349
Teaching Grammar, 202
Teaching Manuscript Writing, 159–160
Teaching the Standard Dialect, 311
Teaching the Writing Process, 135–136
Teaching Writing to Young Children, 139–142
Telegraphic Speech, 28
Telephoning, 83–84
Tennyson, A., 83, 270
Tone, 11
Tongue, 6
Trachea, 4
Transformational-Generative Grammar, 14
Transformations, 16

U

Ulfila, 55
Unaspirated, 7
Uralic-Altaic, 53
Usage, 18

V

Variation in the Classroom, 303–306
Verb, 15
Verbal Output (Stages), 24
Verb Phrase, 14
Vocabulary, Basic Sight, 241
Vocabulary Development, 131–132
Vocabulary Growth, 27
Vocal Tract (diagram), 5
Voice, 5
Voice Disorders, 324–325
Vowels, 9–10

W

Weak-Syllable Deletion, 46
WH-Questions, 35
Word Attack Skills, 233–246
Word Frequency List, 185–190
Word Games, 354–366
Wordsworth, W., 266
Writing, 120–152
Writing, Development of, 154–156
Writing Letters, 144
Writing, Manuscript, 158–159
Writing, Origin of, 154–156
Writing Poetry, 145–147
Writing Program, 128–139
Writing Reports, 147–149
Writing Stories, 143–144
Writing Systems, 102–117

Y

Yes/No Questions, 35